EVEREST

EVEREST

THE BEST WRITING AND PICTURES FROM SEVENTY YEARS OF HUMAN ENDEAVOUR

Edited by

PETER GILLMAN

Foreword by

SIR EDMUND HILLARY

Picture research by

AUDREY SALKELD

LITTLE, BROWN AND COMPANY

BOSTON · TORONTO · LONDON

A Little, Brown book
First published in Great Britain and the
United States of America in 1993
by Little, Brown and Company

Compilation copyright © Peter Gillman
Ltd 1993
See page 205 for copyright details and
original publication of extracted material

The moral right of the author has been
asserted

A CIP catalogue record is available for
this book.

Designed by : Clive Hayball

Typeset by: Avocet Typesetters, Launton,
Bicester, Oxon.

Printed and bound in UK by
Butler & Tanner

ISBN 0-316-90489-9

Page 1: *The North Face of Everest under heavy post-monsoon snow, photographed by Roger Mear.*

Page 2: *The long and winding trail: in Doug Scott's photograph, taken during his 1987 attempt on the North-east or Pinnacles Ridge, Rick Allen (foreground) and Sandy Allan toil through heavy snow near the top of Bill's Buttress at 23,200 feet. Scott and his colleagues reached the First Pinnacle at around 26,000 feet, with the summit still 3,000 feet beyond.*

Contents

'THE FINEST CENOTAPH IN THE WORLD': 1921–1939

'ED, MY BOY, THIS IS EVEREST': 1950–1969

'ALL THE WORLD LAY BEFORE US': 1970–1979

'A DREAMLIKE SENSE OF DISBELIEF': 1980–1993

APPENDICES

Foreword

Sir Edmund Hillary

Climbing on Mount Everest has covered an astonishingly short period in human history – a mere 70 years, all of it within the course of my lifetime. For me George Leigh Mallory epitomized all that was best in adventure in the 1920s and he remains my most heroic figure in the 70-year saga. I read Frank Smythe's *Camp Six* a dozen times and as I became increasingly involved in mountaineering, Eric Shipton became my hero. When we climbed Everest in 1953 I really believed that the story had finished. I supposed that it would be recorded in Alpine club publications the world over – but that was all.

How wrong I was! The media and public reaction was far beyond anything I had naively expected. Every country, every mountaineering club, every enthusiastic climber wants to set foot on the summit too. Formidable expeditions battled with the toughest routes; those who wanted only to get to the summit tried our South-east Ridge route or the North Col – but few found it easy. Even on the obvious routes it's a long way to the top! The weather is so often unpredictable, the thin air a constant challenge. Our climb in 1953 became a start rather than a finish. The skills and equipment developed in Alpine regions were adapted for use at extreme altitude. Climbing Everest without oxygen became a further bonus – pushing the limits of human endurance ever closer to the edge. Many have died in the process.

I am thankful that I climbed Everest in the days of innocence, when everything was new and a constant challenge, and for me at least publicity was a bit of a laugh. I feel sorry for today's climbers trying to find something new and interesting to do on the mountain, something that will get both the public attention and the respect of their peers. Up and down the mountain in 24 hours, a race to the top – what will they think of next?

Happily the commercial deals are soon forgotten and the recent ascents of Mount Everest include some great and heroic efforts – I am sure there will be more in the future. These are the things worth remembering and these are the stories told so well in this anthology. Techniques, equipment and skills change rapidly over the decades but nothing can replace courage, a resounding motivation and that little bit of luck. These are the qualities which separate failure and disaster from the moments of triumph and success. The great stories on Mount Everest have not always concluded with the party reaching the summit, of course. The climbers who inspired me – Mallory, Smythe, Shipton – all failed, but their attempts involved them in taking on considerable odds with a vast amount of effort. I was one of the fortunate ones, who reached the top and got down safely again.

No one succeeds alone. We all, in a sense, climb on the shoulders of those hardy characters who have gone before. Even on the summit of Mount Everest I felt surprise that Tenzing and I should have been the lucky ones. And certainly for me the summit of Everest was a beginning, not an end. There are so many adventures to meet and challenges to overcome. Long may it be that way!

SIR EDMUND HILLARY

Introduction

Galen Rowell's photograph (right) shows Everest from the Pang La, the 17,200 foot pass 40 miles to the north in Tibet. Clearly visible is the North Face, bisected by the Norton (or Great) Couloir. To its left is the North Ridge which rises diagonally to join the North-east Ridge at 27,630 feet.

Page 6: Chris Curry's photograph was taken looking east from 23,442 foot Pumori in Nepal, with the North Face now appearing as the slanting, slabby terrain to the left of the summit. To the right of Everest are the Khumbu Glacier and Icefall, beyond them the Western Cwm which proved the key to the first ascent in 1953. The British expedition climbed the Lhotse Face above the Western Cwm to reach the South Col, the snow-saddle to Lhotse's left, and from there followed the South-east Ridge to the summit.

I first became aware of Everest's power to inspire awe when I was eleven. In the autumn of 1953 I was in one of the lines of schoolchildren taken to watch *The Conquest of Everest*, the film of the triumphant British first ascent. The shot which above all held that potentially unruly cinema audience spellbound was cameraman Tom Stobart's epic pan, seeming to last for several minutes, from the snow-covered floor of the Western Cwm to the corniced crest of the Summit Ridge.

That shot often returned to me as I luxuriated in my task of compiling this book. It served as a reminder of the odds its contributors faced, from the prewar pioneers who battled to within a thousand feet of the summit, to their latterday counterparts, forging routes of increasing audacity. I felt special admiration for the photographers, summoning their determination to take pictures in the most hostile of environments.

I was still in the throes of my work when I saw Everest for the first time, rising from the brown plateau of Tibet. When I returned my task seemed to have become even harder, the problem being what to omit from the hundreds of extracts, articles and photographs we had gathered. In the end we resolved on a mix of old and new, of familiar icons and unpublished material which will, I trust, convey the awe I first felt 40 years before.

Some explanations are necessary. Some pieces have been published in full while others have been extracted from longer articles or books – a list of sources appears on page 205. Some pieces have been slightly trimmed for reasons of space. A few have been subject to minor editing but only in the case of living authors and with their consent. We have endeavoured to make proper names consistent but have left other stylistic variations intact. On the vexed question of whether to convert feet to metres and/or vice versa, we decided it was simplest to follow the authors' choice, but a conversion table appears on page 201.

In compiling this anthology I have received help from a remarkable number of people – a list appears on page 206. To them, as to all the authors and photographers, I should like to express my profound thanks.

Peter Gillman

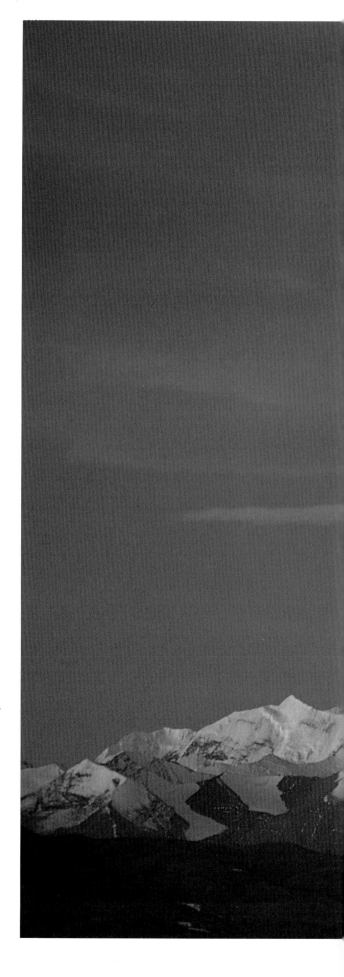

A Household Word

Sir George Everest, the son of a London solicitor, was Surveyor General of India from 1830 to 1843. It was Everest's successor, Andrew Waugh, who proposed naming the world's highest mountain after him as a tribute to his pioneering work in mapping India. Everest, who believed that mountains should be known by their local names, opposed Waugh's suggestion. But Waugh won the argument and the name Everest was officially adopted by the Royal Geographical Society in 1865, just one year before Everest died.

It was in 1808 that the British began the process which was to locate and name the world's highest mountain. It was undertaken by the India Survey, staffed by army officers charged with providing reliable maps to help the British maintain their rule in the era of the Raj. Their goal was to survey the entire Indian sub-continent, and it was a formidable task.

The survey officials began by laying out a series of triangular grids which would eventually cover the whole country and provide a series of fixed points on which to base their maps. They were also plotting the Great Arc of India, a no less ambitious project by which they hoped to be able to calculate the true shape of the earth, suspected of being flattened at the poles rather than a perfect sphere.

With their calibrated chains and measuring rods, their giant theodolites so heavy that they had to be carried by 12 men, the survey teams gradually worked their way north. By the 1830s they had reached the foothills of the Himalayas. Across the border into Nepal, they could glimpse snowy peaks rising beyond lines of intervening ranges, although for much of the time they were obscured by cloud.

The British already suspected that these distant peaks were the highest on earth. Infantry officers had been encouraged to map the territories they visited, and in 1803 Captain Charles Crawford, a trained surveyor, compiled several maps while posted to the British residency in Kathmandu. One, based on his own observations and measurements, showed 'the valley of Nepal', the first formal map of the region. A second, compiled from reports of 'merchants, religious mendicants and other travellers', depicted the entire kingdom of Nepal, and showed a line of peaks named as 'the snow mountains', with one marked as 'highest in the range'.

Crawford's findings had particularly intrigued the Surveyor General himself, Lt Col Robert Colebrook, who had already seen the 'snow peaks' from some 150 miles away. In 1807 Colebrook saw them again from near the Indian town of Gorakhpur: 'a scene which for grandeur can scarcely be rivalled – every part of the stupendous range appeared to be covered with snow.' Colebrook calculated that two of the mountains were at least five miles high, putting

them above any peak in the Andes, then considered the highest range. 'If that is the case,' Colebrook concluded, 'they must be the highest mountains in the known world.'

The surveyors of the 1830s were equally impressed by what one termed these 'stupendous pinnacles' and resolved to establish just how high they were. To their dismay, all further northward travel was barred. The obstacle stemmed from Nepal's suspicion of British intentions: as an autonomous state which had escaped British rule, it was determined to remain that way. It had expelled the British resident in 1803 and, so a British diplomat observed, 'nothing will dissuade the Nepalis from the belief that topographical surveys, geological examinations and botanical collections are either the precursors of political aggression, or else lead to complications which end in annexation.' The surveyors sought permission on several occasions to cross into Nepal but were turned down.

The British were thus compelled to make their observations from the Terai, a tract of country parallel to the Himalayas south of Nepal. They began by marking out a new series of base lines, interspersed with observation posts, 30 feet high, built from mud bricks. Conditions were hideous: part-covered in jungle, the Terai was subject to torrential rains and malaria was rife. Of five successive survey officers, two died and two were forced to retire through ill-health. The fifth contracted malaria too and a stretcher party set off

To measure heights as accurately as possible, Everest deployed giant theodolites weighing 1100lbs and needing 12 men to carry them. In 1849 survey officer James Nicolson used this theodolite to observe what was then known as peak 'b' from distances of more than 100 miles. Nicolson's sightings established that the peak was the highest in the world.

to carry him to hospital in Darjeeling, but he died before it arrived.

Undaunted, the British team began detailed observations of the great Himalayan peaks in 1847. The difficulties remained immense. The distances were enormous, up to 150 miles between the observation stations and the peaks. The weather restricted work to the final three months of each year, when the clouds which habitually obscured the peaks were most likely to clear. But they persevered, and in November the Surveyor General, Andrew Waugh, made a series of observations from Sawajpore station at the eastern end of the range.

One of the peaks which most interested Waugh was Kangchenjunga, hitherto regarded as most likely to be the world's highest peak, and for which the surveyors were already using a version – Kanchanjinga – of the local Nepalese name. Beyond it, some 140 miles away, Waugh sighted another snow-covered mountain which looked higher still. One of Waugh's officials, John Armstrong, saw the same snowy summit – 'perceptible but rather indistinct' – from further west, and called it peak 'b'. Afterwards Waugh wrote that the observations of the peak 'indicate an altitude higher even than that of the great Kanchanjinga . . . but on account of the great distance the observations require further verification from a station less remote.'

Waugh sent a survey officer to the Terai in 1848 to obtain closer sightings, but peak 'b' remained hidden by clouds. The following year he dispatched another officer, James Nicolson, who made two observations over a distance of 118 miles from Jirol station before the clouds closed in again. Taking the largest theodolite, Nicolson headed east and in two months obtained 36 observations from five different stations, the closest 108 miles from the peak.

Although Nicolson did not yet know it, he had just completed the observations which were to establish peak 'b' as the highest mountain in the world. But a hiatus occurred. When the rains came, Nicolson withdrew to a town near Patna on the River Ganges where he was due to make the calculations based on his sightings. His raw data were impressive: he had obtained an average height for peak 'b' of around 30,200 feet, and although that made no allowance for light refraction, which exaggerated heights, it placed it substantially higher than Kangchenjunga.

However Nicolson was in no position to claim that he had just discovered the world's highest

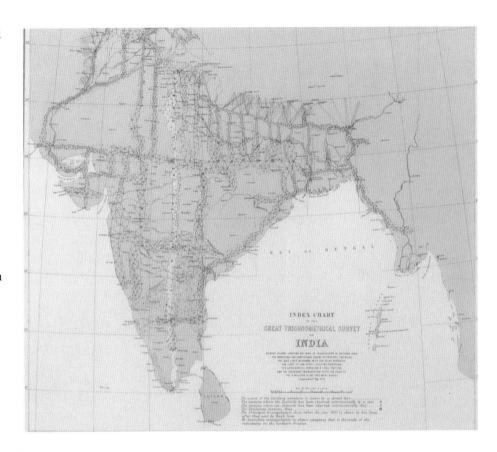

mountain, as he had no idea what heights his colleagues might have obtained elsewhere. Then he too was struck down by malaria, and had to be invalided home. Only in 1854 did Andrew Waugh begin work on Nicolson's figures at the survey headquarters in Dehra Dun. One of Waugh's assistants, Michael Hennessy, had given new designations to the peaks, based on Roman numerals: Kangchenjunga was Peak IX, peak 'b' became Peak XV.

Waugh and his staff spent almost two years on their calculations, wrestling with the problem of refraction which was notoriously difficult to calculate, particularly as they had no idea what allowances to make for temperature and barometric pressure over the enormous distances of Nicolson's sightings. They were also concerned in case the vast gravitational pull of the Himalayas had distorted their equipment. But in March 1856 Waugh finally announced his findings in a letter to his deputy in Calcutta. 'I am now in possession of the final values of the peak designated XV,' Waugh wrote. 'We have for some years known that the mountain is higher than any hitherto measured in India.'

Waugh then gave the crucial figures: Peak IX, Kangchenjunga (now known to be the world's third highest mountain – the second is K2) was 28,156 feet; Peak XV was 29,002 feet. It was,

The officials of the British India Survey covered the country with a series of triangular grids to give them fixed points on which to base their maps. Starting at India's southern tip in 1808, they gradually worked their way north, taking 30 years to reach the Himalayas – known to the early map-makers as the 'snow mountains'.

Waugh concluded, 'most probably the highest in the world.'

There remained the question of what the highest peak should be named. Partly to deflect the accusation that it was merely an appendage of British rule, the survey had been anxious to preserve local names: hence its use of Kangchenjunga – 'the Five Treasure-Houses of the Snows' – and other names such as Dhaulagiri, 'the White Mountain'. But for Peak XV – so Waugh now argued – no obvious name existed.

There was in fact a plethora of existing names. Best-established was Chomolungma, which had been current in Tibet for several centuries and had appeared on a map published in Paris by the geographer D'Anville in 1733. Based on information from Tibetan lamas which was passed on by Jesuit missionaries in Peking, D'Anville's map rendered the name as Tschoumou-Lanckma, Tibetan for 'Goddess Mother of the World', clearly indicating the reverence accorded to the mountain. The name had echoes of another Tibetan phrase, Lhochamalung, which meant 'the district where birds are kept' and had been used from around 650 AD, when the early Tibetan kings had the birds in the region fed at their own expense. There were at least three other candidates, including Devadhunka and Chingopamari, which were well-known in the ancient literature of Nepal, and Gaurisankar, although that turned out to be the name of another mountain.

Despite the claims for Chomolungma, Waugh was set on another name entirely. With some sophistry, he argued that since there were so many local names it would be invidious to choose any of them, and proposed instead that Peak XV should be named after his predecessor as India's Surveyor General – George Everest.

Everest had first arrived in India in 1806. Born in London, he was then a 16-year-old artillery cadet set on a career as an army officer. After a spell in Java he returned to India where he was appointed chief assistant to William Lambton, the current Surveyor General. When Lambton died in 1823, Everest took charge of the Great Trigonometrical Survey, rising to become Surveyor General in 1830. He also completed the Great Arc of India, and it was he who supervised the building of the giant theodolites vital in obtaining the decisive measurements of the Himalaya range, including Peak XV itself.

To Waugh, Everest was the obvious candidate after whom Peak XV should be named. He had set exacting standards for his officials but he too had fallen victim to India's unforgiving climate, being invalided home in 1825. He had returned to India in 1830, extending the Great Arc northwards and building new observatories. His first request to survey inside Nepal in 1840 was turned down, and he returned to Britain three years later.

The British India Survey continued its work into the 20th century. The picture, right, taken in 1904, shows officials taking zenith observations: the British officer at the telescope is observing a star, calling out readings which are noted by his assistant at the table. The observations helped fill in the map of India which began with the triangulations of the Great Trigonometrical Survey.

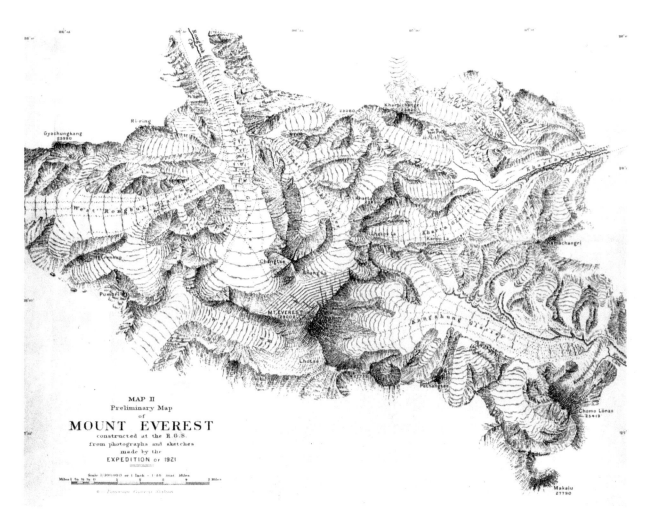

MAP II
Preliminary Map
of
MOUNT EVEREST
constructed at the R.G.S.
from photographs and sketches
made by the
EXPEDITION of 1921

The first detailed map of Everest was constructed from photographs and sketches produced by the British reconnaissance expedition of 1921. Since the expedition approached Everest through Tibet, the map focuses on the northern side of the mountain. It was published in the journal of the Royal Geographical Society the following year.

Waugh was well aware that in nominating the name Everest for what he termed 'this noble peak', he was selecting what was bound to become 'a household word'. Waugh judged that Everest deserved such a privilege, 'in testimony of my affectionate respect for a revered chief, and to perpetuate the memory of that illustrious master of accurate geographical research.'

There were several ironies in Waugh's determination to use Everest's name. The first was that Everest himself was chary of accepting honours; he turned down a knighthood when he retired and was only persuaded to accept one shortly before his death. The second was that Everest had been among the most insistent that the Himalayan peaks should retain their local names, and objected vigorously when he heard Waugh's proposal. The word Everest, he told the Royal Geographical Society in 1857, could not be pronounced by 'the native of India', nor could it be written in Hindi. But Waugh prevailed and in 1865 – just one year before Everest himself died – the Society officially adopted Mount Everest as the name of the world's highest mountain.

While Waugh was keen to commemorate the name of Everest against other deserving claims – and Chomolungma is increasingly used today – his own reputation deserves to be perpetuated. His calculation of Everest's height, 29,002 feet, based on observations made in the face of such intractable problems, remained the agreed figure for almost 100 years. In the 1950s Indian surveyors established a new chain of triangles into Nepal, going much nearer to the mountain than the Victorians and establishing higher observation points. Their new figure of 29,028 feet (8,848 metres) was less than 0.1 per cent higher than Waugh's.

Even with new survey methods using satellites in the 1980s the old figures have held. The most recent calculations have been made by the US cartographer, Bradford Washburn. In May 1992 a US expedition placed a prism on the summit, enabling him to take laser measurements which produced figures very close to the previous height. 'We all have immense admiration and respect for the achievements of the 19th century pioneers,' Washburn says.

The cartographer's art was consummated in this superb 1:50,000 map compiled by Bradford Washburn of the Boston Museum of Science. A renowned geophysicist and photographer, Washburn based his map on his aerial survey and on satellite images. It was drafted by the Swiss Federal Office of Topography and published by the US National Geographical Society in 1988. Washburn then embarked on a 1:2500 Everest map and has also built a computerised model of Everest measuring seven feet high.

THE SPOTLESS PINNACLE OF THE WORLD

In 1903 the British government dispatched a top secret mission to Tibet. Led by Colonel Francis Younghusband, its aim was to secure favour with Tibet's leader, the Dalai Lama, in a bid to prevent Russia from occupying a country from which it could threaten Britain's rule over India. Attempts at negotiation failed and Younghusband marched on Lhasa, beating back attacks by Tibetan forces en route. The British finally achieved their goal in a treaty signed in September 1904.

Among Younghusband's staff, and accorded the rank of Joint Commissioner, was the intriguing figure of J. Claude White. As Britain's political officer in Sikkim, White had considerable experience of the tangled politics of India's north-east frontier, and was fascinated with what he termed 'the mysterious, unknown land of Tibet'. In his account of the mission, Younghusband portrayed White as the quintessential exile; he and his wife were devoted to their garden in Sikkim, finding 'a never-ending interest with all the English flowers – narcissus, daffodils, pansies, iris – in the spring.'

Younghusband did not mention another of White's interests – photography. White took to Tibet a cumbersome plate camera with which he recorded a remarkable series of photographs. Some captured scenes of daily life which had so enthralled him; others clearly had a more practical purpose, showing roads, passes and river-crossings – landmarks of undoubted strategic interest to the British.

Whether from his personal interests or wider British aims, White also photographed Mount Everest, doing so from the fortress town of Khamba Dzong, 94 miles to the north-east. Precisely when is not clear: the photograph is now in the Curzon Collection in the India Office archives in London, dated 1904. But both White and Younghusband were first in Khamba Dzong in July 1903, Younghusband later describing how he could see from his tent 'the first streaks of dawn gilding the snowy summits of Mount Everest, poised high in heaven as the spotless pinnacle of the world.'

Everest had previously appeared as a distant lump in pictures taken from around Darjeeling, most notably in a

The first true portrait of Everest? In Claude White's photograph, taken during the British mission to Tibet of 1903–4, Everest, with the East or Kangshung Face prominent, is the snow-covered peak at the centre of the range.

sequence by the Italian Vittorio Sella during a journey with the British explorer Douglas Freshfield in 1899, but even they were uncertain at the time as to what they had photographed. White's was almost certainly the first definitive portrait of Everest as such and it was precisely the grandeur of the mountain rising above its neighbours, as Younghusband described, that White captured.

After the mission, White returned to the north-east frontier. The mountain state of Bhutan was added to his territory, bringing him continuing delight in 'scenery unparalleled anywhere in the world for magnificence and grandeur'. Although when he retired White wrote a book – *Twenty-one Years on the North-East Frontier* – about his service in Sikkim and Bhutan, he included not a word about the mission to Tibet, clearly still regarded by the British as too sensitive a matter. He died in 1918.

'THE FINEST CENOTAPH IN THE WORLD'

1921–1939

Pages 16/17: *Somervell's photograph shows the 1922 team gazing at Everest, left, from the Pang La Pass. To the right are the peaks of Gyang Chang and Cho Oyu. The 'cenotaph' remark was Somervell's, made after the deaths of Mallory and Irvine.*

THE DREAM OF EVEREST

The first person to publicly raise the question of climbing Mount Everest was the surgeon and mountaineer Clinton Dent. In his book *Above the Snowline*, published in 1885, Dent drew comparisons with polar expeditions to assert that since matters of supplies, expense and risk had not hindered Arctic explorers, there was no reason why they should prove insuperable to Himalayan mountaineers. Dent, who had studied the effects of altitude on balloonists and believed that the problem could be solved through acclimatization, concluded: 'I do not for a moment say that it would be wise to ascend Mount Everest, but I believe most firmly that it is humanly possible to do so; and, further, I feel sure that even in our time, perhaps, the truth of these views will receive material corroboration.'

The first full-scale British expedition to the Himalayas came when Martin Conway climbed a 22,600 foot peak near K2 in the Karakoram Range in 1892. Duly encouraged, Dent wrote an article for *Nineteenth Century* magazine entitled: 'Can Mount Everest be climbed?' and several British explorers and climbers took up the challenge. Chief among them was a Gurkha officer, the Hon. Charles Granville Bruce, who had taken part in Conway's Karakoram venture and now suggested an Everest expedition to Francis Younghusband, who was to lead the celebrated mission to Tibet in 1903–4. Younghusband was enthusiastic. During a reconnaissance trip into western Tibet after the Lhasa treaty was signed, two of his officers came within 60 miles of Everest from the north, close enough for them to conclude that the North Ridge offered a clear way to the summit.

From that moment all attempts to organize expeditions to Everest became mired in the unforgiving politics of the region. The chief obstacle was the Secretary of State for India, one John Morley, who blocked all bids out of 'consideration of high Imperial policy', and probably personal animosity towards the mountaineers besides. The nearest any westerner came to Everest in the next ten years was an illicit foray into Tibet by the British adventurer and photographer Captain John Noel in 1913 with his skin and hair darkened as a disguise. He too came within 60 miles of Everest from the east and obtained one magical glimpse of its top 1,000 feet, a 'glittering spire of rock fluted with snow'. To Noel's bitter disappointment – he later blamed the high wind 'which prevented proper exposures' – he was unable to obtain a photograph.

The First World War put a stop to any further ventures for the next five years. In 1919 Noel took up the idea once more, describing his Tibetan journey in a lecture to the Royal Geographical Society. There was a ready response from the RGS and the Alpine Club, although at an RGS meeting the following year, the former Gurkha Lieutenant, Charles Bruce – now Brigadier General Bruce – warned how little about the mountain was known. 'We have a distant view of its northern ridge, far the most promising part of the mountain that has yet been seen,' Bruce declared. 'It however causes one to think; there are evidently portions of it which are steep, and we have to think out the camps. Very much will depend on what the ridge usually is. Will it be ice, or firm snow, or soft snow? This last is terrible at great heights.'

In January 1921, taking due heed of Bruce's warnings, the RGS and the Alpine Club formed an 'Everest Committee' to launch an expedition with eight members and costing £4,000. Once again the politicians objected – this time for fear of disturbing Japan – but the Everest Committee stuck to its guns and by April 1921 the expedition was on its way to Darjeeling. Its aim was, first and foremost, to find a route up Everest. If possible, it was to climb the mountain as well, although if it failed, that task would be taken up by a full-scale expedition the following year.

The expedition leader was an army officer, Lieutenant Colonel Charles Howard-Bury, a traveller of independent means who owned an estate in Ireland and a string of race-horses, and who had made several exploratory trips into the Himalayas some 20 years before. The most charismatic figure was George Mallory, another Great War veteran and former school-master with socialist leanings and impressive literary talents.

The expedition faced difficulties from the moment it left Darjeeling in May. Their supplies and equipment were carried on Army mules, but these proved to have such poor stamina that they had to be replaced with hill mules and yaks. The climate was exhausting, with heat in the morning, a dust-laden wind by midday, and bitter cold at night. The expedition's food was rudimentary and gastro-enteritis was rife.

Under the strain, relationships between the more strong-willed members began to fracture, with Howard-Bury and Mallory forming a particular dislike of each other. Mallory described his leader as 'too much the landlord with not only Tory prejudices, but a very highly developed sense of hate and contempt for other sorts of people than his own.' The culminating misfortune came when the senior doctor, Alexander Kellas, a man in his fifties, died of a heart attack brought on by exhaustion and dysentery. Mallory meanwhile was plunged into further bouts of depression. 'I sometimes think of this expedition as a fraud,' he later wrote to a friend. 'The prospect of ascent in any direction is almost nil.'

By early June the expedition was

little more than 50 miles from Everest. It had passed Khamba Dzong, from where Claude White had obtained his famous photograph, and was at the edge of the territory explored at the time of the Younghusband mission. Mallory noted: 'We are just about to walk off the map.' On 13 June, after entering a spectacular landscape of limestone cliffs and gorges, Mallory and two colleagues decided to climb a cliff above the Yaru Gorge in the hope of obtaining a view of Everest. It seemed a frail chance, as the Himalayas were still shrouded by the clouds of the monsoon. Later Mallory described what he saw. Gone are the frustration and doubts; in their place is the rapture of the moment when he and his companions became the first westerners to observe Everest in its full awesome glory.

'We were able to make out almost exactly where Everest should be; but the clouds were dark in that direction. We gazed at them intently through field glasses as though by some miracle we might pierce the veil. Presently the miracle happened. A whole group of mountains began to appear in gigantic fragments. Mountain shapes are often fantastic seen through a mist; these were like the wildest creation of a dream. A preposterous triangular lump rose out of the depths; its edge came leaping up at an angle of about 70 degrees and ended nowhere. To its left a black serrated crest was hanging in the sky incredibly. Gradually, very gradually, we saw the great mountainsides and glaciers and arêtes, now one fragment now another

The members of the 1921 reconnaissance expedition were the first to pursue the dream of Everest, so graphically described by Mallory. Front row, left to right: Mallory, Wheeler, Bullock, Morshead; back row: Wollaston, Howard-Bury, Heron, Raeburn.

through the floating rifts, until far higher in the sky than imagination had dared to suggest the white summit of Everest appeared. And in this series of partial glimpses we had seen a whole; we were able to piece together the fragments, to interpret the dream. . . .'

Within a few weeks, having completed their demanding walk from Darjeeling, Mallory and his colleagues were also to become the first mountaineers to attempt to fulfil that dream.

We have established the way

by *George Mallory*

After the five-week walk from Darjeeling, the 1921 reconnaissance expedition arrived at the Tibetan village of Tingri, 50 miles north of Everest, at the end of June. It spent the next three months in search of a way on to the mountain, exploring the valleys, glaciers and cols in the northern section of the Everest massif. For George Mallory, the only person to take part in all three British Everest trips of the 1920s, it was the opportunity of a lifetime. Since returning from the Great War he had become increasingly frustrated by the petty restrictions of a schoolmaster's life and had resigned to join the expedition, with little thought of what he would do afterwards. He wrote prodigiously – to use one of his own favourite words – of his discoveries to his family and friends, revealing far more of his feelings than in his official expedition bulletins. Most of the following extracts are from letters to his wife Ruth.

28 June
First camp under Everest: This is a busier life than might be imagined even on an off day. It is after 9 pm and I have only just finished my lengthy but necessary despatch to Howard-Bury, and I shall have to be up at 5 am . . . I'll tell you about Everest in my next letter. Suffice it to say that it has the most steep ridges and appalling precipices that I have ever seen, and that all the talk of an easy snow slope is a myth.

We are completely cut off from civilization here. There is a monastery quite close to us; it's rather convenient as supplies come up the valley for the monks and we can arrange for fuel to come for us with theirs, so we shall probably keep the base camp here for some weeks. It's a fairly sheltered spot and just near a beautiful little spring, but the wrong side of the valley for the morning sun. Everest is just a little east of south from us.

Yesterday we made a first mountaineering expedition, started at 3.25 am with five coolies; one and a half hours to the terminal moraine of the glacier; 5.45, crossed a torrent with difficulty; then across a flat basin to the end of the glacier, which is covered with stones and made of enormous hummocks; bore across to the true left bank of the glacier and worked up a dry stream bed. Breakfast at 7 am near a great stone, just as the sun hit us. An hour's fast walking brought us to a corner where a glacier comes in from the west. We worked round this corner and up on to a shelf on the mountainside.

I found it pretty hot on the glacier; there is no doubt the sun tends to take the heart out of one, but not unbearably so. I must confess to a degree of tiredness after the glacier work which I have never quite reached in the Alps, but in all I was very pleased with myself from a physical point of view. My darling, this is a thrilling business altogether. I can't tell you how it possesses me, and what a prospect it is. And the beauty of it all!

6 July, climbing Ri-Ring
An early start at 4.15 am, straight up the stony slopes above our camp. After about an hour's going, I took some photos of Everest and some of his neighbours, all looking magnificent in the early sun. It was about 2,500 feet to the crest of our ridge: Bullock and coolies rather tired at this point; 40 minutes' halt and some food. Roped up for snow towards 8 am. A long upwards traverse to a snow col, where we halted, 9.30 to 10.10.

From this point we had to follow a long snow ridge and then rock and snow. Two coolies dropped out here, and the other three after an hour and a half more. Bullock and I plugged on, climbing now and then little steep bits of slaty rock, treading carefully along snow crests, occasionally cutting a few steps in ice to reach the arête again after a short traverse. Our interest was partly in what we saw, partly in the sheer struggle of getting on. We moved very slowly, keeping up muscular energy and overcoming lassitude by breathing fast and deep. It was a colossal labour. We reached the top at 2.45. The aneroid, which reads about 400 feet low, registered 23,500. After a week at our camp I consider this a good performance – a rise of 5,500 feet in the day. I have no doubt when we get better acclimatised and start from a higher camp we shall be able to go a great deal higher. It is a remarkable fact about mountaineering here, so far as our experience goes, that the descent is always very tiring. It is only possible to keep oneself going by remembering to puff like a steam-engine.

19 July, to the col between Lingtren and Pumori

An exciting walk. I so much feared the cloud would spoil all. It was just light enough to get on without lanterns after the moon went down. At dawn almost everything was covered, but not by heavy clouds. Like guilty creatures of darkness surprised by the light, they went scattering away as we came up, and the whole scene opened out. The North Ridge of Everest was clear and bright even before sunrise. We reached the col at 5 am, a fantastically beautiful scene; and we looked across into the West Cwm at last, terribly cold and forbidding under the shadow of Everest. It was nearly an hour after sunrise before the sun hit the West Peak.

But another disappointment: it is a big drop, about 1,500 feet down to the glacier, and a hopeless precipice. I was hoping to get away to the left and traverse into the cwm – that, too, was quite hopeless. However, we have seen this western glacier and are not sorry we have not to go up it. It is terribly steep and broken. In any case, work on this side could only be carried out from a base in Nepal, so we have done with the western side. It was not a very likely chance that the gap between Everest and the South Peak could be reached from the west. From what we have seen now, I do not much fancy it would be possible, even could one get up the glacier.

28 July, to Kharta

I have been half the time in ecstasy. My first thought on coming down was that the world was green again. A month had made all the difference to the appearance of the hillsides. As we have come down lower, and nearer to the Arun valley,

Mallory was assiduous in writing to his wife, Ruth, during his expeditions. They met in 1914 and married three months later; Ruth, an architect's daughter from Surrey, was then 22; George, a vicar's son from Cheshire, 28. Although separated for much of the Great War – Mallory served as an artillery officer in France – they had three children, a son and two daughters. In his letters home, Mallory revealed far more of his feelings than in his official expedition reports.

the appearance of greenness has steadily increased. We have crossed two passes on the way, and we have slept near two clear bubbling streams; and all that we have seen of snow mountains has been of interest, but none of that counts with me. To see things grow again as though they liked growing, enjoying rain and sun – that has been the real joy.

I collected in a beautiful ramble a lovely bunch of wild flowers. The commonest were a pink geranium and a yellow potentilla and a little flower that looked for all the world like a violet but turned out from its leaf to be something quite different; and there was grass of Parnassus, which I really love, and in places a carpet of a little button flower, a brilliant pink, which I think must belong to the garlic tribe. But most of all I was delighted to find kingcups, a delicate variety rather smaller than ours at home, but somehow especially reminding me of you – you wrote of wading deeply through them in the first letter I had from you in Rome.

7 August, to the summit of Kartse

We walked for about three-quarters of an hour by candlelight up a moraine. Even before the first glimmer of dawn, the white mountains were somehow touched to life by a faint blue light – a light that changed, as the day grew, to a rich yellow on Everest and then a bright grey blue

before it blazed all golden when the sun hit it, while Makalu, even more beautiful, gave us the redder shades, the flush of pink and purple shadows. But I'm altogether beaten for words. The whole range of peaks from Makalu to Everest far exceeds any mountain scenery that ever I saw before.

Then we plugged on over the glacier, well covered with fresh snow, till we took off our snow shoes and for the first time the party (four coolies) found themselves on steep rocks – not a very formidable precipice, but enough to give us all some pleasure. The rocks took us to a pass which was our first objective. Below on the far side was a big glacier but we couldn't yet see whether it led to the North Col of our desire.

We had already taken time to observe the great Eastern Face of Mount Everest, and more particularly the lower edge of the hanging glacier; it required but little further gazing to know that almost everywhere the rocks below must be exposed to ice falling from this glacier; that if, elsewhere, it might be possible to climb up, the performance would be too arduous, would take too much time and would lead to no convenient platform; that, in short, other men, less wise, might attempt this way if they would, but emphatically, it was not for us.

We now wanted to see over a high ridge to the col itself. The next section was exceedingly

steep. Bullock thought it would prove impossible, and it was stiff work; I had a longish bit of cutting in good snow. We then reached a flat plateau, put on snow shoes, and hurried across to the far edge. The party then lay down and slept in various postures while I took photographs and examined the North Peak through my glass. It was clearly visible down to the level of the col, but no more than that – so that, though the view was in many ways wonderful, the one thing we really wanted to see was still hidden. Eventually I asked for volunteers to come on to the top, and two coolies offered to come with me. It was only a matter of 500 feet, but the snow was very deep and lying at a terribly steep angle. One coolie refused to come on after a time; the other struggled on with me.

And then suddenly we were on the summit. As the wind blew rifts in the snow I had glimpses of what I wanted to see, glimpses only, but enough to suggest a high snow cwm under this North-east Face of Everest, finding its outlet somehow to the north. It is this outlet that we have now to find – the way in and the way up. We are going back to the valley junction, the glacier stream we left, with the idea that at the head of one of its branches we shall find the glacier we want.

17 August, to the Lhakpa La
When we started at 3 am, our hope was to reach

our snow col while the snow was still hard, in four or five hours from the camp. It was a dim hope, because we knew fresh snow had fallen. After a few steps on the glacier, we found it necessary to put on our snow shoes – blessed snow shoes in that they save one sinking in more than a few inches, but a dismal weight to carry about on one's feet on a long march.

We reached the col at 12.30 pm. Apart from a couple of hours on snow-covered rocks above the icefall, this time was all spent in the heavy grind on soft snow. It is no use pretending that this was an agreeable way of passing time. Once we had regained the glacier from the rocks and eaten breakfast at about 8.15 am, we were enveloped in thin mist which obscured the view and made one world of snow and sky – a scorching mist, if you can imagine such a thing, more burning than bright sunshine and indescribably breathless. One seemed literally at times to be walking in a white furnace. Morshead, who knows the hottest heat of the plains in India, said that he had never felt any heat so intolerable as this. It was only possible to keep plodding on by a tremendous and continually conscious effort of the lungs; and up the steep final slopes I found it necessary to stop and breathe as hard as I could for a short space in order to gain sufficient energy to push up a few more steps.

The clouds of course hid the peaks when we got there, but in the most important sense the expedition was a success: we saw what we came to see. There, sure enough, was the suspected glacier running north from a cwm under the North-east Face of Everest. How we wished it had been possible to follow it down and find out the secret of its exit! There we were baffled. But the head of this glacier was only a little way below us, perhaps 700 feet at most; and across it lay our way, across easy snow up into the other side of the cwm, where the approach to the North Col, the long-wished-for goal, could not be difficult nor even long. And so, whatever may happen to the glacier whose exit we have yet to find, we have found our way to the great mountain. In such conditions as we found it, it cannot of course be used; but there it is, revealed for our use when the weather clears and the snow hardens.

15 September

Pour out your pity, dearest, pull it up from your deep wells – and be pleased to hear that I read myself agreeably to sleep, and slept, slept bountifully, deeply, sweetly from 9 pm to 6 am and woke to see the roof of my tent bulging ominously inwards and a white world outside. It was easy enough to make out that conditions for climbing were entirely hopeless. Every visible mountain face was hung with snow, incredibly

The 1921 expedition leader, Charles Howard-Bury, took a series of photographs with a panoramic camera as the expedition probed for a route on to Everest. This picture, formed by joining two of Howard-Bury's shots and sadly damaged since, was taken when the team reached the Lhakpa La Pass on 17 August. As Mallory described, the route to Everest lay before them at last. In the far right of the photograph the East Rongbuk Glacier is seen leading to the North Col, the dip on the skyline ridge. To the left the North Ridge rises to its junction with the North-east Shoulder, while the summit lies unseen beyond.

more so than when we last were there three weeks ago. The glacier presented an even surface of soft snow and everything confirmed what everybody had previously said – that it was useless to attempt carrying loads up to our col until we had a spell of real fair weather.

I ordered the whole party to pack up and go down. We were still pulling down tents and covering stores when the clouds came up with a rush and the sizzle of hard-driving snow was about us again. We sped down the hillside, facing wind and snow, down the long valley, dancing over the stones half-snow-covered and leaping the grey waters of many streams, and so at length to the humpy grass in the flat hollow where the big tents are pitched . . .

Just now we are all just drifting as the clouds drift, forgetting to number the days so as to avoid painful thoughts of the hurrying month. For my part I'm happy enough; the month is too late already for the great venture; we shall have to face great cold, I've no doubt; and the longer the delay, the colder it will be. But the fine weather will come at last. My chance, the chance of a lifetime, I suppose, will be sadly shrunk by then; and all my hopes and plans for seeing something of India on the way back will be blown to wherever the monsoon blows. I would willingly spend a few weeks longer here, if only for the sake of seeing Everest and Makalu and the excitement of new points of view. I would like to undertake a few other ascents, less ambitious but perhaps more delightful. And it will be a loss not to see again that strangely beautiful valley over the hills, and the green meadows dominated by the two greatest mountains.

Of the pull the other way I needn't tell you. If I picture the blue Mediterranean and the crisp foam hurrying by as the ship speeds on to Marseilles or Gibraltar where I shall expect to see

you smiling in the sunshine on the quayside – my dear one, when such pictures fill my mind, as often enough they do, I'm drawn clean out of this tent into a world not only more lovely, more beautifully lit, but signifying something.

17 September

Wonder of wonders! We had indication that the weather intended to change. We woke and found the sky clear and remaining clear, no dense white clouds drifting up the valley, but a chill wind driving high clouds from the north. I had a good walk yesterday with Morshead and Bullock and we were rewarded by a beautiful view of Everest. Today Morshead, Bury and I started at 2 am to ascend a snow peak on the boundary ridge between this valley and the next one to the south. We had a glorious view, unimaginably splendid – Kangchenjunga and all the higher mountains to the East were standing up over a sea of fleecy cloud: Makalu straight opposite across the valley was gigantic, and Everest at the head of the valley – very fine too. But the snow was in bad condition and it's not melting as it should; above 20,000 feet or so it was powdery under a thin crust and it was impossible to get along without snow shoes, and if it doesn't melt properly on the glacier we might as well pack up our traps at once. In addition to this cause of despair, Morshead was going badly and I must admit to feeling the height a good deal. I'm clearly far from being as fit as I ought to be. It's very distressing, my dear, just at this moment and altogether my hopes are at zero.

After ten weeks' exploration, culminating in a frustrating three weeks pinned down by bad weather, Mallory believed he had finally found a way. His goal was the North Col, on Everest's North-east Ridge, which he believed would open the way to the summit. On 22 September he and his colleagues crossed the Lhakpa La and descended to pitch their tents on the Rongbuk Glacier, ready to attempt to reach the col – and perhaps even to push on for the summit – the next morning.

23 September

After a late start and a very slow march we pitched our tents on the open snow up towards the col. It might have been supposed that in so deep a cwm and sheltered on three sides by steep mountain slopes, we should find a tranquil air and the soothing, though chilly calm of undisturbed frost. Night came clearly indeed, but with no gentle

The map (right) shows the journeys described by Mallory in these extracts from his letters. The 1921 expedition also went to the head of the central spur of the Rongbuk Glacier, without finding a route on to the North Col, and along the Kangshung Glacier from Kharta, where they concluded that the East or Kangshung Face was 'emphatically not for us'.

intentions. Fierce squalls of wind visited our tents and shook and worried them with the disagreeable threat of tearing them away from their moorings, and then scurried off, leaving us in wonder at the change and asking what next to expect. It was a cold wind at an altitude of 22,000 feet, and however little one may have suffered, the atmosphere discouraged sleep. Again I believe I was more fortunate than my companions, but Bullock and Wheeler fared badly. It was an hour or so after sunrise when we left the camp and half an hour later we were breaking the crust on the first slopes under the wall. We had taken three coolies who were sufficiently fit and competent, and proceeded to use them for the hardest work. Apart from one brief spell of cutting when we passed the corner of a bergschrund it was a matter of straightforward plugging, firstly slanting up to the right on partially frozen avalanche snow and then left in one long upward traverse to the summit. Only one passage shortly below the col caused either anxiety or trouble; here the snow was lying at a very steep angle and was deep enough to be disagreeable. About 500 steps of very hard work covered all the worst of the traverse and we were on the col shortly before 11.30 am.

By this time two coolies were distinctly tired, though by no means incapable of coming on; the third, who had been in front, was comparatively fresh. Wheeler thought he might be good for some further effort, but had lost all feeling in his feet. Bullock was tired, but by sheer will power would evidently come on – how far, one couldn't say. For my part I had had the wonderful good fortune of sleeping tolerably well at both high camps and was now finding my best form; I supposed I might be capable of another 2,000 feet, and there would be no time for more. But what lay ahead of us? My eyes had often strayed, as we came up, to the rounded edge above the col and the final rocks below the North-east Arête. If ever we had doubted whether the arête were accessible, it was impossible to doubt any longer. For a long way up those easy rock and snow slopes was neither danger nor difficulty. But at present there was wind. Even where we stood under the lee of a little ice cliff it came in fierce gusts at frequent intervals, blowing up the powdery snow in a suffocating tourbillion.

On the col beyond it was blowing a gale. And higher was a more fearful sight. The powdery fresh snow on the great face of Everest was being swept along in unbroken spindrift and the very ridge where our route lay was marked out to receive its unmitigated fury. We could see the blown snow

deflected upwards for a moment where the wind met the ridge, only to rush violently down in a frightful blizzard on the leeward side. To see, in fact, was enough; the wind had settled the question; it would have been folly to go on. Nevertheless, some little discussion took place as to what might be possible, and we struggled a few steps further to put the matter to the test. For a few moments we exposed ourselves on the col to feel the full strength of the blast, then struggled back to shelter. Nothing more was said about pushing our assault any further.

29 September

My dearest Ruth,

This is a mere line at the earliest moment, in the midst of packing and arrangements to tell you that all is well. It is a disappointment that the end should seem so much tamer than I hoped. But it wasn't tame in reality; it was no joke getting to the North Col. I doubt if any big mountain venture has ever been made with a smaller margin of strength. I carried the whole party on my shoulders to the end, and we were turned back by a wind in which no man could live an hour. As it is we have established the way to the summit for anyone who cares to try the highest adventure.

Oliver Wheeler, pictured with his plate camera and two of his native assistants, was both an expert surveyor and an accomplished mountaineer. From Canada, where he had climbed in the Rockies, he was one of the three-man party, led by Mallory, which reached the North Col on 24 September and established that it offered a route to the summit.

The tortures of Tantalus

by George Finch

The first full-scale expedition to Everest was like a moonshot of its day. The climbers who arrived in the Rongbuk Valley in April 1922 after their long trek across the Tibetan Plateau were venturing into the unknown, uncertain of the effects of altitude and with clothes and equipment better suited to the Alps. The first summit attempt met near-disaster when three climbers started sliding down an ice slope and George Mallory held them on his rope. The second came on 25 May, when a party of three set off from the North Col. They consisted of a Gurkha officer, Geoffrey Bruce (not to be confused with expedition leader General Charles Bruce) who had never climbed before; his regimental field aide, Tejbir Bura; and the Australian-born George Finch, the most accomplished mountaineer on the expedition.

On 24 May, Captain Noel, Tejbir, Geoffrey Bruce, and I, all using oxygen, went up to the North Col. Bent on a determined attack, we camped there for the night. Morning broke fine and clear though somewhat windy, and at eight o'clock we sent off up the long snow-slopes leading towards the North-east Shoulder of Mount Everest, 12 porters carrying oxygen cylinders, provisions for one day, and camping gear. An hour and a half later, Bruce, Tejbir, and I followed, and, in spite of the fact that each bore a load of over

George Finch, 34 in 1922, was the strongest climber on the expedition. Born in Australia, brought up in Switzerland, he was never entirely accepted by the British mountaineering establishment; he was turned down for the 1921 reconnaissance and not invited in 1924. As well as writer and photographer, Finch was a pioneer of mountaineering equipment. He rejected the Alpine clothing recommended for the 1922 team and, as shown right, designed his own jacket from balloon cloth with a quilt lining filled with eiderdown.

30lb, which was much more than the average weight carried by the porters, we overtook them at a height of about 24,000 feet. They greeted our arrival with their usual cheery, broad grins. Leaving them to follow, we went on, hoping to pitch our camp somewhere above 26,000 feet. But shortly after one o'clock the wind freshened up rather offensively, and it began to snow. Our altitude was 25,500 feet, some 500 feet below where we had hoped to camp, but we looked round immediately for a suitable camping site, as the porters had to return to the North Col that day, and persistence in proceeding further would have run them unjustifiably into danger. This I would under no circumstances do, for I felt responsible for these cheerful, smiling, willing men, who looked up to their leader and placed in him the complete trust of little children. As it was, the margin of safety secured by pitching camp where we did instead of at a higher elevation was none too wide; for before the last porter had departed downwards the weather had become very threatening. A cheerful spot in which to find a space to pitch a tent it was not; but though I climbed a couple of hundred feet or so further up the ridge, nothing more suitable was to be found. Our porters arrived at 2 pm, and at once all began to level off the little platform where the tent was soon pitched, on the very edge of the tremendous precipice falling away to the East Rongbuk and main Rongbuk Glaciers, over 4,000 feet below. Within 20 minutes the porters were scurrying back down the broken, rocky ridge towards

the snow-slopes leading to the North Col, singing, as they went, snatches of their native hillside ditties. What splendid men! Having seen the last man safely off, I looked to the security of the guy-ropes holding down the tent, and then joined Bruce and Tejbir inside. It was snowing hard. Tiny, minute spicules driven by the wind penetrated everywhere. It was bitterly cold, so we crawled into our sleeping-bags, and, gathering round us all available clothing, huddled up together as snugly as was possible.

With the help of solidified spirit we melted snow and cooked a warm meal, which imparted some small measure of comfort to our chilled bodies. A really hot drink was not procurable, for the simple reason that at such an altitude water boils at so low a temperature that one can immerse the hand in it without fear of being scalded. Over a *post-prandium* cigarette, Bruce and I discussed our prospects of success. Knowing that no man can put forward his best effort unless his confidence is an established fact, the trend of my contribution to the conversation was chiefly, 'Of course, we shall get to the top'. After sunset, the storm rose to a gale. Terrific gusts tore at our tent with such ferocity that the ground-sheet with its human burden was frequently lifted up off the ground. On these occasions our combined efforts were needed to keep the tent down and prevent its being blown away. Although we had blocked up the few very small openings in the tent to the best of our powers, long before midnight we were all thickly covered in a fine

frozen spindrift that somehow or other was blown in upon us, insinuating its way into sleeping-bags and clothing. Sleep was out of the question. We dared not relax our vigilance, for ever and again all our strength was needed to hold the tent down and to keep the flaps of the door, stripped of their fastenings by a gust that had caught us unawares, from being torn open. We fought for our lives, realising that once the wind got our little shelter into its ruthless grip, it must inevitably be hurled, with us inside it, down on to the East Rongbuk Glacier, thousands of feet below.

And what of my companions in the tent? To me, who had certainly passed his novitiate in the hardships of mountaineering, the situation was more than alarming. About Tejbir I had no concern; he placed complete confidence in his sahibs, and the ready grin never left his face. But it was Bruce's first experience of mountaineering, and how the ordeal would affect him I did not know. I might have spared myself all anxiety. Throughout the whole adventure he bore himself in a manner that would have done credit to the finest of veteran mountaineers, and returned my confidence with a cheerfulness that rang too true to be counterfeit. By one o'clock on the morning of the 26th the gale reached its maximum. The wild flapping of the canvas made a noise like that of machine-gun fire. So deafening was it that we could scarcely hear each other speak. During lulls we took it in turn to go outside to tighten up the tent more firmly with our Alpine rope. It was impossible to work in the open

Breakfast at Base Camp: the 1922 expedition ate impressively, their supplies ranging from cans of Heinz spaghetti, for use on the mountain, to tinned quails truffled in pâté de foie, reserved as a treat for climbers returning to base. Seated left to right: expedition doctor Arthur Wakefield; John Morris; the expedition leader, General Bruce; Karma Paul, the local interpreter; Edward Norton, who partnered Finch on his summit attempt; an unnamed Gurkha; and Geoffrey Bruce, after whom the Norton Couloir was named. The picture was taken by the official expedition photographer, Captain John Noel.

for more than three or four minutes at a stretch, so profound was the exhaustion induced by this brief exposure to the fierce cold wind. But with the Alpine rope taking some of the strain, we enjoyed a sense of security which, though probably only illusory, allowed us all a few sorely needed moments of rest.

Dawn broke bleak and chill; the snow had ceased to fall, but the wind continued with unabated violence. Once more we had to take it in turns to venture out and tighten up the guy-ropes, and to try to build on the windward side of the tent a small wall of stones as an additional protection. The extreme exhaustion and chill produced as a result of each of these little excursions were sufficient to indicate that, until the gale had spent itself, there could be no hope of either advance or retreat. As the weary morning hours dragged on, we believed we could detect a slackening off in the storm. And I was thankful, for I was beginning quietly to wonder how much longer human beings could stand the strain. We prepared another meal. The dancing flames of the spirit stove caused me anxiety bordering on anguish lest the tent, a frail shelter between life and death, should catch fire. At noon the storm once more regained its strength and rose to unsurpassed fury. A great hole was cut by a stone in one side of the tent, and our situation thus unexpectedly became more desperate than ever.

But we carried on, making the best of our predicament until, at one o'clock, the wind dropped suddenly from a blustering gale to nothing more than a stiff breeze. Now was the opportunity for retreat to the safety of the North Col camp. But I wanted to hang on and try our climb on the following day. Very cautiously and tentatively I broached my wish to Bruce, fearful lest the trying experience of the last 24 hours had undermined his keenness for further adventure. Once again might I have spared myself all anxiety. He jumped at the idea, and when our new plans were communicated to Tejbir, the only effect upon him was to broaden his already expansive grin.

It was a merry little party that gathered round to a scanty evening meal cooked with the last of our fuel. The meal was meagre for the simple reason that we had catered for only one day's short rations, and we were now very much on starvation diet. We had hardly settled down for another night when, about 6 pm, voices were heard outside. Our unexpected visitors were porters who, anxious as to our safety, had left the North Col that afternoon when the storm subsided. With them they brought thermos flasks of hot beef tea and tea provided by the thoughtful Noel. Having accepted these most gratefully, we sent the porters back without loss of time.

That night began critically. We were exhausted by

When the 1922 expedition
had to ford a river during
its approach march, Arthur
Wakefield (centre in picture
left) removed his walking
boots, while Howard
Somervell (left) took off his
shorts as well. George
Mallory (right in group)
clearly felt no inhibitions.
The picture right, taken by
Finch, shows his climbing
partner Geoffrey Bruce
trying out the expedition's
primitive oxygen
equipment. Although some
expedition members were
sceptical about using
supplementary oxygen,
Finch was in no doubt.
After he and Bruce had
spent a frightening night
struggling to breathe at
25,500 feet, Finch
declared that it had saved
their lives.

our previous experiences and through lack of sufficient food. Tejbir's grin had lost some of its expanse. On the face of Geoffrey Bruce, courageously cheerful as ever, was a strained, drawn expression that I did not like. Provoked, perhaps, by my labours outside the tent, a dead, numbing cold was creeping up my limbs – a thing I had only once before felt and to the seriousness of which I was fully alive. Something had to be done. Like an inspiration came the thought of trying the effect of oxygen. We hauled an apparatus and cylinders into the tent, and, giving it the air of a joke, we took doses all round. Tejbir took his medicine reluctantly, but with relief I saw his face brighten up. The effect on Bruce was visible in his rapid change of expression. A few minutes after the first deep breath, I felt the tingling sensation of life and warmth returning to my limbs. We connected up the apparatus in such a way that we could breathe a small quantity of oxygen throughout the night. The result was marvellous. We slept well and warmly. There is little doubt that it was the use of oxygen which saved our lives during this second night in our high camp.

Before daybreak we were up. Putting on our boots was a struggle. Mine I had taken to bed with me, and a quarter of an hour's striving and tugging sufficed to get them on. But Bruce's and Tejbir's were frozen solid, and it took them more than an hour to mould them into shape by holding them over lighted candles. Shortly after six we assembled outside. Some little delay was incurred in arranging the rope and our loads, but

at length at 6.30 am, soon after the first rays of the sun struck the tent, we shouldered our bundles and set off. What with cameras, thermos bottles, and oxygen apparatus, Bruce and I each carried well over 40lb; Tejbir with two extra cylinders of oxygen shouldered a burden of about 50lb.

Our scheme of attack was to take Tejbir with us as far as the North-east Shoulder, there to relieve him of his load and send him back. The weather was clear. The only clouds seemed so far off as to presage no evil, and the breeze, though intensely cold, was bearable. But it soon freshened up, and before we had gone more than a few hundred feet the cold began to have its effect on Tejbir's sturdy constitution, and he showed signs of wavering. Bruce's eloquent flow of Gurumuki, however, managed to boost him up to an altitude of 26,000 feet. There he collapsed entirely, sinking face downwards on to the rocks and crushing beneath him the delicate instruments of his oxygen apparatus. I stormed at him for thus maltreating it, while Bruce exhorted him for the honour of his regiment to struggle on; but it was all in vain. Tejbir had done his best; and he has every right to be proud of the fact that he has climbed to a far greater height than any other native. We pulled him off his apparatus and, relieving him of some cylinders, cheered him up sufficiently to start him with enough oxygen on his way back to the high camp, there to await our return.

After seeing him safely off and making good progress, we loaded up Tejbir's cylinders, and, in view of the easy nature of the climbing, mutually agreed to dispense with the rope, and thus enable ourselves to proceed more rapidly. Climbing not very steep and quite easy rocks, and passing two almost level places affording ample room for some future high camp, we gained an altitude of 26,500 feet. By this time, however, the wind, which had been steadily rising, had acquired such force that I considered it necessary to leave the ridge and continue our ascent by traversing out across the great Northern Face of Mount Everest, hoping by so doing to find more shelter from the icy blasts. It was not easy to come to this decision, because I saw that between us and the shoulder the climbing was all plain sailing and presented no outstanding difficulty. Leaving the ridge, we began to work out into the face. For the first few yards the going was sufficiently straightforward, but presently the general angle became much steeper, and our trials were accentuated by the fact that the stratification of the rocks was such that they shelved outward and downward, making the securing of adequate footholds difficult. As I led out over these steeply sloping, evilly smooth slabs, I carefully watched Bruce to see how he would tackle the formidable task with which he

Geoffrey Bruce (ahead) and George Finch on the North Col. Carrying 30 lb loads, they set off from the col on 25 May to make their summit attempt. Accompanied by Bruce's regimental aide, Tejbir Bura, and supported by 12 Sherpas who carried supplies to Camp V, they were, Finch wrote, 'bent on a determined attack'.

Frost-bitten and exhausted, Bruce (left) is assisted by Sherpas as he descends to Camp II on 28 May, following his failed summit bid with Finch (right, with scarf). 'We were deplorably tired,' Finch wrote. 'Knees did not alway bend and unbend as required. At times they gave way altogether.' They had none the less reached a record height of 27,300 feet before turning back. 'Ours were truly the tortures of Tantalus,' wrote Finch. 'Weak from hunger and exhausted by that nightmare struggle for life, we were in no fit condition to proceed.'

was confronted on this his first mountaineering expedition. He did his work splendidly and followed steadily and confidently, as if he were quite an old hand at the game. Sometimes the slabs gave place to snow – treacherous, powdery stuff, with a thin, hard, deceptive crust that gave the appearance of compactness. Little reliance could be placed upon it, and it had to be treated with great care. And sometimes we found ourselves crossing steep slopes of scree that yielded and shifted downwards with every tread. Since leaving the ridge we had not made much height although we seemed to be getting so near our goal. Now and then we consulted the aneroid barometer, and its readings encouraged us on. 27,000 feet; then we gave up traversing and began to climb diagonally upwards towards a point on the lofty North-east Ridge, midway between the shoulder and the summit.

Soon afterwards an accident put Bruce's oxygen apparatus out of action. He was some 20 feet below me, but struggled gallantly upwards as I went to meet him, and, after connecting him on to my apparatus and so renewing his supply of oxygen, we soon traced the trouble and effected a satisfactory repair. The barometer here recorded a height of 27,300 feet. The highest mountain visible was Cho Oyu, which is just short of 27,000 feet. We were well above it and could look across it into the dense clouds beyond. The great West Peak of Everest, one of the most beautiful sights to be seen from down in the Rongbuk Valley, was hidden, but we knew that our standpoint was nearly 2,000 feet above it. Everest itself was the only mountaintop which we could see without turning our gaze downwards.

The point we reached is unmistakable even from afar. We were standing on a little rocky ledge, just inside an inverted V of snow, immediately below the great belt of reddish-yellow rock which cleaves its way almost horizontally through the otherwise greenish-black slabs of the mountain. Though 1,700 feet below, we were well within half a mile of the summit, so close, indeed, that we could distinguish individual stones on a little patch of scree lying just underneath the highest point. Ours were truly the tortures of Tantalus; for, weak from hunger and exhausted by that nightmare struggle for life in our high camp, we were in no fit condition to proceed. Indeed, I knew that if we were to persist in climbing on, even if only for another 500 feet, we should not both get back alive.

The decision to retreat once taken, no time was lost, and, fearing lest another accidental interruption in the oxygen supply might lead to a slip on the part of either of us, we roped together. It was midday. At first we returned in our tracks, but later found better going by aiming to strike the ridge between the North-

east Shoulder and the North Col at a point above where we had left it in the morning. Shortly after 2 pm we struck the ridge and there reduced our burdens to a minimum by dumping four oxygen cylinders. The place will be easily recognised by future explorers; those four cylinders are perched against a rock at the head of the one and only large snow-filled couloir running right up from the head of the East Rongbuk Glacier to the ridge.

The clear weather was gone. We plunged down the easy, broken rocks through thick mists driven past us from the west by a violent wind. For one small mercy we were thankful – no snow fell. We reached our high camp in barely half an hour, and such are the vagaries of Everest's moods that in this short time the wind had practically dropped. Tejbir lay snugly wrapped up in all three sleeping-bags, sleeping the sleep of exhaustion. Hearing the voices of the porters on their way up to bring down our kit, we woke him up, telling him to await their arrival and to go down with them. Bruce and I then proceeded on our way, met the ascending porters and passed on, greatly cheered by their bright welcomes and encouraging smiles.

But the long descent, coming as it did on the top of a hard day's work, soon began to find out our weakness. We were deplorably tired, and could no longer move ahead with our accustomed vigour. Knees did not always bend and unbend as required. At times they gave way altogether and forced us, staggering, to sit down. But eventually we reached the broken snows of the North Col, and arrived in camp there at 4 pm. A craving for food, to the lack of which our weakness was mainly due, was all that animated us. Hot tea and a tin of spaghetti were soon forthcoming, and even this little nourishment refreshed us and renewed our strength to such an extent that three-quarters of an hour later we were ready to set off for Camp III. An invaluable addition to our little party was Captain Noel, the indefatigable photographer of the expedition, who had already spent four days and three nights on the North Col. He formed our rearguard and nursed us safely down the steep snow and ice slopes on to the almost level basin of the glacier below. Before 5.30 pm, only 40 minutes after leaving the col, we reached Camp III. Since midday, from our highest point we had descended over 6,000 feet; but we were quite finished.

That evening we dined well. Four whole quails truffled in pâté de foie gras, followed by nine sausages, left me asking for more. The last I remember of that long day was going to sleep, warm in the depths of our wonderful sleeping-bag, with the remains of a tin of toffee tucked away in the crook of my elbow.

THE LAMA'S TALE

In the third month of the Tibetan year once again a group of 13 Britishers with 100 coolies and 300 pack-charges pitched their camp in front of the mantra house and stayed one day. The representative from the authorities at Ding-Ri [Karma Paul, interpreter to all British expeditions of the 1920s and 1930s] also came as guide and assistant. He said to me, 'The best thing would be to meet the leaders and all their servants or at least the principal sahib. There is no means of avoiding it.'

I said, 'If one meets one heretic, there is no point in keeping all the others back'; but I was feeling very sick.

The next day I greeted the General, three other sahibs and their interpreter. The leader gave me a photo of the Dalai Lama and a length of gold brocade with a ceremonial scarf. I had tea and rice-with-curds served.

'Where are you going?' I asked.

'As this snow peak is the biggest in the world, if we arrive on the summit we will get from the British government a recompense and high rank,' he said.

I replied, 'As our country is bitterly cold and frosty, it is difficult for others than those who are devoted to religion not to come to harm. As the local spirits are furies, you must act with great firmness.'

'Thank you. As we shall also come under the Lama's protection, we trust you will allow us to collect a little brushwood for firewood. Moreover we won't harm the birds and the wild animals in this area. I swear we have no weapons apart from this little knife.'

After saying this, they took their leave. According to the custom of the country, I had conveyed to them a carcass of meat, a brick of tea, and a platterful of roasted wheat flour. After they had left, they established a big camp near the mountain. They stayed about a month and a half. Making use of instruments such as iron pegs, wire

ropes and crampons they strove to ascend the mountain.

They climbed with the most extreme difficulty. Two sahibs got frost-bitten feet. Meanwhile the others climbed on ahead. When they had reached about a third of the way up the mountain, one day, with a roar, an avalanche occurred and some men were projected over the cliff face. Seven or eight coolies died. The leader of the expedition sent 15 silver coins with a request to say prayers for the dead. I was filled with compassion for their lot who underwent such suffering on unnecessary work. I organised very important dedications for the dead.

At the time of the yearly prayer-dance five sahibs and many coolies arrived back. They took photos of the dance, etc. I asked them to stay the night. The following day I met eight sahibs and all the servants.

The leader started by saying, 'Previously I sent money with a request for a special prayer for the seven coolies who died. Just now I sent rice and a cook-box for the Shel-rdzong representative. Did they arrive?'

I asked, 'Are you not weary?'

'Me? I'm all right. A few men died,' he replied, and was a little ashamed.

The chief Lama of Rongbuk Monastery: although he viewed the 1922 climbers as 'heretics', he supplied them with meat and tea.

I gave him a wooden tubful of breads and a new gold and copper image of Tara; I resolved to pray for his conversion to Buddhism. Then, as he left, as is the custom in Tibet, he took off his hat and said: 'Be seated, be seated,' and so saying went away.

After that, learning that there remained much roasted barley flour, rice and oil, etc in the places where the Britishers had stayed near the mountain, about 20 youngsters passed by secretly at midnight and arrived at the base of the mountain. From a cleft in the scree, seven bears came out. At first one man caught sight of them; after that they all saw them and in a great panic they all ran away. When they came back they asked: 'Is not this inauspicious sight terrible and will not our lives be harmed?'

I said, 'It is a sign that at the moment the guardian spirits of the valleys are not pleased. But if we do our prayer rituals in order, no harm will come.'

From the Chronicles of the Lama of Rongbuk Monastery, 1922.

Two frail mortals

by T. Howard Somervell

The second summit bid of the 1924 expedition was made by Major Edward Norton, a serving Army officer, and Howard Somervell, a surgeon in a London hospital. On the first attempt, Mallory and Bruce had established Camp V at 25,300 feet / 7,710 metres on the North Ridge. On 2 June, Somervell and Norton left the North Col with six porters, passing Mallory and Bruce on the way down. Climbing without supplementary oxygen, they reached Camp V that evening and prepared for their attempt. As well as writing about their climb, Somervell recorded it on a vest-pocket 'Autographic' Kodak camera, obtaining a remarkable sequence of pictures culminating in the highest photograph yet taken.

Howard Somervell, aged 34 in 1924, was the polymath of the expedition. As well as surgeon, photographer and mountaineer, he was a talented artist and musician with a love of literature. He and Mallory read Shakespeare to each other in their tent.

Norton and I settled down to melt snow for tonight's supper and tomorrow's breakfast, looking out from time to time at our porters bucketing down the mountainside, and far beyond them at a sunset all over the world, as it seemed – from the rosy fingers of Kangchenjunga in the east, past the far-distant peaks of mid-Tibet, separated from us by several complete ranges of mountains, to Gaurisankar and its satellites in the west, black against the red sky. I remember a curious sensation while up at this camp, as if we were getting near the edge of a field with a wall all round it – a high, insuperable wall. The field was human capacity, the wall human limitations. The field, I remember, was a bright and uniform green, and we were walking towards the edge – very near the edge now, where the whitish-grey wall said: 'Thus far, and no farther'. This almost concrete sense of being near the limit of endurance was new to me, and though I have often felt the presence of a Companion on the mountains who is not in our earthly party of climbers, I have only on this single occasion had this definite vision of limitation. With it I went to sleep, and slept remarkably well, though I woke up at 5 am with my extremely sore throat even worse than before, and with the unwelcome announcement by Norton that the cork had come out of the thermos flask and there was nothing for it but to melt some more snow and make more coffee.

So it was 6.40 am before we started, taking with us a few cardigans, a thermos flask of coffee and a vest-pocket Kodak: nothing else save ice-axes and a short rope.

The ground over which we started was easy but trying; scree, which slipped while we were trying to mount it, and rocks, which provided simple scrambling. It was intensely cold, but ahead of us we saw a patch of sunlight, and strained every nerve to reach this and get warm. There was one broad patch of snow across which Norton chipped steps, and once over this the slippery scree ended and we climbed for the rest of the day on rocks – easy rocks, though all the ledges sloped outwards and many of them were covered with small stones which made one feel rather insecure. The sun, however, was kind to us, and cheered us on our way. Even the wind was not so bad as it had been the day before. We had, in fact, the best possible weather conditions; if only we had not started on our climb already a couple of invalids, emaciated and enfeebled by the bad weather of the last few weeks.

About 700 or 800 feet above our camp the effects of height seemed to assert themselves quite suddenly. From going 300 feet or so of vertical height in an hour, we suddenly found ourselves cut down to little more than 100. From taking three or four breaths to a step we were reduced to having to take ten or more. Even then we had to stop at frequent intervals to get our breath. As Norton said in the account he wrote afterwards: 'Every five or ten minutes we had to sit down for a minute or two, and we must have looked

a sorry couple.' The imaginative reader must not picture a couple of stalwarts breasting the tape, but a couple of crocks slowly and breathlessly struggling up, with frequent rests and a lot of puffing and blowing and coughing. Most of the coughing, and probably most of the delay, came from me; Norton was, as ever, infinitely patient, and never so much as suggested that I was keeping him back. Finally, as we approached the level of 28,000 feet, the summit being only half a mile away or less, I felt that, as far as I was concerned, it was hopeless to continue. I told Norton that he had no chance of the summit with me. My throat was not only extremely painful, but was getting almost blocked up – why, I knew not. So, finding a suitable ledge on which to sit in the sun and pull myself together, I told Norton to go on. If the remainder of the mountain were as easy in general angle as what we had already done, there was no particular danger in climbing it alone; we two had not yet used the rope at all.

So, at 28,000 feet, I sat down and watched Norton. But he, too, was not far from the limit of his endurance, and after proceeding for some distance horizon-

tally, but not a hundred feet in vertical height above me, he stopped in the big couloir, looked at the rocks around its tip (which are rather steeper than we had thought) and turned back. Soon he was shouting to me to come on and bring a rope, as he was beginning to be snow-blind and could not see where to put his feet. So I went on and joined him, not forgetting to put a specimen of the rock from our highest point in my pocket. We roped up. Norton went down first and myself last, ready to hold him if at any time he slipped owing to his failing eyesight.

We sat down for a bit and worked out our chances of reaching the top – 900 feet above us, nine hours of climbing at our present rate, including the difficult bit that was just above Norton when he was at his nearest point to the summit, where two climbers, properly roped up, were essential for success and safety. Obviously, we could not get up to the top before midnight, and we realized that, in the moonless night which almost certainly required a few stops to find the way down, that meant almost certain death by freezing. We had been willing always to risk our lives, but we did not believe in throwing them away, so

The world from 25,000 feet: Somervell's photograph, one of the series he took during his attempt with Norton, shows the view to the north-west of Everest, dominated by the Rongbuk Glacier.

The highest photographs on earth: the picture right is Somervell's shot of the summit of Everest, taken at 27,000 feet with the vest-pocket Kodak camera shown above. Norton can be seen bent over his ice-axe as he struggles for breath. Somervell took another picture (far right) of the summit from just above 28,000 feet. Hardly able to breathe because of the obstruction in his throat, Somervell gave up at this point. But Norton, centre left, struggled on for another 100 feet before giving up. Somervell's photograph remained the highest taken by anyone on earth for the next 29 years.

we decided that we must go down the mountain and own ourselves beaten in fair fight. No fresh snow, no blizzards, no intense cold had driven us off the peak. We were just two frail mortals, and the biggest task Nature has yet set to man was too much for us. Moving slowly and resting frequently, and so far from normal that for the first time in my climbing experience I dropped my ice-axe, we carefully retraced our steps down the rocky ledges, Norton, in spite of his eyes, making no mistake nor slip.

One thing we had plenty of time to survey, and that was the view. In its extent it was, of course, magnificent. Great peaks that had towered over us with their impressive and snow-clad heads a week ago were now but so many waves on the ocean of mountains below us. Except for Everest itself there was nothing within view so high as we were ourselves. The colossal bastion of Cho Oyu and Gyachung Kang was a wall over which we could see the low limestone hills of Tibet, and far away in the distance beyond them a few snowy summits, maybe 200 miles away. Mountain peaks are nearly always at their best when one is below their level: but whilst they lose their individual glory when seen from above, there is an exhilaration about a view of tremendous extent such as was ours that day.

In a country which has the clearest atmosphere in the world, we were lucky in being up on Everest on an exceptionally clear day. We simply saw everything there *was* to see; the experience of a lifetime, but quite indescribable. At so great a height, one's psychical faculties are dulled, and, just as this amazing extent of landscape failed to give us its full impressiveness, so, when we turned from it to descend, we had but little feeling of disappointment that we could not go on. We realized that it would be madness to continue, and we were somehow quite content to leave it at that, and to turn down with almost a feeling of relief that our worst trials were over.

We called at our camp, and took away a tent-pole as a substitute for my axe. Below this, the going was easier, so we unroped. Alas, that we did so! Somewhere about 25,000 feet high, when darkness was gathering, I had one of my fits of coughing and dislodged something in my throat which stuck so that I could breathe neither in nor out. I could not, of course, make a sign to Norton, or stop him, for the rope was off now; so I sat in the snow to die whilst he walked on, little knowing that his companion was awaiting the end only a few yards behind him. I made one or two attempts to breathe, but nothing happened. Finally, I pressed my chest with both hands, gave one last almighty push – and the obstruction came up. What a relief! Coughing up a little blood, I once more breathed really freely – more freely than I had done

for some days. Though the pain was intense, yet I was a new man, and was soon going down at a better pace than ever to rejoin Norton. He had thought I was hanging back to make a sketch before the light went completely, and fortunately had not been worried. Shuffling along in the dark with the aid of an electric torch, we at last got into touch with Camp IV, for Mallory and Odell came out to meet us. Though the oxygen they carried for our use was a kind thought, it was not what we wanted at all; but the news they brought of Irvine in the camp below brewing hot tea and soup cheered us up and brought us home in good temper. What a contrast to our arrival in the same camp two years before, with Morshead not far from dying, and no food nor drink for us, nor any living soul nearer than Camp III. This time we entered the camp soon after 9 pm, and within an hour were warmed and fed and asleep.

The height Norton had reached was later calculated as 28,126 feet. In so doing, he had passed the mark set by George Finch in 1922 and set a record, the highest point achieved by any climber, which was to last until the first Swiss attempt of 1952. Norton was also the first to reach the giant gully, or couloir, which runs down the face from close to the foot of the summit pyramid. It was named the Norton Couloir, although it is often called the Great Couloir.

MT. EVEREST TRAGEDY.

Times—31/6/24

TWO CLIMBERS KILLED.

——

FATE OF MR. MALLORY AND MR. IRVINE.

The Mount Everest Committee have received with profound regret the following telegram from Lieut.-Colonel E. F. Norton, the leader of the expedition, dispatched from Phari Dzong on June 19, at 4.50 p.m.:—

"Mallory and Irvine killed on last attempt. Rest of party arrived at base camp all well."

The Committee have telegraphed to Colonel Norton expressing their deep sympathy with the expedition in the loss of their two gallant comrades, which must have been due to the most unfavourable conditions of weather and snow which have from the first arrival at the scene of operations impeded the climbing this year. The last message from Colonel Norton, dated May 26, told how the party had been driven out of their high camp for the second time by heavy snow. It seems probable that they had been able to return to the assault early in this month, and that the lamentable accident which has cost the lives of two of the best climbers occurred about June 6.

The tragic death of these two men—George Leigh Mallory, who alone of all those engaged in the present attempt had also taken part in the two previous expeditions, and A. C. Irvine, one of this year's band of recruits—is a terribly sad ending to the story of the assaults on the mountain that began three years ago. It is only a few days since we published Mr. Mallory's own account of the second reverse suffered by the present expedition.

About the middle of last month they had been driven back by the exceptional severity of the weather, "discomfited, but very far from defeated," from their first attempt to establish the chain of camps necessary for the final effort to reach the summit. After a very short stay at the base camp, for the rest that was indispensable after their exhausting labours, they returned once more to the charge, only to be driven back again by a blizzard, which lasted for 26 hours, and a temperature which for five nights averaged 50deg. of frost. It was this second attempt which Mr. Mallory, at Colonel Norton's request, so graphically described in the dispatch published on Monday last.

The story which he was commissioned to tell was that of the twofold operation carried out on May 24—the evacuation

The Riddle of Mallory and Irvine

The fate of Mallory and Irvine remains the most tantalizing of Everest mysteries. How far were they below the summit when last seen on 8 June 1924? Could they have reached the top – 29 years ahead of Hillary and Tenzing? How and where did they die? These are questions the mountaineering world has long pondered.

The pairing of Mallory and Irvine for the second summit bid of 1924 was an intriguing one. At 38, Mallory was manifestly the senior partner, and it was he who, to his colleagues' surprise, selected Irvine for the summit bid. A more dependable choice would have been the geologist Noel Odell, who was both fitter and more experienced, but Mallory favoured the 22-year-old undergraduate Andrew Irvine, an Oxford rowing Blue, both for his ingenuous enthusiasm and for his expertise with the hideously heavy oxygen apparatus they had decided to carry.

Four days after Norton and Somervell had retreated from their summit bid, Mallory and Irvine left the tenuous shelter of Camp VI at 26,800 feet. In a final note, Mallory declared that the oxygen was 'a bloody load for climbing' but that they had 'perfect weather for the job'. Climbing in support of Mallory and Irvine that day was Odell. At some 2,000 feet below the two men, he had seen nothing of them since leaving Camp V and during mid morning clouds drifted across their route on the North-east Ridge.

At 12.50 pm the clouds suddenly cleared. In a dispatch to *The Times* which has become one of the classic texts of mountaineering, Odell described what he saw:

'The entire Summit Ridge and final peak of Everest were unveiled. My eyes became fixed on one tiny black spot silhouetted on a small snow-crest beneath a rock step in the ridge; the black spot moved. Another black spot became apparent and moved up the snow to join the other on the crest. The first then approached the great Rock Step and shortly emerged at the top; the second did likewise. Then the whole fascinating vision vanished, enveloped in cloud once more.'

Mallory and Irvine were never seen again. Three days later, it fell to Odell to lay out a cross in the snow with sleeping-bags – the pre-arranged signal to his colleagues below that a catastrophe had occurred. Four days later, with heavy hearts, they cleared Base Camp and embarked on the long journey home.

Ever since then there has been speculation about the significance of Odell's sighting. Had Mallory and Irvine reached the summit or not? And what had happened to them afterwards? At first, Odell believed he had seen the two men surmount the Second Step, the prominent buttress at 28,200 feet on the North-east Ridge. As this was believed to be the last major obstacle, Odell concluded there was 'a strong possibility' that they had succeeded, only to die from a fall or from exhaustion and exposure during their descent.

Later Odell changed his mind. In this he was heavily influenced by reports from the next British expedition in 1933. Climbers who approached the Second Step found it a formidable obstacle: Percy Wyn Harris described it as a 'dark grey precipice, smooth and holdless'. Odell now accepted that it was doubtful whether Mallory and Irvine could have climbed it at all, let alone in the five minutes he had described, and concluded that he must have seen them on the First Step, some 300 feet lower down the ridge. This made it far less likely that Mallory and Irvine could have reached the summit as there would not have been enough time left that day to do so.

A second discovery in 1933 seemed to clinch the matter. Above Camp VI Percy Wyn Harris found an ice-axe, probably Irvine's, close to the

George Mallory and Andrew Irvine (right) on board the SS California *which carried the 1924 expedition from Liverpool to Bombay. When the time came for Mallory's summit attempt, most of his colleagues expected him to choose Noel Odell as his partner but Mallory opted for youth over experience in selecting Irvine instead. It was while climbing in support of Mallory and Irvine that Odell glimpsed them for the last time through a brief parting of the clouds shrouding the North-east Ridge. But were they on the First Step or the Second? The question was crucial in judging whether they could have reached the summit – but Odell could never be sure. The discovery of Irvine's ice-axe further down the ridge in 1933 seemed to show that they must have failed.*

Ice-Axe · First Step · Second Step

In a note written before he and Irvine left Camp VI on 8 June, Mallory advised the photographer, Captain John Noel, where he should look out for them (8pm is an obvious error for 8am). Two days earlier Noel Odell had taken the last photograph of Mallory (left) and Irvine as they set off from the North Col.

crest of the North-east Ridge and some 250 yards below the First Step. The best guess was that it marked the site of a fatal slip by one or both of the men during their descent. It appeared to follow that they must have failed, for if they had been on the First Step when last seen, they could not have reached the summit and returned to the site of the ice-axe before nightfall. Nor could they have reached the ice-axe location the following day as their primitive equipment would not have enabled them to survive a night out so high. The mountaineering world, Odell among them, reluctantly concluded that Mallory and Irvine must have met their deaths in gallant defeat.

There the matter rested for some 40 years. Then new perspectives were brought to bear. The first argument to be reconsidered concerned where Mallory and Irvine had last been sighted. For a long time the North-east Ridge had been barred to western mountaineers by virtue of the Chinese occupation of Tibet. But when western climbers finally reached the crest of the ridge they reported that when approached from above the Second Step was far less formidable than it appeared from below. They also looked along Odell's sight-path and reported that the Second Step fitted his description, while the First Step was scarcely in view.

The second issue to be re-examined was oxygen. One of the revisionists, American climber and writer Tom Holzel, recalled the hostility among colleagues of Mallory and Irvine to the use of oxygen, which they condemned as burdensome, unreliable and unethical (see page 101). He argued that this had led them to underestimate its benefits and produced calculations to show that the summit was within reach from above the Second Step after all. There was a twist to Holzel's theory, for he also argued that the two men must have split up as there was only enough oxygen left by then for one. He suggested that Mallory went on for the summit while Irvine retreated down the ridge. Both men died in separate falls, Mallory near the summit, Irvine at the point where his ice-axe was found.

Since then the controversy has raged. Holzel's opponents argued that it was deeply implausible to suggest that Mallory and Irvine would split up, since Mallory would never have abandoned his inexperienced partner. Others have countered that Mallory and Irvine need not have split up after all. Instead they could have pushed on for the summit together despite running out of oxygen, afterwards struggling back down the ridge only to fall at the site of the ice-axe find.

Holzel hoped that the argument could be resolved by finding the bodies of one or both men, perhaps with their camera intact which could contain the ultimate proof. Holzel even went to Everest himself to conduct a search, without success. There, for the moment, the matter rests.

THE WRONG MOUNTAIN

The headline says Everest; the photograph shows the distinctive West Ridge of Makalu, Everest's neighbour and the fifth highest mountain in the world. The Times later corrected its mistake. In the picture left, the leading Westland was photographed by the second plane as they reached Everest's summit.

OVER EVEREST
FIRST PICTURES OF THE HOUSTON MOUNT EVEREST FLIGHT

In March 1933 a new Everest expedition arrived in India. Equipped with two Westland biplanes fitted with plate cameras, its aim was to make the first flight over the mountain and obtain the first aerial photographs. The Westlands took off from 150 miles south of Everest on 3 April. As the leading pilot, Squadron Leader Lord Clydesdale, headed up to 31,000 feet, his navigator and photographer, Colonel Blacker, saw Everest appear as a 'tiny triangle of whiteness, so white as to appear incandescent'. An immense snow plume was streaming from its crest – the sign of 'a mighty wind raging across the summit'.

Blacker began exposing his plates, some through a floor hatch, others from the open cockpit. 'The scene was superb and beyond description,' he recalled. As the plane approached the South-west Face it hit a downdraught and plunged 2,000 feet.

Clydesdale managed to lift the plane

and cleared the summit by 100 feet. It was promptly caught in the snow-plume, ice fragments rattling into the cockpit. Undaunted, Blacker 'crammed plate after plate into the camera, releasing the shutter as fast as I could.'

The results were superb, some shots showing Everest rising above its neighbours, Makalu and Cho Oyu, others revealing the mountain's most intimate rock and snow scenery. The photographs were dispatched to *The Times*.

The outcome was somewhat unfortunate. On 24 April, *The Times* published the best of the photographs, the first captioned: 'a vivid impression of the awe-inspiring summit of Everest.' Filling the entire front page, however, was a picture not of Everest but of Makalu. Reports soon appeared elsewhere gleefully pointing out *The Times*'s mistake.

At first Clydesdale gallantly shouldered blame, saying that he might

have changed course to Makalu while Blacker was changing a plate, but Blacker was adamant he knew which mountain he had photographed. The mistake was corrected at an exhibition of the pictures which opened on 18 May. 'I want to assure everyone,' Blacker joked, 'that we did not go to the Andes'.

My nastiest moment

by Jack Longland

The four British expeditions of the 1930s were dispiriting affairs, beset by rows and battling against heavy snow and poor conditions. The most valiant bid came in 1933, when three climbers reached approximately 28,100 feet / 8,565 metres, the height achieved by Edward Norton in 1924. It was also in 1933 that Jack Longland faced the most alarming predicament of his mountaineering career. An experienced Alpinist, later to become a distinguished broadcaster, Longland, together with two companions and eight Sherpa porters, helped establish Camp VI at 27,500 feet / 8,380 metres on 29 May. Longland had set off to lead the Sherpas back to Camp IV when the group was hit by a storm.

We gave the party a day's rest, and then at 5 am on 28 May set off again up the weary ridge to Camp V. It is a slow grind up easy rocks and scree – easy, that is, if there's not a wind to throw you off your balance. Scree is always exhausting, for your feet slip back at every step. It's specially beastly above 24,000 feet, when each step needs three or four breaths. We must have looked a strange bunch of asthmatic crocks, but after five hours we had worked our way to the little sloping shelf, and found the tents at Camp V intact.

You don't stay long to admire the view at that height; after seeing the porters safely packed away, we crawled into our sleeping-sacks and started the laborious game of cooking. Cooking is a courtesy title – what we really did was to fill our cooking-pots with snow, and wait for an hour or more till the water grew faintly warm, and we could produce something that was a mockery of soup or tea. At that height even boiling water is not hot enough to scald your hand. Then an uncomfortable night, trying to keep warm inside double sleeping-sacks with all our clothes on. It must have been cold, because at 5 am when I tried to pour the water out of the vacuum flask that had been filled with lukewarm water the night before, several small pieces of ice came out with it. We found a bitter wind blowing outside, and decided to send the porters back to their tents, then cooked more warm drinks to fortify ourselves for the job ahead. At last, when the wind dropped a trifle and the sun was out, we set off at half-past eight.

We aimed to hit the long East Ridge of Everest near a tower at about 28,000 feet – the 'First Step'. The route took us over great slabs of outward-shelving rock, reminiscent of the tiles of a roof, and mostly coated with new snow and varied by belts of steep scree. We found no flat ledges to rest on, and there were long periods of difficult balancing where we had to depend on the friction of our bootnails against the smoothly sloping rock.

Birnie had to stay behind at Camp V – he'd crocked a leg. So I had to give up the idea of joining Wyn Harris and Wager in their attempt on the summit next day, and concentrate on seeing the porters safely down from Camp VI. On the way up Wyn Harris and Wager prospected the route, while I brought up the rear: but all the porters climbed magnificently, like seasoned mountaineers, on ground where a slip would often have been fatal. The going was treacherous, particularly where the rocks were covered with loose pebbles, and a slither would have been hard to check – and if it *wasn't* it would only have ended when you reached the glacier, 8,000 feet below.

At the end of every 50 minutes we called a ten-minute halt, and I could encourage the most exhausted porters when I had breath to spare to try out my few Nepalese phrases. I was as glad of the halts as they were, though they were carrying 10lbs or more on their backs and we were unloaded. At last, just about mid-day, we struggled up over a steeper band of yellowish rocks, and found a sloping snow-clogged ledge at about 27,500 feet. This was to be Camp VI – but there wasn't

even room to pitch our tent until the porters had cleared away the snow and built up a platform of small stones at the lower edge. Even then the tent sloped drunkenly downwards, and those who slept in it always found the man who had the upper berth slipping down on his companion during the night. Still, there it was – the final jumping-off place for the top, now not much more than 1,500 feet above. Our eight porters had done a magnificent piece of work. They had carried up the highest camp that has ever been pitched, 700 feet higher and nearly a quarter of a mile nearer the summit than a tent had been before – or since.

There wasn't much time for resting – the porters had to be got down to safety at Camp IV before night came. I remember catching a glimpse of the Rongbuk Monastery 10,000 feet below, and thinking how odd it was to see it across those great depths after nearly six weeks' absence. We set off just before one o'clock, after the briefest of goodbyes to Wyn Harris and Wager in their tent, and one final glance towards the summit,

which looked invitingly close.

I decided not to try and take the porters directly down the steep and slippery slabs by which we had climbed up from Camp V. Looking back, I have never blessed any decision more – if I had decided otherwise I doubt if I should be alive now. Instead we worked along horizontally, following a break in the steep Yellow Band and aiming to hit the top of the main North Ridge, which I thought would be safer for the tired porters to descend. As I was helping them down a steep section just before the ridge, I had a moment to look at the view. You are more than ordinarily stupid at that height – the brain is starved of oxygen, and so neither eyes nor ears nor any of the senses do their job properly. But I told myself that this was the best view I was ever likely to see, and managed to take in the fact that I was seeing peaks that must have been more than 250 miles away: and all the high summits that had looked so proud from Camp IV were now insignificant humps below.

Jack Longland set up Camp VI, perched on a narrow ledge 1,500 feet below the summit on the North Face, with the help of Percy Wyn Harris, Lawrence Wager and eight Sherpas. The group, minus one Sherpa, posed afterwards for a photograph in the safety of Base Camp. Wyn Harris, Wager and Longland are in the centre row, left to right.

The 1933 expedition suffered from atrocious weather which confined the climbers to their camps for weeks on end and helped cause a host of ailments, including laryngitis, gastric ulcers and pneumonia. Frost-bite was yet another problem: Frank Smythe's photograph (left) shows a climber examining a colleague's foot for symptoms. Smythe also took the photograph (right) of Camp V at 25,700 feet in deceptively good weather. It was to reach here a few days later that Longland and a Sherpa team battled for their lives through a storm.

These glimpses of the view had a sudden and nasty interruption. Without any warning that I remember a storm blew up out of the west. There were no more distant horizons – the most I could see was a snow-swept circle of 20 or 30 yards. A mountain storm is always unnerving, but its effect at 27,000 feet on cold and exhausted men is devastating. Worst of all I was responsible for the safety of eight men who had trustingly followed us to this height, and who had somehow to be got safely down to Camp IV. Even worse, we were now at the top of the North Ridge, and the whole length of it down to Camp V was entirely unknown to me, as our diagonal route of the morning had missed it out. That wouldn't have mattered on some ridges, even in an Everest hurricane, for a sharp ridge is easy to follow, even if you can't

see more than a few paces. But the North Ridge of Everest is broad and badly defined – you can miss the best way even in calm weather – and here I was trying to collect my wits and mountaineering experience to follow it correctly when it was all I could do to stagger downhill at all, and when all the rest of my mind was occupied with keeping the porters together, urging on the stragglers, and seeing that they kept away from the steep rocks where a fatal slip might occur.

The snow began to cover the holds on the rocks and give a slippery coating to the patches of scree, and the wind came in terrifying gusts, forcing us to cling or cower against the rocks to avoid being blown bodily away. My snow-goggles soon became useless, choked with snow. I took them off, only to find that eyelids and eyelashes coated up as well, forming an opaque film which had to be rubbed away every few minutes before I could peer out and get a glimpse of the next few yards.

Every ten minutes I called a halt to count up my band and collect them together, and then with a few shouted words of encouragement in what I hoped was Nepalese, off we pushed again, fighting our way down against the bitterly driving snow.

We had a moment's respite in the lee of a small cliff, where we happened on the tattered remains of a green tent. It must have been the old Camp VI from which Mallory and Irvine left in 1924 for their attempt on the summit. For a minute or two the least tired porters rummaged among the wreckage. One brought out a candle lantern and another an electric torch – the kind that worked with a press-button. Even after nine years of storm and cold the torch still worked, so we pushed on rather heartened by these signs of human occupation, many years old as they were.

But the finding of the 1924 tent gave me my nastiest moment. I had a photograph in my pocket on which the position of Mallory's camp was marked. I was going to use it to mark the position of our own new Camp VI for Smythe and Shipton, who were to follow up Wyn Harris and Wager if the first attempt failed. I pulled the photograph out of my pocket and discovered to my horror that Mallory's camp was marked as being not on the main North Ridge, but on a subsidiary spur further east. This must mean that, in spite of all my care, we were not on the main ridge, and worse still, this second spur ran out on steep ice-slopes overhanging the East Rongbuk Glacier thousands of feet below. If I led the party on to these slopes there was no escape – it would at best mean a night in the open, and to spend a night out at this height, even without a storm, would be fatal.

I had to think desperately quickly – and it was a problem I couldn't possibly share with the porters, though if I went wrong they were equally involved in an unpleasant death. Looking at the photograph again I saw that if we *were* on the wrong ridge, I ought soon to see signs of a steep ice couloir on the left. Equally, if I *wasn't* wrong, that couloir ought not to appear. So the next half-hour or more was full of desperate anxiety, as I peered through the snow expecting and yet hoping not to see that steep funnel of ice on my left. When minute after minute of painful stumbling and struggling with the wind went by and no couloir appeared, I began to hope that the marking of the photograph was wrong and that my mountain experience had led me right. It was a pretty desperate chance – nine times out of ten map or photograph is bound to be right, and the climber lost in a storm is as certainly wrong.

Meanwhile the storm was telling: the more exhausted porters were beginning to sit down, even between our frequent halts. It took a lot of urging to get them to their feet again – it was so much easier to lie down and die! And perhaps they were right – if I really was leading them down the wrong ridge, why not die quietly now rather than after hours of struggle and cold? That was the problem that made these two hours the worst I have spent – worse even than the storm and the effort of fighting on down against it.

All this time I was hoping for some pause in the storm – just a minute of clearer view which would give me a glimpse of the North Peak and a chance of fixing our position. I believe I carried my compass in my gloved hand during most of the descent, but without a single landmark to be seen beyond the driving snow it was as much use as a sick headache. The weaker porters were beginning to sit down more often now. More than once I had to lift a man up and set him going again: anything seemed better than continuing in the face of that unrelenting storm. Still I hoped it was the right ridge – surely, if I was wrong, we ought to have come to the tip of those ice-slopes by now. I don't remember much about the last bit of the descent – it was all slipping and staggering down icy screes and round little snowed-up cliffs. Then suddenly, down through the snow-scud, appeared a little patch of green. I rubbed the ice off my eyelashes and looked again: and it *was* a tent, three, four tents – the little cluster that meant Camp V and safety, and an end to the tearing anxiety of two hours.

Only two hours of storm – less than three since I'd left Wager and Wyn Harris at Camp VI; but I seemed to have crowded a lifetime of fear and struggle and responsibility into that short time. And it wasn't till a day or two later that I learnt that it was careless marking of the photograph that had made me think that Mallory's camp was not on the main North Ridge.

MIRAGES AT 28,000 FEET

by Frank Smythe

During my solitary climb two curious phenomena were experienced. The first was one that is by no means unique, and has been experienced in the past by solitary wanderers, not only on mountains but on desert wastes and in polar regions. All the time that I was climbing alone I had a strong feeling that I was accompanied by a second person. This feeling was so strong that it completely eliminated all loneliness I might otherwise have felt. It even seemed that I was tied to my 'companion' by a rope, and that if I slipped 'he' would hold me. I remember constantly glancing back over my shoulder, and once, when after reaching my highest point, I stopped to try and eat some mint cake, I carefully divided it and turned round with one half in my hand. It was almost a shock to find no one to whom to give it. It seemed to me that this 'presence' was a strong, helpful and friendly one, and it was not until Camp VI was sighted that the link connecting me, as it seemed at the time to the beyond, was snapped, and, although Shipton and the camp were but a few yards away, I suddenly felt alone.

Frank Smythe (with Himalayan lily, left) was one of the most prolific writers and photographers of pre-war mountaineering. He took part in all three principal Everest expeditions of the 1930s and in 1933 made a solo attempt on the summit, reaching just over 28,100 feet on the North Face and equalling Norton's height record from 1924. Smythe climbed without supplementary oxygen and later described the hallucinations which were to become familiar to other climbers at that altitude.

The second phenomenon may or may not have been an optical illusion – personally I am convinced that it was not. I was still some 200 feet above Camp VI and a considerable distance horizontally from it when, chancing to glance in the direction of the North Ridge, I saw two curious-looking objects floating in the sky. They strongly resembled kite-balloons in shape, but one possessed what appeared to be squat, under-developed wings, and the other a protuberance suggestive of a beak. They hovered motionless but seemed slowly to pulsate, a pulsation incidentally much slower than my own heart-beats, which is of interest supposing that it was an optical illusion. The two objects were very dark in colour and were silhouetted sharply against the sky, or possibly a background of cloud. So interested was I that I stopped to observe them. My brain appeared to be working normally, and I deliberately put myself through a series of tests. First of all I glanced away. The objects did not follow my vision, but they were still there when I looked back again. Then I looked away again, and this time identified by name a number of peaks, valleys and glaciers by way of a mental test. But when I looked back again, the objects still confronted me. At this I gave them up as a bad job, but just as I was starting to move again a mist suddenly drifted across. Gradually they disappeared behind it, and when a minute or two later it had drifted clear, exposing the whole of the North Ridge once more, they had vanished as mysteriously as they came.

It may be of interest to state that their position was roughly midway between the position of the 1924 Camp VI and the North-east Shoulder. Thus, they were at a height of about 27,200 feet, and as I was at about 27,600 feet when I saw them, a line connecting their approximate position with my position would not bring them against a background of sky, but against lower and distant mountains. It is conceivable, therefore, that it was some strange effect of mist and mountain magnified by imagination. On the other hand, it may have been a mirage.

The mad Yorkshireman

by Audrey Salkeld

During the British 1935 expedition, Charles Warren was resting on a rock in the upper East Rongbuk Glacier, waiting for his companions to catch up, when his eyes lit on a boot sticking out of the snow. Beside it was what he took to be the remains of a tent.

'I say,' Warren called, 'There's a perfectly good pair of Lawrie boots and a tent up here.' Only when Warren approached more closely did he see a body lying huddled in the snow. It had to be Maurice Wilson, dubbed 'the mad Yorkshireman',

who had disappeared while making an audacious solo attempt on Everest the previous year.

Wilson had made no secret of his plans. Born in Bradford in 1898, he had served with distinction in the trenches during the Great War, winning a Military Cross at Ypres, and surviving a spray of machine gun fire which left his left arm permanently weak. He had then embarked on a spell of globe-trotting, including several years in New Zealand. After recovering from a serious illness through a combination of fasting and

Wilson bought his Gipsy Moth, which he promptly named Ever-Wrest, before he could even fly. His feat in piloting it to India in 1933 was impressive enough but he overreached himself in making a solo bid to climb Everest.

prayer, he became imbued with a sense of divine purpose which convinced him he could climb Everest. True, he lacked the resources of the previous British attempts; but these would be more than compensated for by his faith and his belief in the power of the human mind.

'When I have accomplished my little work,' he declared, 'I shall be somebody. People will listen to me, and I shall be allowed to do the tests I want on the experimental machine I want to build.' (Beyond Everest lay an even grander project to ascend into the stratosphere.)

Just how Wilson intended to accomplish his feat seemed utterly far-fetched. He bought a second-hand Gipsy Moth which he christened *Ever-Wrest*. With this he intended to fly to Tibet, crash-land on Everest's lower slopes, then step out for the summit. It did not matter that he had never flown a plane or climbed a mountain in his life; he took a holiday in the Lake District and booked a course of flying lessons at the London Aero Club. He tested his nerve by making a parachute jump and to build up his stamina regularly walked from London to Bradford, where his parents lived.

By the spring of 1933, Wilson was almost ready. There was a last-minute hitch when he flew to Bradford to say goodbye to his parents, crashing en route and costing him a three-week delay. Then the British Air Ministry sent a telegram forbidding him to take off. Wilson tore it up and departed. After an impressive solo flight, he reached northern India two weeks later.

Here Wilson had to modify his plans. Having been definitively refused permission to fly over Nepal or Tibet, he sold the Gipsy Moth and headed for Darjeeling. There, early in 1934, he engaged three Sherpas and made his way to Tibet, travelling in disguise and often by night, arriving in the Rongbuk Valley in mid-April.

On 16 April, carrying a 45lb rucksack, Wilson embarked on his attempt. Nine days later,

With macabre regularity, Wilson's remains surface periodically from the slopes below the North Col. This photograph was taken in 1989 by Roger Mear.

defeated by storms and fatigue, he returned without even having reached the top of the East Rongbuk Glacier. He remained undaunted. 'I still know I can do it,' he wrote in his diary.

Eighteen days later Wilson tried again. This time two of his porters accompanied him to the traditional site of Camp III near the foot of the North Col. From there he made several fruitless attempts to surmount the Col. The Sherpas tried to persuade him to give up, in vain. On 31 May he set off for his last attempt. The final entry in his diary reads: 'Off again, gorgeous day'.

After finding Wilson's last remains a year later, Warren and his two companions, Eric Shipton and Edwin Kempson, wrapped his body in a tent and interred it in a crevasse. That night they sat together under an overhanging rock, reading aloud from Wilson's diary. The three men were moved by his account of his struggles. 'A moving and gallant document,' Kempson recalled. Warren called it 'an extraordinary documentary revelation of monomania and determination of purpose,' while Shipton declared: 'We cannot fail to admire his courage.'

Yet questions obtruded. If Wilson had set off for the North Col, how was it that he had died in his camp back on the Rongbuk Glacier? Where was his sleeping-bag, when most of his other equipment, including his notebook, rucksack, stove and Union Jack, was found in the snow beside him? And what of the Sherpas, supposedly camped a few hundred yards away? Had they not seen his hapless efforts to reach the North Col, or realized he was dying close by?

Some speculated that the Sherpas had retreated to wait for Wilson at a more amenable altitude. Perhaps they knew he had died but were so frightened of having lost their sahib that they did not tell the authorities the full story. Perhaps they even took his sleeping-bag for themselves.

Wilson has advocates, however, who believe he reached the North Col, maybe even higher, before being compelled to descend, abandoning his equipment en route. As with Mallory and Irvine, they hope that one day the missing items will be discovered to prove their case.

Mountaineers continue to stumble across Wilson's remains, spewed with macabre regularity from the glacier. His diary has a permanent home at the Alpine Club archives in London. It perhaps reveals the ultimate truth: that Wilson could never have returned from Everest empty-handed, obliged to admit that his faith had been unfounded.

ONE DAY MOUNT EVEREST WILL BE CLIMBED
by Eric Shipton

The wide interest which the Mount Everest expeditions aroused among the non-climbing public, the great confidence of each successive expedition in its ability to reach the summit and the fact that several parties have been forced to turn back when success was apparently almost within their grasp, have caused a good deal of perplexity and perhaps have made the repeated failures seem rather foolish. To see the matter in its true perspective it is well to remember that in spite of all the attempts that have been made during the last 60 years upon the giants of the Himalayas by climbers of many nations, not a single mountain of 26,000 feet has yet been climbed. Most prominent among these attempts were the repeated, desperate and sometimes disastrous German efforts to climb Kangchenjunga and Nanga Parbat. There were no fewer than five German expeditions to Nanga Parbat in the 1930s. On the first of these, in 1932, the climbers appeared to come so close to their goal that when I discussed the prospects of the second attempt in 1934 with the leader, he appeared to regard its success almost as a foregone conclusion, in much the same way as we had assessed our chances on Everest in 1933. It would seem almost as though there were a cordon drawn round the upper part of these great peaks beyond which no man may go. The truth, of course, lies in the fact that, at altitudes of 25,000 feet and beyond, the effects of low atmospheric pressure upon the human body are so severe that really difficult mountaineering is impossible and the consequences even of a mild storm may be deadly, that nothing but the most perfect conditions of weather and snow offer the slightest chance of success, and that on the last lap of the climb no party is in a position to choose its day.

In this connection it is not irrelevant

Eric Shipton made his prediction that Everest would eventually be climbed in Upon that Mountain, published in 1942. Seven years earlier a young Sherpa porter named Tenzing (third from left) had queued to sign on for his first Everest expedition.

to reflect upon the countless attempts to climb the Matterhorn before the summit was finally reached in 1865 – attempts by the best mountaineers, amateur and professional, of the day. Compare the two problems. The Matterhorn could be attempted on any day in each successive summer; attempts upon the summit of Everest have been launched on, at the most, two days of a few arbitrarily chosen years. The upper part of the Matterhorn could be reached in a single day from a comfortable hotel in the valley, so that the same party could set out day after day to attempt the climb, gaining personal knowledge and experience of the problem with each successive effort; no man has yet succeeded in making more than one attempt upon the summit of Everest in any one year – few have tried more than once in a lifetime. Climbing on the Matterhorn is an experience of supreme mental and physical enjoyment; mountaineering on the upper part of Everest is a heavy, lifeless struggle. The actual climbing on the Matterhorn is no more difficult than that on the last 2,000 feet of Everest. Today the Matterhorn is regarded as an easy climb for a competent party in reasonably good conditions. And yet year after year it resisted all the efforts of the pioneers to climb it; many proclaimed it to be unclimbable. It was certainly not that

these men were incompetent. The reason must be sought in that peculiar, intangible difficulty presented by the first ascent of any peak. How much more should we expect this factor to play a part in the defence of the great peaks of the Himalayas!

No, it is not remarkable that Everest did not yield to the first few attempts; indeed, it would have been very surprising and not a little sad if it had, for that is not the way of great mountains. Perhaps we had become a little arrogant with our fine new technique of ice-claw and rubber slipper, our age of easy mechanical conquest. We had forgotten that the mountain still holds the master card, that it will grant success only in its own good time. Why else does mountaineering retain its deep fascination?

It is possible, even probable, that in time men will look back with wonder at our feeble efforts, unable to account for our repeated failure, while they themselves are grappling with far more formidable problems. If we are still alive we shall no doubt mumble fiercely in our grey beards in a desperate effort to justify our weakness. But if we are wise we shall reflect with deep gratitude that we seized our mountaineering heritage, and will take pleasure in watching younger men enjoy theirs.

Great Couloir. They were all deep in powder snow as when I had last seen them in 1938.'

But the 'most remarkable and unexpected aspect of the view,' Shipton went on, was that he and Hillary could see the length of the Western Cwm and beyond, to the West Face of Lhotse, the South Col and the slopes between them. Guessing that the head of the cwm was around 23,000 feet, some 2,000 feet higher than they had predicted, they saw a 'perfectly straightforward route' to 25,000 feet on Lhotse and from there a traverse to the South Col. 'The sudden discovery of a practicable route from the West Cwm to the South Col was most exciting.'

There remained the small matter of the Icefall. For the next month, interspersed with trips to neighbouring valleys and peaks, the team probed for a route through. It was a daunting place, 'a wild labyrinth of ice-walls, chasms and towers', Shipton wrote, with hip-deep snow, rarely a clear view ahead, and constant apprehension that the

pinnacles around them would collapse or that the ice-blocks they walked on would drop away.

On their final foray, at the end of October, they reached the far side of the Icefall and were on the very lip of the Western Cwm, a sanctuary no human had ever visited, leading gently onwards to the heart of Everest and Nuptse. But it lay beyond reach for a giant crevasse blocked their way. Bill Murray considered the crevasse the biggest he had ever seen, between 100 feet and 300 feet wide, splitting the glacier from side to side, at least 100 feet deep, and with a sheer ice-wall on the far side. 'We were defeated,' Murray wrote, and the team withdrew.

Shipton himself concluded: 'The fact that we had climbed the Icefall without mishap made the decision all the more difficult. But there was nothing for it but to submit, hoping that we would get another chance in the spring.'

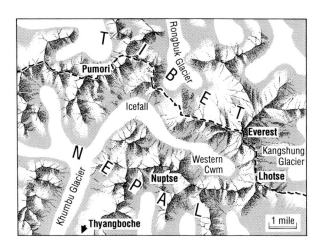

THE MYSTERY OF THE YETI

The 1951 reconnaissance expedition returned home not only with dramatic reports of a potential route to the summit; it also brought news of the yeti.

Otherwise known as the abominable snowman, the yeti had featured in Himalayan folklore for centuries. Stories of a creature, half-human, half-beast, which inhabited the kingdom of the snows were embedded in legends of the mountain kingdoms of Tibet and Nepal. 'Yeti' is a Nepalese word, while its alternative name derives from an imaginative translation of the Tibetan *metohkangmi* – literally 'filthy snowman'. There had been tales of the yeti from Himalayan travellers but most were second-hand and none had any satisfactory evidence.

This time it was different: for the 1951 expedition had photographs. The principal picture appeared quite convincing. It showed, clearly delineated in the snow, the single footprint of a creature with a large outer toe, three smaller ones alongside, and a well-defined heel. Judged against the head of an ice-axe, it measured 13 inches by 8 inches. There was a second photograph showing a line of footprints in the snow. They were published in *The Times* on 6 December 1951 under the dramatic headlines: FOOTPRINTS OF THE 'ABOMINABLE SNOWMAN'.

Of all the purported evidence of the existence of the yeti, the 1951 footprints remain the single most persuasive item. But are they all they seem? When zoologists scrutinized the photographs, they found it hard to imagine what kind of creature could have left such tracks. The Natural History Museum suggested they could have been made by a giant monkey; another expert theorized that the creature in question was a cross between an ape and a bear – a species as yet unknown. Other curiosities intruded: from the print in the snow it appeared that the ball of the creature's foot was concave, whereas in all known bipeds, including humans, it is convex.

Those who doubted the authenticity of the prints have focused their attentions on the man who took the photographs, Eric Shipton. Renowned for his part in the attempts of the 1930s, Shipton attracted respect and controversy in equal measure. He had led the 1951 reconnaissance and was originally nominated to lead the 1953 bid. But his lack of organizational abilities and his prejudice against large expeditions told against him, and he was replaced by John – later Lord – Hunt.

Shipton was renowned for a mischievous sense of humour and for his liking for travellers' tales. Among his adversaries was the geologist Noel Odell, a colleague on the 1938 expedition. Shipton liked to tell how in 1924 Odell had collected some rock specimens which, befuddled by altitude, he had mistaken for sandwiches: the story, Odell said later, was 'complete nonsense'. Shipton also told of finding a notorious 'sex diary' beside the body of the solo climber Maurice Wilson; that too has proved untrue.

The sceptics suspect, in short, that Shipton fabricated the crucial 1951 print. There *was* a line of prints in the snow that day, made by a conventional animal such as a goat. By the sceptics' theory, Shipton embellished one of these prints, adding the thumb-like big toe, and etching the outline of the heel. He had conceived it as a joke on his colleagues but once the photographs had been published in *The Times* it was too late to admit the truth.

Curiously, no one remarked at first on the fact that the single print was markedly different from the prints in the line of tracks. Shipton himself ignored this difference in his own writings, but when finally challenged claimed that the pictures had been wrongly captioned by *The Times*.

Shipton's contemporaries are divided in their views. Two colleagues from the expedition, Bill Murray and Dr Mike Ward, insist that he would not have perpetrated such a hoax; others, such as Sir Edmund Hillary, believe he could have done so. Shipton himself supplied a wry and possibly revealing comment in his account of the footprints for *The Times*. He conceded that they had 'aroused a certain amount of public excitement' but added that it was 'interesting, and perhaps a little sad, that the British Museum appears to have taken the matter more seriously than the Society for Psychical Research.'

The picture (left) shows Mike Ward against a clear line of tracks; but the tracks are markedly different from the close-up of a supposed single footprint, shown beside an ice-axe (right).

A new world

by Raymond Lambert

The first climbers to take advantage of the Western Cwm approach, pioneered in 1951, were the Swiss, awarded permission by the Nepalese Government in 1952. Having tried to stage an expedition since the 1920s, the Swiss seized their chance. After camping by the Khumbu Glacier they pushed a route through the hazardous Icefall, becoming the first humans to stand in the Western Cwm. They climbed the Lhotse Glacier to reach the next historic landmark, the South Col, from where they embarked on their summit bid on 27 May. There were four men in the summit party: Raymond Lambert, an outstanding Alpinist, climbing with Tenzing Norgay, the Sirdar (leader) of the expedition Sherpas, who had been to Everest three times with the British; and the all-Swiss pair of René Aubert and Léon Flory.

The Khumbu Icefall, shown in Doug Scott's 1972 photograph (left), was the barrier which stopped the British in 1951. Perpetually shifting, scored by monstrous crevasses, it has presented a perpetual hazard since. After negotiating it safely in 1952, the Swiss prepared for a summit bid headed by Raymond Lambert (left in picture, right) and Tenzing, who had added Norgay – 'the fortunate one' – to his name.

At ten in the morning, after the three Sherpas had vanished beyond the hump above the Col, we set out on two ropes of two men each, Aubert and Flory, Tenzing and myself, carrying one tent and food for one day. As soon as we left the zone of ice and stone, we broke into sheets of crusted snow. We made towards the base of the South-east Ridge, at the foot of a large rock buttress. The weather was clear, the intensity of the wind had diminished, as if it concentrated its anger upon the col itself.

Having reached the foot of the buttress, we were disillusioned. It was too steep. The rocks that overlooked us were undoubtedly negotiable at 13,000 feet, but not at 26,000 feet. Flory and Aubert pushed on 100 yards to make sure that the Eastern Face offered no way out, and they ran up against a slope of more than 60 degrees, which vanished into the sky.

So we returned in our steps, moved along the base of the large buttress and attacked the couloir which runs down it. The snow was good and the ascent easy. We made steps between the snow and the rock. We constantly relieved each other in the lead, we gained height quickly and the tents on the col already seemed small. Soon we reached the top of the couloir but the dry rocks allowed us to continue by moving over to the right. We waited for Aubert and Flory while taking oxygen like some precious liqueur; then we continued the climb straight up.

Suddenly I emerged on to the ridge above the large buttress and there discovered a new world, the whole Eastern Face of the mountain, plunging for more than 16,000 feet to the Kharta Valley and Tibet. And in the mist, on the far horizon, other chains of mountains broke through. Behind us the summit of Lhotse had fallen away; it was now no more than 300 or 400 feet above us. We were at about 27,500 feet.

It was fine and there was no wind. Both of us were fit. Should we sleep there without a primus and without sleeping-bags? Perhaps the next day . . .? Tenzing interrupted my reflections.

'Sahib, we ought to stay here tonight!' He indicated the tent he had been carrying since the start. I smiled, for our thoughts had been pursuing the same course.

Flory and Aubert joined us. Like us they were in good shape. They too might stay and try their luck the next day. This is doubtless what they desired. But

It took the Swiss five days to find a route through the Icefall. After passing through a couloir menaced by avalanches which they called 'Suicide Passage', they came to the giant crevasse just below the Western Cwm which stopped the British in 1951. They climbed down 60 feet into it and crossed it via a snow bridge, and then erected a rope bridge (above) which proved precarious but effective. Four weeks later they climbed to 26,000 feet on Lhotse and then, with Everest's South-east Ridge looming before them (picture far right), began the descending traverse to the South Col.

there was only one tent and very little food. We had only set out to make a reconnaissance and to fix the site of Camp VII. In an undertaking like that, the party matters more than the individual; the individual is nothing without the party. In order that the privileged pair should have not only a chance of success but a possibility of returning, it has to be supported at the last camp by the second pair. Though its task might appear to be less brilliant, it needs men who are just as determined and in equally good physical shape – perhaps in better shape, since they should be capable of going to seek and bring back, whatever the risk, those who have taken their lives in their hands.

Between the four of us there was no argument. Aubert, who was one of those who found and saved me in the Combe Maudite in 1938, and Flory, reliable, cautious and determined, agreed to leave us. 'You two stay. We will wait for you at the col.'

We watched them move off, growing smaller and ever smaller down the slope, until they reached the col an hour later. Now we were only two! How many men and how much effort had been necessary to bring us to this farthest point of the expedition!

We pitched our tent with great difficulty. The altitude and the wind made our movements awkward. Our legs would not obey us and our brains scarcely functioned. Our hands were more skilful without gloves, but to take them off would cost us dear. The sun had gone down behind Nuptse and the temperature fell instantly. We took a last look towards Kangchenjunga and Tibet. Tenzing extended an arm westwards, pointing to a disquieting sea of clouds. The horizon reddened.

In this improvised bivouac there were no sleeping-bags, no equipment, no primus. Only a tent which slapped in the wind like a prayer-flag. It was a glacial

night. The whole being curled up as if seeking to create a mattress of air between its skin and itself. Our muscles stiffened and those of the face became fixed as if from an injection of anaesthetic. Slowly the cold penetrated the bones themselves. There was no question of sleep: the wind and the growling avalanches kept us awake. Which was just as well.

We were overtaken by a consuming thirst, which we could not appease. There was nothing to drink. An empty tin gave us an idea: a fragment of ice and the candle-flame produced a little lukewarm water. The gusts of wind made our heads whirl; it seemed to us that we took off with them into space, like those houses one thinks one sees moving when watching clouds in flight. To resist this vertigo, I tried to fix my thoughts on the next day's attack, and I mused on those who at all the stages were thinking of us: Aubert and Flory at the col, Dittert at Camp V, Wyss at the Base Camp. In a state of semi-hallucination the entire expedition seemed to me to be a stretched bow and ourselves the arrow. A poor blunted arrow at that. Could it reach its target?

This was the boundary between waking and sleeping. I dared not sleep, must not sleep. Tenzing shook me and I awoke, and I shook him in my turn. Amicably we beat one another and pressed close together throughout the night. In the sky the stars were so brilliant that they filled me with fear.

The shadows became clearer. The shape of Tenzing, rolled up like a ball, began to stand out from the background of the tent-cloth, which gradually grew lighter. Dawn entered the half-open tent and with it came anxiety. The wind hurled a handful of ice-needles into my face. Nevertheless, we had to open our eyes. The weather was not reassuring, for the sky was clear to the north, but very dark to the west and south. The summits of Lhotse and Nuptse were hidden in a mass of dark clouds, and the valley was drowned in fog.

What should we do? We looked at each other, undecided, but once more we understood each other without speaking. I indicated the ridge with a wink and Tenzing answered by nodding his head. We had gone too far to give up. Our preparations were quickly made, for we had worn everything, except the crampons, from fear of frost-bite. They took longer to put on again, for our numbed hands were clumsy and bending over literally took our breath away. Laden with the last three canisters of oxygen, sufficient for six hours, we set off below the ridge on sheets of snow broken by bands of rock. One step, three breaths, one step . . . when we rested for a moment, we slobbered at the inhaler; it could only be used during a halt because the resistance of the valves was too great for our lungs when the effort of moving was added. At about every 20 yards we relieved each other in the lead to economize our strength and in order to inhale while letting the other pass. When the slope steepened we advanced like dogs following a scent, sometimes on all fours.

But the weather grew worse. Waves of mist passed, carried along on the south-west wind. Showers lashed at us in passing, leaping over the crest. Then the sun reappeared and reassured us. We rose slowly, terribly slowly. Nevertheless, we still rose.

In the clear intervals Lhotse emerged from the storm clouds and it was already below us. The whole landscape and all the summits fell away. The peaks which had seemed monstrous from the lower camps had lost their splendour; they became hills, like the Verte or the Jorasses, seen from Mont Blanc. But the clear intervals did not last; the dense fog, filled with a drift of frozen snow, enveloped us again. All our vital functions were slowed down. There was a confused impression of being on some other planet. Asphyxia destroyed our cells and our whole beings deteriorated.

At about eleven o'clock we came out again, on to the ridge, sinking deeply into the wind-crusted snow. There were no technical difficulties; the slope was rather easy and not too steep. We were rather fearful of the cornices to our right and we instinctively kept our distance.

Our pace became still slower. Three steps, a halt, oxygen. Three steps, a halt. Then came a clearing and we saw that the South Summit was at least 200 metres above us. Three steps, oxygen. I watched Tenzing. He seemed well but at moments he swayed a little, trying to find his balance. I tried to keep a watch on myself and asked myself: 'How do you feel? All right, quite all right.' This was euphoria, the worst of all dangers. I remembered the fifth and last bivouac on the Aiguilles du Diable: there, too, I felt well. How did Mallory and Irvine feel when they dissolved into the rarefied air of the North Ridge? Was this not the reason why they did not return?

Granulated snow struck our left cheeks increasingly hard. The wind became more evil. The South Summit was so close: just this band of rock where we were now engaged, the last; just that snow-crest. But no; it was impossible to go on. This was the end. We had taken five hours to gain 200 metres.

Once more the decision was taken without words. One long look and then the descent. Was it an altitude record? No. Failure. That is what we thought. But did we think? Our bodies were of lead, almost without spirit. There was no trace of automatism, for our muscles no longer obeyed our orders. Pick up your

left foot and put it in front; now the other. Our tracks had almost entirely vanished. We stopped as often as on the ascent.

We passed the tent. The wind had begun to do its work; it was torn in two places. Would it last till the others could occupy it?

'Leave it there. Perhaps they will have better luck than us.'

And we went on, kept in motion only by the will to resist the lethargy that was invading us. We crouched as we dragged along, descending the couloir and the slope towards the col.

From the col to the tents there were a dozen yards uphill, an insignificant hummock of snow. We could do no more. Flory and Aubert dragged us into our tents, inert, at the limit of exhaustion. Tenzing sank into a deep sleep and did not move until the hour of departure.

For us the adventure was ended.

It seemed like a lifetime

by Sir Edmund Hillary

After the Swiss failure of 1952, the British prepared their bid – to take place in Coronation year – with due determination. The mercurial Eric Shipton, who had headed the 1951 reconnaissance, was replaced as leader by Colonel John Hunt, an experienced Himalayan mountaineer and a brilliant organizer. After finding a new route through the ever-shifting Icefall, the team traversed the South Face of Lhotse to reach the South Col, while support climbers and Sherpas ferried equipment, supplies and oxygen behind them. On 26 May Tom Bourdillon and Charles Evans pushed beyond the Swiss high point to the South Summit, at 28,750 feet less than 300 feet below the final summit. Two days later the second assault began. George Lowe, Alf Gregory and Ang Nyima carried supplies up the South-east Ridge, followed by the New Zealand bee-keeper Ed Hillary and Tenzing Norgay, by now an Everest veteran. After helping to find a precarious camp site at 27,900 feet / 8,500 metres, the support climbers returned to the South Col, leaving Hillary and Tenzing to await the dawn.

An Everest icon: Charles Evans photographed by Tom Bourdillon at the South Summit of Everest, the first climbers ever to reach it. No more than 300 feet above them, the final summit seemed tantalizingly close, but they were too tired to go on.

At 4 am it was very still. I opened the tent door and looked far out across the dark and sleeping valleys of Nepal. The icy peaks below us were glowing clearly in the early morning light and Tenzing pointed out the Monastery of Thyangboche, faintly visible on its dominant spur 16,000 feet below us. It was an encouraging thought to realize that even at this early hour the Lamas of Thyangboche would be offering up devotions to their Buddhist gods for our safety and well-being.

We started up our cooker and in a determined effort to prevent the weaknesses arising from dehydration we drank large quantities of lemon juice and sugar, and followed this with our last tin of sardines on biscuits. I dragged our oxygen sets into the tent, cleaned the ice off them and then completely rechecked and tested them. I had removed my boots, which had become a little wet the day before, and they were now frozen solid. Drastic measures were called for, so I cooked them over the fierce flame of the Primus and despite the very strong smell of burning leather managed to soften them up. Over our down clothing we donned our windproofs and on to our hands we pulled three pairs of gloves – silk, woollen and windproof.

At 6.30 am we crawled out of our tent into the snow, hoisted our 30lb of oxygen gear on to our backs, connected up our masks and turned on the valves to bring life-giving oxygen into our lungs. A few good deep breaths and we were ready to go. Still a little worried about my cold feet, I asked Tenzing to move off and he kicked a deep line of steps away from the rock bluff which protected our tent out on to the steep powder snow-slope to the left of the main ridge. The ridge was now all bathed in sunlight and we could see our first objective, the South Summit, far above us. Tenzing, moving purposefully, kicked steps in a long traverse back towards the ridge and we reached its crest just where it forms a great distinctive snow-bump at about 28,000 feet. From here the ridge narrowed to a knife-edge and as my feet were now warm I took over the lead.

We were moving slowly but steadily and had no need to stop in order to regain our breath, and I felt that we had plenty in reserve. The soft unstable snow made a route on top of the ridge both difficult and dangerous, so I moved a little down on the steep left side where the wind had produced a thin crust which sometimes held my weight but more often than not gave way with a sudden knock that was disastrous to both balance and morale. After several hundred feet of this rather trying ridge, we came to a tiny hollow and found there the two oxygen bottles left on the earlier attempt by Evans and Bourdillon. I scraped the ice off the gauges and was greatly relieved to find that they still contained several hundred litres of oxygen

- sufficient to get us down to the South Col if used very sparingly. With the comforting thought of these oxygen bottles behind us, I continued making the trail on up the ridge, which soon steepened and broadened into the very formidable snow face leading up for the last 400 feet to the Southern Summit. The snow conditions on this were, we felt, distinctly dangerous, but as no alternative route seemed available, we persisted in our strenuous and uncomfortable efforts to beat a trail up it. We made frequent changes of lead on this very trying section and on one occasion as I was stamping a trail in the deep snow a section around me gave way and I slipped back through three or four of my steps. I discussed with Tenzing the advisability of going on and he, although admitting that he felt very unhappy about the snow conditions, finished with his familiar phrase 'Just as you wish'. I decided to go on.

It was with some relief that we finally reached some firmer snow higher up and then chipped steps up the last steep slopes and cramponned on to the South Peak. It was now 9 am. We looked with some interest at the virgin ridge ahead. Both Bourdillon and Evans had been depressingly definite about its problems and difficulties and we realized that it could form an almost insuperable barrier. At first glance it was certainly impressive and even rather frightening. On the right, great contorted cornices, overhanging masses of snow and ice, stuck out like twisted fingers over the 10,000 foot drop of the Kangshung Face. Any move on to these cornices could only bring disaster. From the cornices the ridge dropped steeply to the left until the snow merged with the great rock face sweeping up from the Western Cwm. Only one encouraging feature was apparent. The steep snow-slope between the cornices and the rock precipices seemed to be composed of firm, hard snow. If the snow proved soft and unstable, our chances of getting along the ridge were few indeed. If we could cut a trail of steps along this slope, we could make some progress at least.

We cut a seat for ourselves just below the Southern Summit and removed our oxygen. Once again I worked out the mental arithmetic that was one of my

On 28 May came Hillary and Tenzing's turn. Photographed high on the South-east Ridge during their attempt, they made a powerful team: the phlegmatic and unassuming Hillary, 33, and Tenzing Norgay, at 39 making his seventh trip to the mountain.

Tenzing to belay me as best he could, I jammed my way into this crack, then kicking backwards with my crampons I sank their spikes deep into the frozen snow behind me and levered myself off the ground. Taking advantage of every little rock hold and all the force of knee, shoulder and arms I could muster, I literally cramponned backwards up the crack, with a fervent prayer that the cornice would remain attached to the rock. Despite the considerable effort involved, my progress although slow was steady, and as Tenzing paid out the rope I inched my way upwards until I could finally reach over the top of the rock and drag myself out of the crack on to a wide ledge. For a few moments I lay regaining my breath and for the first time really felt the fierce determination that nothing now could stop us reaching the top. I took a firm stance on the ledge and signalled to Tenzing to come on up. As I heaved hard on the rope Tenzing wriggled his way up the crack and finally collapsed exhausted at the top like a giant fish when it has just been hauled from the sea after a terrible struggle.

I checked both our oxygen sets and roughly calculated our flow rates. Everything seemed to be going well. Probably owing to the strain imposed on him by the trouble with his oxygen set, Tenzing had been moving rather slowly but he was climbing safely, and this was the major consideration. His only comment on my enquiring of his condition was to smile and wave along the ridge. We were going so well at three litres per minute that I was determined now if necessary to cut down our flow rate to two litres per minute if the extra endurance was required.

The ridge continued as before. Giant cornices on the right, steep rock slopes on the left. I went on cutting steps on the narrow strip of snow. The ridge curved away to the right and we had no idea where the top was. As I cut around the back of one hump, another higher one would swing into view. Time was passing and the ridge seemed never-ending. In one place, where the angle of the ridge had eased off, I tried cramponning without cutting steps, hoping this would save time, but I quickly realized that our margin of safety on these steep slopes at this altitude was too small, so I went on step-cutting. I was beginning to tire a little now. I had been cutting steps continuously for two hours, and Tenzing, too, was moving very slowly. As I chipped steps around still another corner, I wondered rather dully just how long we could keep it up. Our original zest had now quite gone and it was turning more into a grim struggle. I then realized that the ridge ahead, instead of still monotonously rising, now dropped sharply away, and far below I could see the North Col and the Rongbuk Glacier. I looked upwards to see a narrow snow ridge running up to a snowy summit. A few more whacks of the ice-axe in the firm snow and we stood on top.

My initial feelings were of relief – relief that there were no more steps to cut, no more ridges to traverse and no more humps to tantalize us with hopes of success. I looked at Tenzing and in spite of the balaclava, goggles and oxygen mask all encrusted with long icicles that concealed his face, there was no disguising his infectious grin of pure delight as he looked all around him. We shook hands and then Tenzing threw his arm around my shoulders and we thumped each other on the back until we were almost breathless. It was 11.30 am. The ridge had taken us two and a half hours, but it seemed like a lifetime.

THE GREAT MYSTERY
by Tenzing Norgay

The crowning moment: Tenzing Norgay on the summit of Everest, holding aloft his ice-axe bearing the flags of the United Nations, Britain, Nepal and India. This was the second of three summit photographs of Tenzing taken by Hillary – 'hoping that one would come out'. Tenzing wrote afterwards that he had offered to take Hillary's photograph, but Hillary declined.

I have thought much about what I will say now – of how Hillary and I reached the summit of Everest. Later, when we came down from the mountain, there was much foolish talk about who got there first. Some said it was I, some Hillary. Some that only one of us got there – or neither. Still others, that one of us had to drag the other up. All this was nonsense. And in Kathmandu, to put a stop to such talk, Hillary and I signed a statement in which we said 'we reached the summit almost together'. We hoped this would be the end of it. But it was not the end. People kept on asking questions and making up stories. They pointed to the 'almost' and said, 'What does that mean?' Mountaineers understand that there is no sense to such a question; that when two men are on the same rope they are *together*, and that is all there is to it. But other people did not understand. In India and Nepal, I am sorry to say, there has been great pressure on me to say that I reached the summit before Hillary. And all over the world I am asked, 'Who got there first? Who got there first?'

Again I say, 'It is a foolish question. The answer means nothing.' And yet it is a question that has been asked so often – that has caused so much talk and doubt and misunderstanding – that I feel, after long thought, that the answer should be given. As will be clear, it is not for my own sake that I give it. Nor is it for Hillary's. It is for the sake of Everest and the generations after us. 'Why,' they will say, 'should there be a mystery to this thing? Is there something to be ashamed of? To be hidden? Why can we not know the truth?' . . . Very well: now they will know the truth. Everest is too great, too precious, for anything but the truth.

A little below the summit Hillary and I stopped. We looked up. Then we went on. The rope that joined us was 30 feet long, but I held most of it in loops in my hand, so that there was only six feet between us. I was not thinking of 'first' and 'second'. I did not say to myself, 'There is a golden apple up there. I will push Hillary aside and run for it.' We went on slowly, steadily. And then we were there. Hillary stepped on top first. And I stepped up after him.

So there it is – the answer to the 'great mystery'. And if, after all the talk and argument, the answer seems quiet and simple I can only say that that is as it should be. Many of my own people, I know, will be disappointed at it. They have given a great and false importance to the idea that it must be I who was 'first'. These people have been good and wonderful to me, and I owe them much. But I owe more to Everest –

and to the truth. If it is a discredit to me that I was a step behind Hillary, then I must live with that discredit. But I do not think it was that. Nor do I think that, in the end, it will bring discredit on me that I tell the story. Over and over again I have asked myself, 'What will future generations think of us if we allow the facts of our achievement to stay shrouded in mystery? Will they not feel ashamed of us – two comrades in life and death – who have something to hide from the world?' And each time I asked it the answer was the same: 'Only the truth is good enough for the future. Only the truth is good enough for Everest.'

Now the truth is told. And I am ready to be judged by it. We stepped up. We were there. The dream had come true. . . .

The Chinese described their 1975 ascent as extravagantly as in 1960. The summit party (above) 'demonstrate the heroism of the Chinese people, for whom there are no unscalable heights or unvanquishable fortresses.'

After a short stay on the summit, we started to descend. The great excitement overshadowed our extreme fatigue. We were worried about our comrade Liu Lien-man. The day was breaking when we came down from the snow-covered slope. In the distance we could see Liu Lien-man still there alive. We learned that after we had departed, Liu found out that he still had some oxygen left, but he didn't take any for himself. He thought of his comrades battling towards the summit of Chomolungma, and wrote in his diary that the oxygen was reserved specially for them. Finally

he fell into a state of semi-consciousness. As soon as we found out what he had done, and as he offered us his breathing apparatus and a piece of candy which he had saved for a long time, we were all moved to tears by his noble character and embraced him and kissed him. Soon the red sun rose slowly from the east behind the mountains, and shed its shining rays upon us. Ah, it was the shining light of our motherland! It was the shining light of the Party and Chairman Mao Tse-tung. It was the Party and Chairman Mao Tse-tung who gave us boundless strength and wisdom.

RIDICULOUSLY FAR-FETCHED?

The Chinese portrayed their ascent of Everest in 1960 as a triumph not merely of the human spirit but also of a political system. 'Summing up our conquest of Everest,' wrote expedition leader Shih Chan-Chun, 'we must in the first place attribute our victory to the leadership of the Communist Party and the unrivalled superiority of the socialist system of our country.'

It was in part assertions like these – even more ideological in content than the account by the summiteers, Wang Fu-chou and Chu Yin-hua – that inspired unrestrained scepticism among western mountaineers over whether the Chinese had reached the summit at all. 'Propaganda is always suspect,' snorted the *Alpine Journal.*

The Chinese accounts were deficient in other respects valued by mountaineers. It seemed inherently unlikely that a series of high-altitude Party meetings could compensate for the apparent inexperience of the climbers. It also seemed improbable that the Chinese party should have managed to climb through the cold and darkness of night to reach the summit. Whether or not the propaganda was to blame, all the accounts were short on technical details. Nor was there a summit photograph – although that was a self-fulfilling corollary of the Chinese claim to have finished their ascent in the dark. A further commentary in the *Alpine Journal* concluded that 'the Chinese claim, though not impossible, must be considered as non-proven.'

Over the years, however, the mountaineering world has softened its view. There had been doubts over a photograph which the Chinese had said was taken soon after dawn at 8,700 metres during their descent; on closer analysis, their claim proved credible. The Chinese account of reaching the summit in semi-darkness without oxygen seemed far more likely when western climbers accomplished the same

GUARDIAN

Wednesday September 5 1962

Price 4d

The Chinese looking at the remains of Camp 5 used by the British expedition in 1933

Everest climbers of 1933 say Chinese claim unsure

NO DETAILS OF CRITICAL STEPS

BY OUR OWN REPORTER

Three British veterans of the North face of Mount Everest agreed last night that the film the Chinese claim records a successful assault on the mountain does not, in fact, substantiate that claim. On the evidence of the film alone, the verdict must remain "not proven."

Sir Percy Wyn-Harris, former Governor of Gambia, Professor Lawrence Wager, of the chair of geology at Oxford, and Mr Jack Longland, director of education for Derbyshire, saw the film at a special showing arranged by the "Guardian" in London last night.

To refresh their memories of their own climb in 1933 (Sir Percy alone of the three returned to Everest in 1936) they also saw film taken during that attempt.

The two sets of film tallied right up to the point where the fifth camp of the 1933 expedition was reached by the Chinese. Their film showed the ruins of the camp, which the earlier film showed the British mountaineers repitching.

The Guardian's front-page story reflected scepticism over the 1960 ascent. But most experts later accepted the Chinese claim, and the summit climbers appear in official lists of ascents.

feats. Then there was Chu Yin-hua's heroic tale of removing his boots and socks to climb the Second Step: surely not even the most determined Party member would take self-sacrifice to such lengths. That, too, became plausible when he showed visiting American climbers his toe-less feet. Finally Chris Bonington went to Peking and talked at length with the 1960

leader, Shih Chan-Chun, returning to declare that he had 'no shadow of a doubt' about the Chinese ascent.

Some western authorities remained sceptical, even when the Chinese claimed a second ascent in 1975. *Mountain* magazine described this as 'ridiculously far-fetched' but the last word was with the Chinese. Four months later the British South-west Face expedition reached the summit to find a six-foot tripod defiantly anchored there as evidence of the Chinese success.

Promises to keep

by Tom Hornbein

In 1963 it was the Americans' turn. Led by Norman Dyhrenfurth, their expedition had two aims: to reach the summit by the British South Col route; and to forge a new route up Everest's West Ridge, with the bonus of descending via the South Col to make the first traverse of the mountain. The divided objectives soon caused conflict in the expedition, with most of its resources being pledged to the South Col teams. But two men clung to the vision of climbing the West Ridge: US anaesthesiologist Dr Tom Hornbein and philosopher and mountain guide Willi Unsoeld. After Jim Whittaker and Nawang Gombu reached the summit via the South Col on 1 May, Hornbein and Unsoeld battled through storms on the West Ridge to reach a tenuous bivouac site at 27,250 feet / 8,300 metres on 21 May, where they prepared for their bid the next morning.

Everest's West Ridge soars 4,000 feet from the West Shoulder, with Tom Hornbein and Willi Unsoeld shown in the foreground of Barry Bishop's photograph. After climbing 1,000 feet up the ridge, the team struck out on to the North Face and followed the deep cleft now known as the Hornbein Couloir. Hornbein took the title of his account from lines from a poem by Robert Frost: '. . . . And I have promises to keep/And miles to go before I sleep.'

At four the oxygen ran out, a most effective alarm clock. Two well-incubated butane stoves were fished from inside our sleeping-bags and soon bouillon was brewing in the kitchen. Climbing into boots was a breathless challenge to balance in our close quarters. Then overboots, and crampons.

'Crampons, in the tent?'

'Sure,' I replied, 'It's a hell of a lot colder out there.'

'But our air mattresses!'

'Just be careful. We may not be back here again, anyway. I hope.'

We were clothed in multilayer warmth. The fishnet underwear next to our skin provided tiny air pockets to hold our body heat. It also kept the outer layers at a distance which, considering our weeks without a bath, was respectful. Next came Duofold underwear, a wool shirt, down underwear tops and bottoms, wool climbing pants, and a lightweight wind parka. In spite of the cold, our down parkas would be too bulky for difficult climbing, so we used them to insulate two quarts of hot lemonade, hoping they might remain unfrozen long enough to drink during the climb. Inside the felt inner liners of our reindeer-hair boots were innersoles and two pairs of heavy wool socks. Down shells covered a pair of wool mittens. Over our oxygen helmets we wore wool balaclavas and our parka hoods. The down parka lemonade-muff was stuffed into our packs as padding between two oxygen bottles. With camera, radio, flashlight, and sundry mementos (including pages from Emerson's diary), our loads came close to 40lb. For all the prior evening's planning it

was more than two hours before we emerged.

I snugged a bowline about my waist, feeling satisfaction at the ease with which the knot fell together beneath heavily mittened hands. This was part of the ritual, experienced innumerable times before. With it came a feeling of security, not from the protection provided by the rope joining Willi and me, but from my being able to relegate these cold grey brooding forbidding walls, so high in such an unknown world, to common reality – to all those times I had ever tied into a rope before: with warm hands while I stood at the base of sun-baked granite walls in the Tetons, with cold hands on a winter night while I prepared to tackle my first steep ice on Longs Peak. This knot tied me to the past, to experiences known, to difficulties faced and overcome. To tie it here in this lonely morning on Everest brought my venture into contact with the known, with that which man might do. To weave the knot so smoothly with clumsily mittened hands was to assert my confidence, to assert some competence in the face of the waiting rock, to accept the challenge.

Hooking our masks in place we bade a slightly regretful goodbye to our tent, sleeping-bags, and the extra supply of food we hadn't been able to eat. Willi was at the edge of the ledge looking up the narrow gully when I joined him.

'My oxygen's hissing, Tom, even with the regulator turned off.'

For the next 20 minutes we screwed and unscrewed regulators, checked valves for ice, to no avail. The hiss

Of its twin targets, the 1963 US expedition completed a South Col ascent first. Above, the South Col team traverses the Lhotse Face, with the Geneva Spur immediately ahead, the South Col and South-east Ridge beyond. The first South Col pair, James Whittaker and Nawang Gombu, reached the summit on 1 May. A second South Col pair, Barry Bishop and Lute Jerstad, made their bid on 22 May, the day when Hornbein and Unsoeld went for the summit from the West Ridge.

Pages 72/73: Sherpas photographed by Al Auten as they skirt a series of crevasses in the Western Cwm, with the plunging buttresses of Nuptse in the background.

continued. We guessed it must be in the valve, and thought of going back to the tent for the spare bottle, but the impatient feeling that time was more important kept us from retracing those 40 feet.

'It doesn't sound too bad,' I said. 'Let's just keep an eye on the pressure. Besides if you run out we can hook up the sleeping T and extra tubing and both climb on one bottle.' Willi envisioned the two of us climbing Everest in lockstep, wed by six feet of rubber hose.

We turned to the climb. It was ten minutes to seven. Willi led off. Three years before in a tent high on Masherbrum he had expounded on the importance of knee-to-toe distance for step-kicking up steep snow. Now his anatomical advantage determined the order of things as he put his theory to the test. Right away we found it was going to be difficult. The couloir, as it cut through the Yellow Band, narrowed to 10 or 15 feet and steepened to 50 degrees. The snow was hard, too hard to kick steps in, but not hard enough to hold crampons; they slid disconcertingly down through this wind-sheltered, granular stuff. There was nothing for it but to cut steps, zigzagging back and forth across the gully, occasionally finding a bit of rock along the side up which we could scramble. We were forced to climb one at a time with psychological belays from axes thrust a few inches into the snow. Our regulators were set to deliver two litres of oxygen per minute, half the optimal flow for this altitude. We turned them off when we were belaying to conserve the precious gas, though we knew that the belayer should always be at peak alertness in case of a fall.

We crept along. My God, I thought, we'll never

get there at this rate. But that's as far as the thought ever got. Willi's leads were meticulous, painstakingly slow and steady. He plugged tirelessly on, deluging me with showers of ice as his axe carved each step. When he ran out the 100 feet of rope he jammed his axe into the snow to belay me. I turned my oxygen on to '2' and moved up as fast as I could, hoping to save a few moments of critical time. By the time I joined him I was completely winded, gasping for air, and sorely puzzled about why. Only late in the afternoon, when my first oxygen bottle was still going strong, did I realize what a low flow of gas my regulator was actually delivering.

Up the tongue of snow we climbed, squeezing through a passage where the walls of the Yellow Band closed in, narrowing the couloir to shoulder-width.

In four hours we had climbed only 400 feet. It was 11 am. A rotten bit of vertical wall forced us to the right on to the open face. To regain the couloir it would be necessary to climb this 60 foot cliff, composed of two pitches split by a broken snow-covered step.

'You like to lead this one?' Willi asked.

With my oxygen off I failed to think before I replied, 'Sure, I'll try it.'

The rock sloped malevolently outward like shingles on a roof – rotten shingles. The covering of snow was no better than the rock. It would pretend to hold for a moment, then suddenly shatter and peel, cascading down on Willi. He sank a piton into the base of the step to anchor his belay.

I started up around the corner to the left, crampon points grating on rusty limestone. Then it became a snowploughing procedure as I searched for some sort of purchase beneath. The pick of my axe found a crack. Using the shaft for gentle leverage, I moved carefully on to the broken strata of the step. I went left again, loose debris rolling under my crampons, to the base of the final vertical rise, about eight feet high. For all its steepness, this bit was a singularly poor plastering job, nothing but wobbly rubble. I searched about for a crack, unclipped a big angle piton from my sling, and whomped it in with the hammer. It sank smoothly, as if penetrating soft butter. A gentle lift easily extracted it.

'Hmmm. Not so good,' I mumbled through my mask. On the fourth try the piton gripped a bit more solidly. Deciding not to loosen it by testing, I turned to the final wall. Its steepness threw my weight out from the rock, and my pack became a downright hindrance. There was an unlimited selection of hand-holds, mostly portable. I shed my mittens. For a few seconds the rock felt comfortably reassuring but cold. Then not cold any more. My eyes tried to direct sensationless fingers. Flakes peeled out beneath my crampons. I leaned out from the rock to move upward, panting like a steam engine. Damn it, it'll go; I know it will, T, I thought. But my grip was gone. I hadn't thought to turn my oxygen up.

'No soap,' I called down. 'Can't make it now. Too pooped.'

'Come on down. There may be a way to the right.'

I descended, half rappeling from the piton, which held. I had spent the better part of an hour up there. A hundred feet out we looked back. Clearly we had been on the right route, for above that last little step the gully opened out. A hundred feet higher the Yellow Band met the grey of the summit limestone. It had to get easier.

'You'd better take it, Willi. I've wasted enough time already.'

'Hell, if you couldn't make it, I'm not going to be able to do any better.'

'Yes you will. It's really not that hard. I was just worn out from putting that piton in. Turn your regulator clear open, though.'

Willi headed up around the corner, moving well. In ten minutes his rope was snapped through the high piton. Discarding a few unsavoury holds, he gripped the rotten edge with his unmittened hands. He leaned out for the final move. His pack pulled. Crampons scraped, loosing a shower of rock from beneath his feet. He was over. He leaned against the rock, fighting for breath.

'Man, that's work. But it looks better above.'

Belayed, I followed, retrieved the first piton, moved up, and went to work on the second. It wouldn't come. 'Guess it's better than I thought,' I shouted. 'I'm going to leave it.' I turned my oxygen to four litres, leaned out from the wall, and scrambled up. The extra oxygen helped, but it was surprising how breathless such a brief effort left me.

'Good lead,' I panted. 'That wasn't easy.'

'Thanks. Let's roll.'

Another rope-length and we stopped. After six hours of hiss Willi's first bottle was empty. There was still a long way to go, but at least he could travel ten pounds lighter without the extra cylinder. Our altimeter read 27,900. We called base on the walkie-talkie.

Willi: West Ridge to Base. West Ridge to Base. Over.

Base (Jim Whittaker, excitedly): This is Base here, Willi. How are you? How are things going? What's the word up there? Over.

Willi: Man, this is a real bearcat! We are nearing the top of the Yellow Band and it's mighty tough. It's too damned tough to try to go back. It would be

too dangerous.

Base (Jim): I'm sure you're considering your exits. Why don't you leave yourself an opening? If it's not going to pan out, you can always start working your way down. I think there is always a way to come back.

Willi: Roger, Jim. We're counting on a further consultation in about 200 or 300 feet. It should ease up by then! Goddammit, if we can't start moving together we'll have to move back down. But it should be easier once the Yellow Band is passed. Over.

Base (Jim): Don't work yourself up into a bottleneck, Willi. How about rappeling? Is that possible, or don't you have any reepschnur or anything? Over.

Willi: There are no rappel points, Jim, absolutely no rappel points. There's nothing to secure a rope to. So it's up and over for us today . . .

While the import of his words settled upon those listening 10,000 feet below, Willi went right on:

Willi (continuing): . . . and we'll probably be getting in pretty late, maybe as late as seven or eight o'clock tonight.

As Willi talked, I looked at the mountain above. The slopes looked reasonable, as far as I could see, which wasn't very far. We sat at the base of a big, wide-open amphitheatre. It looked like summits all over the place. I looked down. Descent was totally unappetizing. The rotten rock, the softening snow, the absence of even tolerable piton cracks only added to our desire to go on. Too much labour, too many sleepless nights, and too many dreams had been invested to bring us this far. We couldn't come back for another try next weekend. To go down now, even if we could have, would be descending to a future

The key to the West Ridge ascent proved to be the Hornbein Couloir, which carved a way up the North Face, parallel to the ridge, for almost 2,000 feet. In Al Auten's photograph it is steep but broad, with the Rongbuk Glacier below and the flanks of Changste visible through cloud to the right. Higher up, where it sliced through the Yellow Band, the couloir became so narrow that the climbers had to squeeze through.

Another icon: Lute Jerstad of the South Col team, photographed by his partner Barry Bishop, approaches the summit, marked by the US flag placed there by the first South Col team three weeks before. Jerstad and Bishop reached the summit at 3.15 pm on 22 May. Unsoeld and Hornbein followed them three hours later. The four bivouacked together at 28,000 feet during the descent, the highest Everest bivouac yet. Unsoeld and Bishop suffered frost-bite injuries. In the morning support climbers Dave Dingman and Girme Dorje helped them down.

marked by one huge question: what might have been? It would not be a matter of living with our fellow man, but simply living with ourselves, with the knowledge that we had had more to give.

I listened, only mildly absorbed in Willi's conversation with Base, and looked past him at the convexity of rock cutting off our view of the gully we had ascended. Above – a snowfield, grey walls, then blue-black sky. We were committed. An invisible barrier sliced through the mountain beneath our feet, cutting us off from the world below. Though we could see through, all we saw was infinitely remote. The ethereal link provided by our radio only intensified our separation. My wife and children seemed suddenly close. Yet home, life itself, lay only over the top of Everest and down the other side. Suppose we fail? The thought brought no remorse, no fear. Once entertained, it hardly seemed even interesting. What now mattered most was right here: Willi and I, tied together on a rope, and the mountain, its summit not inaccessibly far above. The reason we had come was within our grasp. We belonged to the mountain and it to us. There was anxiety, to be sure, but it was all but lost in a feeling of calm, of pleasure at the joy of climbing. That we couldn't go down only made easier that which we really wanted to do. That we might not get there was scarcely conceivable.

Willi was still talking.

Willi: Any news of Barry and Lute? Over.

Jim: I haven't heard a word from them. Over.

Willi: How about Dingman?

Jim: No word from Dingman. We've heard nothing, nothing at all.

Willi: Well listen, if you do get hold of Dingman, tell him to put a light in the window because we're

headed for the summit, Jim. We can't possibly get back to our camp now. Over.

I stuffed the radio back in Willi's pack. It was 1 pm. From here we could both climb at the same time, moving across the last of the yellow slabs. Another 100 feet and the Yellow Band was below us. A steep tongue of snow flared wide, penetrating the grey strata that capped the mountain. The snow was hard, almost ice-hard in places. We had only to bend our ankles, firmly plant all 12 crampon points, and walk uphill. At last, we were moving, though it would have appeared painfully slow to a distant bystander.

As we climbed out of the couloir the pieces of the puzzle fell into place. That snow rib ahead on the left skyline should lead us to the Summit Snowfield, a patch of perpetual white clinging to the North Face at the base of Everest's final pyramid. By 3 pm we were on the snowfield. We had been climbing for eight hours and knew we needed to take time to refuel. At a shaly outcrop of rock we stopped for lunch. There was a decision to be made. We could either cut straight to the North-east Ridge and follow it west to the summit, or we could traverse the face and regain the West Ridge. From where we sat, the ridge looked easier. Besides, it was the route we'd intended in the first place.

We split a quart of lemonade that was slushy with ice. In spite of its down parka wrapping, the other bottle was already frozen solid, as were the kippered snacks. They were almost tasteless but we downed them more with dutiful thoughts of calories than with pleasure.

To save time we moved together, diagonalling upward across down-sloping slabs of rotten shale. There were no possible stances from which to belay each other. Then snow again, and Willi kicked steps, fastidiously picking a route between the outcropping rocks. Though still carting my full load of oxygen bottles, I was beginning to feel quite strong. With this excess of energy came impatience, and an unconscious anxiety over the high stakes for which we were playing and the lateness of the day. Why the hell is Willi going so damned slow? I thought. And a little later: he should cut over to the ridge now; it'll be a lot easier.

I shouted into the wind, 'Hold up, Willi!' He pretended not to hear me as he started up the rock. It seemed terribly important to tell him to go to the right. I tugged on the rope. 'Damn it, wait up, Willi!' Stopped by a taut rope and an unyielding Hornbein, he turned, and with some irritation anchored his axe while I hastened to join him. He was perched, through no choice of his own, in rather cramped, precarious quarters. I sheepishly apologized.

We were on rock now. One rope-length, crampons

scraping, brought us to the crest of the West Ridge for the first time since we'd left Camp 4 West yesterday morning. The South Face fell 8,000 feet to the tiny tents of Advance Base. Lhotse, straight across the face, was below us now. And near at hand 150 feet higher, the South Summit of Everest shone in the afternoon sun. We were within 400 feet of the top! The wind whipped across the ridge from the north at nearly 60 miles an hour. Far below, peak shadows reached long across the cloud-filled valleys. Above, the ridge rose, a twisting, rocky spine.

We shed crampons and overboots to tackle this next rocky bit with the comforting grip of cleated rubber soles. Here I unloaded my first oxygen bottle though it was not quite empty. It had lasted ten hours, which obviously meant I was getting a lower flow than indicated by the regulator. Resisting Willi's suggestion to drop the cylinder off the South Face, I left it for some unknown posterity. When I resaddled ten pounds lighter, I felt I could float to the top.

The rock was firm, at least in comparison with our fare thus far. Climbing one at a time, we experienced the joy of delicate moves on tiny holds. The going was a wonderful pleasure, almost like a day in the Rockies. With the sheer drop to the cwm beneath us, we measured off another four rope-lengths. Solid rock gave way to crud, then snow. A thin, firm, knife-edge of white pointed gently towards the sky.

Buffeted by the wind, we laced our crampons on, racing each other with rapidly numbing fingers. It took nearly 20 minutes. Then we were off again, squandering oxygen at three litres per minute, since time seemed the shorter commodity at the moment. We moved together, Willi in front. It seemed almost as if we were cheating, using oxygen; we could nearly run this final bit.

Ahead the North and South Ridges converged to a point. Surely the summit wasn't that near? It must be off behind. Willi stopped. What's he waiting for, I wondered as I moved to join him. With a feeling of disbelief I looked up. Forty feet ahead, tattered and whipped by the wind, was the flag Jim had left three weeks before. It was 6.15. The sun's rays sheered horizontally across the summit. We hugged each other as tears welled up, ran down across our oxygen masks, and turned to ice.

THE WHY OF CLIMBING
by Dr Jim Lester

Try as I will, I am unable to resist speculating about the *why* of climbing; I know better than to attempt it, but the lure of the distant summit is too strong. I speak now only of the American climbers I knew from the 1963 Everest expedition; I must start from there. It has gradually dawned on me that there is possibly a fundamental split within the typical climber in this group, that his life involved some paradoxes, and that out of these paradoxes might come the energy and its channelling that makes the difference between a mountaineer and the rest of us. Some of these paradoxes, darkly glimpsed, are these: that he is basically introspective yet highly active in attempting to master the outside world; that he is basically humanistic but tends to choose a career dealing with abstractions or the impersonal world; that he is assertively individualistic yet showed a distinct tendency to idealize

Frost-bite victims Bishop and Unsoeld wait to be flown from Base Camp to Kathmandu. Bishop lost several finger tips and all his toes; Unsoeld nine toes.

the Buddhist way of life in which Nepal immersed us. These may all be clues to a divided nature, an ambivalence, which most people experience as distinctly undesirable. Ambivalence seeks resolution. I have come to feel that one of the deepest attractions of mountaineering is its potential, for a time at least, to allow us to feel *whole*, pulled together, undivided, undistracted – in a word, *ourselves*. Searching for the right words, I find these of Ortega y Gasset touching and highly relevant:

'Each of us is always in peril of not being the unique and untransferable *self* which he is. The majority of men perpetually betray this *self* which is waiting to be; and to tell the whole truth our personal individuality is a personage which is never completely realized, a simulating Utopia, a secret legend, which each of us guards in the bottom of his heart.'

I was in heaven

by Sonam Gyatso and Sonam Wangyal

The Indians made two strong bids to climb Everest in 1960 and 1962, coming within 500 feet / 150 metres of the summit. They succeeded in 1965, when Captain A.S. Cheema and Nawang Gombu (the first man to make two ascents) reached the summit on 20 May via the South Col. Two days later, Sonam Gyatso and Sonam Wangyal made their attempt.

The leader of the Indian expedition was Mohan Kohli (above right), a navy officer who took part in the two previous Indian attempts. In 1965 there were four successful bids: the fourth consisted of Hari Ahluwalia and Sherpa Phu Dorji (pictured above) together with Harish Rawat.

SONAM WANGYAL

May 22: 5am. This was 'D-Day'. The winds were blowing furiously; their speed I estimated at 140 kilometres per hour. The tent walls were flapping and the whole tent was shivering and trembling. Come what may, we were determined to go ahead; never did we think of abandoning our attempt. Both Gyatso and I prayed fervently. We had, somehow, confidence that we would succeed; our faith in God could not be shaken. Gyatso had a small statue of Karmapa and a few prayer-flags which had been given to him by Rimpoche of Lachung. The prayer-flags had been given specially to ward off the evils of weather and protect us from the wrath of the elements.

Slowly and laboriously, but not reluctantly, we started getting ready. By 5.30 am the sun had come out. Lo and behold, the winds were dying down! We tried to contact the Advance Base Camp but did not succeed. We put on our crampons at 6.40 am and left the camp for the most cherished goal of all mountaineers. Could we make it? The question loomed large in our minds. It kept on recurring all the time. But we never lost hope.

Immediately we were out of the tent, we were on the sharp ridge known as 'the Razor's Edge'. Each step had to be cut carefully lest one was dashed down. One could not help seeing Makalu sparkling in the distance. It stood out in its splendid isolation and its snow-encrusted majestic wall was quite awe-inspiring.

Gyatso was leading but he found it difficult as the pain in his waist was cutting deep into his flesh. I asked him, 'Would you rather that we went back?' He gave a very emphatic, 'No'. He had an unshakeable feeling that he would succeed. He had been told by Karmapa and Rimpoche that he would do so. They could not be wrong.

Gyatso's determination gave me hope and increased my confidence. I took the lead on the rope. Slowly we went up as the moaning of the winds died down to a whine and then to a whisper. Two hours after we had left the last camp we reached the point where Cheema and Gombu had left their second oxygen bottle. We too dumped our half-used oxygen bottles there. We were now carrying only one full oxygen bottle each. Thank God, 13lbs of weight had been removed and we could increase our pace a little.

We kept advancing steadily and cautiously, getting nearer and nearer the South Summit. Occasionally a step had to be whacked out of the snow but mainly we chose to stay on the rocks on the left side of the ridge. Two hours later, we were on top of the ridge. From there we could see the final Summit Ridge which was not as difficult as the one which we had just surmounted. But we could not see the main summit. It was still a long way I thought. We had to continue with our effort, muster all our strength and go on and on till we reached our goal. The main ridge looked full of firm snow. At last there was no wind. The sun was sparkling over the snow and the glare was at times blinding.

We rested for five minutes. We had now to descend about 30 feet and it was a fairly steep slope. The cornices down below looked like ice flowers and looked so real that one had an irresistible desire to go down and pluck them. Gyatso belayed me, and gingerly I walked down the ridge on rock and snow. We were on the main Summit Ridge.

The ridge was not much corniced on its lower portion but we chose to walk on rocks. The Advance

Base could be clearly seen from here. I was sure that I could even make out some of my colleagues moving about in the camp. They looked like tiny pebbles.

Our progress was slow. Gyatso was in severe pain but he would not give up. We reached the rock chimney, called 'Hillary's Chimney'. On one side of it was rock, on the other was snow and a frightening crevasse below. Climbing the chimney was not difficult. After a short rest we were off again. There was a lot of ice and snow ahead of us. Then we came to a hump; we crossed it and saw another hump. This too was surmounted, and. . . .

Joy of joys! We saw the summit hump and the Indian Tricolour fluttering from the American flag-pole. Both of us were excited beyond words. Gyatso forgot his pain. The last few steps to the peak of Everest, we walked side by side. It was 11.30 am when after six hours of trudging, climbing, heaving, belaying, kicking and whacking we reached the top. So this was it. We were on top of the world. When I was selected for the expedition I had asked my family to pray for me. Their prayers had been answered.

Both Gyatso and I fell down on our knees and prayed. We embraced each other, thumped each other on the back and shook hands. I must confess, I was a little frightened. I was new to Everest, the mountain overwhelmed me. The fear of getting back safely was suddenly uppermost in my mind. It was the same fear I had felt when I went first to the Icefall. Gradually that fear had dissolved, but now it came back.

I took out a flag-pole from my rucksack. It was a folding type. I buried it deep in the snow and hoisted the Indian national flag on it. Then I planted a yellow prayer-flag which had been given to me by my father. My father had given seven such flags and six of them had already been planted on other parts of Everest. A ring which my sister had given, I buried in the snow and stones of the summit.

The sun was bright and a gentle wind was streaming by gracefully. I bowed before the prayer-flag and prayed. Gyatso did the same. We got up and took in the view. There were clouds far far below us. The Thyangboche Monastery was glittering in the sun like a diamond in a setting of emeralds. The other peaks, lower down, looked like heaps of flour. Far away in the horizon, on the other side, we could see the verdant patches of the high plains of Tibet.

We stayed on the top for 50 minutes, hoisting various flags given to us by our friends and taking a number of photographs. I collected a few stones and a little snow from the summit as sacred mementoes. The snow I kept in a thermos flask. For a good 20 minutes, while we were on the summit, we did not use oxygen but when breathlessness was overpowering us, we resumed the breathing of oxygen from our oxygen bottles. We firmly put on our oxygen masks as we prepared to leave the summit.

SONAM GYATSO

The dreams of 20 years of my father, Mr Rinzing Ngo Dup, had come true. I looked towards Rongbuk Monastery and saw clouds in the lower valleys. I saw the Rongbuk Glacier and the beautiful green patches. There were plenty of small peaks jutting out of the clouds all around us like thick needle-points. I felt very humble and offered a few Cadbury chocolates and sweets; I offered all I had to Chomolungma.

My approach to the mountains is religious. I revere them and hold the holy peaks in respect. I approach the mountains with humility. I love nature and have a passion for flowers, plants, rocks and snow. Everest has always been sacred to me. In 1957, when I went to Nanda Devi, I had done so without informing my wife. In fact I had told her that I was going on some official duty. When she saw the report of the expedition in the newspapers and read about me, she was hurt and angry. She wrote a long letter of complaint. She was frightened of mountains and did not want any evil to come to me. On my return I had to assure her that mountains were the abode of gods and gods would not be cruel to me. I promised her that whenever I went on an expedition, I would each time collect some holy snow and stones of the mountain for her. So she had looked forward to my climb on Everest and I knew that she was waiting for the *parsad* [a sacred offering]. I took some sacred snow and holy rocks from the top of Everest for my wife. On the Everest peak I felt as if I was in heaven. There was nothing higher than us anywhere.

A scarf given to me by my wife was placed on the summit. Two idols, one of Lord Buddha and the other of Lord Krishna, given to me by my friends were planted there. Kohli had given me two pairs of rosaries, one belonged to Hari Dang, a member of the 1962 Indian Everest expedition, and the other had been given to Kohli by his father. These, too, were placed on the summit. A large Indian national flag on a strong flag-pole was planted permanently on the top of Everest by the side of the American flag-pole of 1963.

Guru Rimpoche had given me a small statue which too I placed on the summit but before leaving I picked it up and brought it back with me for my safety. Later when Guru Rimpoche asked me why I had brought back the icon, I said that I was frightened and needed its protection for the return journey. The Guru smiled and asked me to keep the idol always with me.

Sonam Gyatso (top) and Sonam Wangyal (below) were two of nine members of the Indian expedition who reached the summit. Gyatso wrote: 'When I was selected for the expedition I asked my family to pray for me. Their prayers were answered.' For Wangyal, 'the dreams of my father had come true.'

'ALL THE WORLD
LAY BEFORE US'

1970–1979

Sorry, Harsh, you've had it

by Murray Sayle

The 1971 International Expedition was launched on the idealistic belief that a team of men and women from a dozen different nations could unite to meet a common challenge. Led by Norman Dyhrenfurth, it had two routes as its goals: one, the unclimbed South-west Face, the other, a direct version of the American West Ridge route of 1963. Sadly, the expedition soon fragmented, riven by personal and national rivalries. The highest point achieved, by the British Don Whillans and Dougal Haston, was around 27,400 feet/8,350 metres on the South-west Face. The most tragic incident came when the popular Indian Army officer Harsh Bahuguna, who had nearly reached the summit in 1965, attempted to retreat from the West Ridge during a blizzard on 18 April. Sayle reported the episode for the London Sunday Times.

Companions Wolfgang Axt from Austria and Harsh Bahuguna from India take a breather in the Khumbu Icefall. A few days later Bahuguna was fighting for his life while Axt descended unaware of his plight.

Pages 80/81: Doug Scott's summit shot of Dougal Haston, 1975. The comment is Scott's.

Since we set off on this expedition, I considered Harsh Bahuguna one of my closest friends among the climbers. We often walked together on the march in, and talked about all sorts of things: his wife and two small daughters, his obsession with Mount Everest, and his career with the Indian Army.

Harsh – which in Sanskrit means 'happiness' – came from an Indian tribal group, the Garhwali, who are famous as soldiers and hill climbers (they are first cousins of the Gurkhas of Nepal). His uncle, Major Nandu Jayal, died in 1958 while attempting another Himalayan giant, Cho Oyu.

Harsh himself came within 800 feet of the summit

of Everest as a member of the successful Indian Army expedition of 1965. His own attempt was delayed to the last of the Indian groups because of stomach trouble, and then a sudden break in the weather robbed him of his chance of the summit.

I was not alone in thinking that Harsh was a special friend – after his death, I found that at least two-thirds of the climbers were sure they were particularly close to him. But, if he had a special companion on this expedition, it was undoubtedly the Austrian Wolfgang Axt. They ate together, shared a tent on the march in and another at Base Camp, shared much of the dangerous work of forcing a passage up the Icefall (where they were outstanding) and they spent the last five days of Harsh's life together in a tiny tent perched high on the West Ridge of Everest.

They made odd, but clearly close friends. Axt is 6 feet 3 inches, beautifully built, and his approach to people, to life itself, is in terms of physical strength and endurance. He is married to the former Austrian women's 60 metre sprint champion; and no one has ever heard him discuss any other subjects but health diets, physical fitness, climbing mountains and related topics. He often told us how much he enjoyed climbing with Harsh.

The sequence of events which ended with Bahuguna's death and the subsequent dissensions began on the evening of 17 April, when a deputation called on Norman Dyhrenfurth, our Swiss-American joint leader, in his tent at the Advance Base Camp in the

Western Cwm (Camp II, 21,700 feet), and presented something like an ultimatum. The visitors were Carlo Mauri, the Italian mountaineer and adventurer (he was a member of the Ra voyage), Pierre Mazeaud, the member of the French National Assembly who hopes one day to be Minister for Youth and Sport, and other members of the ridge team.

They said what everyone knew: that, largely because of the weather, the face route was looking hopeful and the ridge route, for which the deputation had opted, was lagging behind. Unless more Sherpa porters were switched to ferrying supplies to the ridge they said, then the whole ridge group should turn their efforts to the classical, 'easy' route – up the South Col.

Dyhrenfurth is a genial man who prefers discussion and consensus to giving orders. He was severely hampered by a bad case of high-altitude laryngitis, which he was trying to treat by inhaling steam from a pan of melted snow; but he did his best to explain that both he and the British joint leader, Colonel Jimmy Roberts (directing the Sherpa lift of supplies up the Icefall from Base Camp), were also disturbed about the supply situation. The Icefall, much trickier than usual, was absorbing a lot of Sherpa labour, and a log-jam of supplies was building up at Camp I, perched on an ice-cliff at the top of the fall. The answer, said Dyhrenfurth tactfully, was for the sahibs themselves to start carrying up some supplies.

The deputation had touched on a sore spot which, sooner or later, was bound to disturb an expedition like ours. No one enjoys the dull work of carrying supplies in support – climbing thousands of feet with a reel of rope, a couple of oxygen cylinders and a box of food, then dumping it and climbing down again. And at those altitudes, everyone seems to have a definite stock of energy, no more and no less, although the amount varies with individuals. Ambitious people who conserve their energies for the glamorous summit push are being no more than human.

Still, a story going around the expedition is that one eminent climber by mistake picked up the rucksack of another during a 'support' climb and found he could easily lift it with his little finger. And, when our chapter of calamities began, there were only two oxygen bottles in the high camps on the face, only one on the ridge.

Base Camp for the 1971 International Expedition was this collection of tents amidst the jumbled moraine of the Khumbu Glacier, photographed by John Cleare under a dusting of snow. Later a five-day storm hit the expedition, compounding the problems with which it was beset.

The South-west Face towers 7,000 feet from the Western Cwm. By 1975, six expeditions had failed in attempts to climb it. The British route goes directly to the vee-shaped couloir, strikes left through the Yellow Band, then traverses right across the upper snowfield to the South Summit.

All the winds of Asia

by Peter Boardman

In 1975 the British, led by Chris Bonington, made a fresh attempt on the South-west Face, following failures by at least six teams including the ill-fated international expedition of 1971. The key lay in overcoming the Rock Band, the formidable black cliff starting at 26,000 feet/7,925 metres. After Nick Estcourt and Tut Braithwaite had found a route via a series of ramps and gullies, Doug Scott and Dougal Haston went to the summit on 24 September – the first British climbers to do so. They were rewarded with stupendous views and survived the highest Everest bivouac yet, at 28,750 feet/8,763 metres. Two days later Peter Boardman and Pertemba followed them to the top. As they started down, they were astonished to meet the climber and cameraman Mick Burke, making a solo attempt. Burke decided to press on and arranged to meet Boardman and Pertemba at the South Summit. Boardman's account of their anguished wait is one of the most affecting passages in mountaineering literature.

Peter Boardman (above) was 23 when Chris Bonington invited him to join the 1975 team. Then working as a climbing instructor in Scotland, he had several bold Himalayan ascents to his name, and had impressed Bonington with his 'quiet maturity'. The climber in the background is Dave Clarke.

All the winds of Asia seemed to be trying to blow us from the ridge. A decision was needed. It was four in the afternoon and the skies were already darkening around the South Summit of Everest. I threw my iced and useless snow-goggles away into the whiteness and tried, clumsily mitted, to clear the ice from my eyelashes. I bowed my head into the spindrift and tried to peer along the ridge. Mick should have met us at least three-quarters of an hour before, unless something had happened to him. We had been waiting for nearly one and a half hours. There was no sign of Doug and Dougal's bivouac site. The sky and cornices and whirling snow merged together, visibility was reduced to ten feet and all tracks were obliterated. Pertemba and I huddled next to the rock of the South Summit where Mick had asked us to wait for him. Pertemba said he could not feel his toes or fingers and mine too were nailed with cold. I thought of Mick wearing his glasses and blinded by spindrift, negotiating the fixed rope on the Hillary Step, the fragile one foot windslab on the Nepal side, and the cornices on the Tibetan side of the ridge. I thought of our own predicament, with the 800 feet of the South Summit Gully – guarded by a 60 foot rock step halfway – to descend, and then half of the 2,000 foot great traverse above the Rock Band to cross before reaching the end of the fixed ropes that extended across from Camp VI. It had taken Doug and Dougal three hours in the dawn sunshine after their bivouac to reach Camp VI

– but we now had only an hour of light left. At 28,700 feet the boundary between a controlled and an uncontrolled situation is narrow and we had crossed that boundary within minutes – a strong wind and sun shining through clouds had turned into a violent blizzard of driving snow, the early afternoon had drifted into approaching night and our success was turning into tragedy.

A mountaineer when he is climbing is doing, seeing and feeling and yet on his return home from the hill he often baulks at recollection in public of these experiences because he treasures the privacy and intensity of his memories. And yet, as Hornbein remarked after being asked to write about his ascent of the West Ridge:

'I soon learned, Everest was not a private affair. It belonged to many men.'

The stories of man's adventures on Everest have almost reached the stature of myth in the popular imaginations of the 20th century. The full record of our expedition will eventually appear to add to these stories. I do not aspire here to document the planning and events of the expedition, nor to presume to evaluate its achievements, nor to predict the future of climbing on Everest. I fear that at such a cold touch the pains and charms that are my memories of Everest will fly.

My memories are of a keen apprehension that

turned into a living nightmare. Even on the leech infested walk-in we dreamt about the climb to come – one morning Tut and Doug confessed, with gallows humour, 'I keep getting stranded above the Rock Band' and, 'Dougal got severe frost-bite last night'. Whilst Nick and Tut were tackling the Rock Band I wrote:

'Everyone is very optimistic that we'll crack it soon, but it's still early days. We've been lucky with the weather and there could easily be a storm at any time to curtail or even set back all movement.'

'Think upwards' always seems to be a good dictum for success in climbing and the Everest summit was in my mind night and day all the time I was moving up the face into position for the second attempt. Aside from the physical effort and practical judgement and worry there is a dreamlike quality in the climbing on Everest. At Camp V I wrote:

'The face is a strange unreal world. All dressed up in one piece oversuits and six layers on the feet, oxygen mask and goggles one seems distanced from where one is and what one is doing, like a sort of moonwalk.'

This half-glimpsed quality was preserved far back in my mind. As a child I used to daydream over a painting in a big picture book, *Adventure of the World*, which depicted the tiny bold figures of Hillary and Tenzing on the top of a summit that thrust out of a sea of clouds.

As Pertemba and I crossed the traverse above the Rock Band in the early dawn of our summit day it felt as if we were on that highest peak above the clouds, as if the sight of the endless cloud sea was joining hands with the dreamland of the past. The weather was changing and the cloud layer was up to 27,000 feet, covering Nuptse and everything beyond it. Only the top of Lhotse peeped out below us, whereas above us the sun sparkled through the snow smoking over the Summit Ridge. For three days I had been jumaring up fixed ropes, counting steps and trying to keep in front of some Sherpas coming up to Camp IV, gasping up to Camp V, and then following Nick and Tut's intricate route through the Rock Band. But now I felt free and untrammelled, and exhilarated as if I had just become committed on the start of a climb in the Alps. Pertemba and I moved, unroped, steadily away from the end of the fixed line and kicked away the spindrift from the tracks that Doug and Dougal had made two days before. Everest, the myth, with its magic and history, seemed to make me feel strong, thinking upwards. Invincible together.

The snow was only a few feet deep on top of the rocks and the route wavered around spurs and over rock steps. The South Summit gully was steep but there was a fixed line hanging over the rock step half way up it. As I reached the South Summit, Pertemba dropped behind and I waited for him. His oxygen mask had stopped working. One and a half hours and several cold fingers later we had slit open the tube and cleared the two inches of ice that were blocking the airway, and patched the mask back into working order. We changed to fresh oxygen cylinders and moved, roped now, along the ridge towards the summit of Everest. Its red ribbons were fading in the strong light and fluttering prayers from the other side of the mountain. The Chinese tripod was catching drifting snow and leaning defiantly in the wind. Its presence was strangely reassuring. Pertemba attached a Nepalese flag to it and I hung a Deadman snow anchor from it. We ate some chocolate and mint cake and I burbled into a tape-recorder. We started down.

We were amazed to see him through the mist. Mick was sitting on the snow only a few hundred yards down an easy angled snow-slope from the summit. He congratulated us and said he wanted to film us on a bump on the ridge and pretend it was the summit, but I told him about the Chinese maypole. Then he

Tension at Base Camp, left: while Haston and Scott go for the summit on 24 September, their colleagues keep watch from Advance Base in the Western Cwm. Expedition doctor Charlie Clarke has the binoculars; Nick Estcourt, who helped forge the route through the Rock Band, is on the telephoto lens. Right: Haston, photographed by Scott, crampons up a 60 degree snow slope as he heads for the South Summit Gully, visible just above his rucksack.

'We were amazed to see him through the mist.' Boardman and Pertemba met Burke a short distance below the summit. Burke wanted his colleagues to go back to the summit with him so that he could film them there, but Boardman was reluctant so Burke said he would go on alone. Before parting, Boardman took the last photograph of Burke (above). The previous day (right) Haston and Scott had gone to the summit in clear conditions. In Scott's photograph, the South Summit is just behind Haston; the main summit is less than 250 feet above them. Lhotse is the peak below and to the left.

asked us to go back to the summit with him. I agreed reluctantly and he, sensing my reluctance, changed his mind and said he'd go up and film it and then come straight down after us. He borrowed Pertemba's camera to take some stills on the top and we walked back 50 feet and then walked past him whilst he filmed us. I took a couple of pictures of him. He had the Blue Peter flag and an auto-load camera with him. He asked us to wait for him by the big rock on the South Summit where Pertemba and I had dumped our first oxygen cylinders and some rope and film on the way up. I told him that Pertemba was wanting to move roped with me – so he should catch us up fairly quickly. I said, 'See you soon' and we moved back down the ridge to the South Summit. Shortly after we had left him the weather began to deteriorate.

A decision was needed. I pointed at my watch and said 'We'll wait ten more minutes'. Pertemba agreed. That helped us – it gave some responsibility to the watch. I fumbled in my sack and pulled out our stove to leave behind. The time was up. At first we went the wrong way – too far towards the South Col. About 150 feet down we girdled back until we found what we thought was the South Summit Gully. There was a momentary lessening in the blizzard, and I looked up to see the rock of the South Summit. There was still no sign of Mick and it was now about half past four. The decision had been made and now we had to fight for our own lives and think downwards.

Pertemba is not a technical climber, not used to moving away from fixed ropes or in bad conditions. At first he was slow. For three pitches I kicked down furiously, placed a Deadman and virtually pulled him down in the sliding, blowing powder snow. But Pertemba was strong and adaptable – he began to move faster and soon we were able to move together. Were we in the gully? I felt panic surge inside. Then I saw twin rocks in the snow that I recognized from the morning. We descended diagonally from there and in the dusk saw Dougal's oxygen cylinder that marked the top of the fixed rope over the rock step.

We abseiled down to the end of the rope and tied a spare rope we had to the end and descended the other 150 feet. From there we descended down and across for 1,000 feet towards the end of the fixed ropes. During our traverse we were covered by two powder snow avalanches from the summit slopes. Fortunately our oxygen cylinders were still functioning and we could breathe. It was a miracle that we found the end of the fixed ropes in the dark, marked by two oxygen cylinders sticking out of the snow. On the fixed rope Pertemba slowed down again and I pulled him mercilessly until he shouted that one of his crampons had fallen off. The rope between us snagged and in

It took exactly half an hour for Reinhold to prepare the tea. My deliberations were also shared by him; we exchanged them wordlessly. We were completely united in our determination to continue the assault on the summit.

Once again we set off. The tracks of our predecessors, which could still be seen in the snow, served as an excellent orientation guide. The clouds were moving over from the south-west, from the bad weather corner of the Himalayas. We had to push ourselves even more because that promised bad news. We found ourselves in the lower area of the jet stream, those raging winds of speeds up to 200 kilometres per hour, upon which the enormous passenger planes are carried from continent to continent. We had traversed the troposphere and were approaching the frontier of the stratosphere. Here cosmic radiation was already noticeable and the intensity of the ultra-violet radiation had multiplied. Only a few minutes without our snow-goggles sufficed, even in the fog, to diminish our powers of vision. In a very short space of time direct insolation would lead to snow-blindness and painful conjunctivitis.

Reinhold and I photographed and filmed as often as we had the opportunity. To do this, we had to take off our snow-goggles and we also had to remove our overgloves. Each time it became more difficult for us to put the gloves back on again. But losing them would have led to the very rapid paralysis and frost-bite of our hands.

Since it was no longer possible to go on in this deep snow, we had made a detour towards the South-east Ridge. Here the wall dropped 2,000 metres down to the south-west. One false step and we would have plunged down into the Valley of Silence. The exposed, very airy climb on brittle rock without any rope demanded extreme concentration. Reinhold was right behind me. I took the lead to the South Summit. Completely without warning, we suddenly found we had passed through the clouds and now stood on the last stage before our goal.

At this point the storm attacked us with all its might. However, in spite of the storm and the fatigue, my fear of the mountain had dissipated with the clouds. I was quite sure of myself. Over there lay the main summit, almost near enough to touch, and at this precise moment I was sure we were going to do it. Reinhold, too, told me later: 'This was the moment in which I was convinced of the success of our adventure.'

A sort of joyful intoxication overcame the two of us. We looked at each other – and shrank back. From Reinhold's appearance I could only conclude that my own was very similar. His face was contorted in a

we climbed up, climbed as we do at home, in the Alps! I dug out a little stance in the snow and drove a weak peg into the brittle rock. I finally took off my gloves and roped myself up, with Andrej belaying, while I tackled an overhanging crack. The cold of the rock bit immediately and ruthlessly into my bare fingers. After a few more moves and touching more rock they became frozen hard and totally numb. I had set the oxygen valve to the maximum supply, but there was nothing that could help to ward off the cold. The 15 kilogram burden on my back threatened to pull me down. There was no time to test the holds, or the frozen fingers would have let go. Suddenly, with a broken-off piece of rock in my hands, I landed in the snow below, held by the rope thanks to Andrej's presence of mind. Knee-deep in the snow I waved my hands to make blood come back to my fingers. The blood obeyed, but, oh, how it hurt! I would have howled with pain if I had had any breath left. Andrej was silent. His faith in me was not shaken. So I tackled the overhang again. A bit higher a foothold broke off. I remained hanging on my fingers for a while, but having lost all support for my feet I slipped again. Bloody hell! What is the time, Andrej? A quarter to twelve. We are damned late! Shouldn't we go back? Andrej asked. No answer. We would talk it over on top of the Grey Step.

I tackled the overhang now slightly more to the left. It was even more arduous there, the rocks hanging even farther out beyond the vertical, but the strain would be limited to a shorter section. I made a loop on the rope, then climbed as high as I could and passed the loop round a hump of rock. But when I stepped into the loop I found that the hump was too small to hold the rope and I started slipping down again. My fingers were fast losing strength, and yet I kept pulling myself up. Somehow I managed to catch a tiny hold with one of my feet, but at the same time I pressed the little tube for the oxygen supply against the rock with my knee and pulled it out of my mask. Oh, God help me! I'll choke! I rallied the last of my will power and dragged myself on to a snow-covered miniature ledge. The tube was pushed back in its place and I paused to take some oxygen. The fingers had long stopped hurting, they were totally numb again. But Andrej, we will win! We will win the battle! Not the battle against the mountain, but against ourselves and our shortcomings. You can't fight against the mountain. There you can only survive or die. There are no more alternatives, and the choice is yours. We two will survive, we two must survive . . . .

I followed a narrow ledge leading as far as the crack on my right-hand side which I had attempted before. It was easier there now, but still impossible with gloves on. At the end of the pitch I hammered in a piton. The crack was shallow, two centimetres only, but I had no choice. I switched off the oxygen. The first bottle was empty. Cloud suddenly descended upon us. But it did not matter. I did not think of Makalu any longer, I did not long to see it any more. I only wished we would escape from this hell safe and sound. While Andrej was climbing, the piton was bending under his weight. We both were literally hanging on it. Would it break off? I did not feel any fear but trusted in my good fortune. Andrej was swinging in mid-air on one jumar, half-choked by the rope and harness. He thought he would never do it.

Finally he touched the rocks and found some support for his feet. Memories of previous hard training in domestic hills crossed my mind. How often had we been running, as if for life, in heat and rain, in snow and mud, with tongues dangling down to our knees, day after day, every day. Now we reaped what we had sown. I was glad that we were together on the hill. Friendship means more than the greatest success.

By now we had used up one bottle of oxygen each. We let the empty shells slip into the abyss. Andrej took over the lead in the following pitch. It was decidedly easier. Belayed by the rope from above I advanced quickly. We were now on top of the Grey Step. The wind had grown into a hurricane. The rope, however, was put back into the rucksack, and only then did we remember to switch on the radio. What impatient moments they must have gone through in the camps below, and we never bothered so much as to come on the air.

'Hello, Tone, come in, please.'
'I'm on the air.'
'We've just managed to climb the Grey Step. It looks easy ahead of us. Three more hours and we reach the top.'
'Bravo, boys!'
'Tone, what's the time? We're late, aren't we?'
'Not at all. It's only twelve. Over and out for now. We'll be continually on the air.'

How was that? At a quarter to twelve we had been at the foot of the Grey Step, it had taken us three hours to climb it, and now it was twelve. Andrej dug out his watch from under his gloves and down jacket – it was truly no more than twelve o'clock. How was that possible? It must have been nine before, but Andrej, upset by my falls must have mixed up the hands and read it as a quarter to twelve. So we were not late – we would manage without a bivouac. Then I realized that my hands were still numb. The fingers were as white as wax, and I did not feel them at all.

I panicked. I had been so preoccupied with climbing that I'd had no eye for anything but hard passages we had had to negotiate. Now I fell to rubbing my fingers, but I could not bring any life back to them. I swung my arms at their full length like a windmill. Finally there was the first trace of pain, the herald of the more severe pain to come. With the blood streaming again through the cramped veins, I calmed down. The skin remained white, though. But that was harmless.

The cloud settled down, totally obstructing our view. Gentle snow-slopes gradually narrowed up into a gully, which rose steeper and steeper towards the final step below the summit. We were now 8,600 metres high. The ridge soared steeply again, vanishing somewhere in the cloud. We did not have to take our gloves off any more. We helped each other now and then on awkward spots, which saved us the trouble of taking out the rope. The ridge assumed the form of a knife-edge, but the rock was firm. I held on to the crest of the ridge with my hands and let the crampons scratch along a vertical slab on the South Face side. Oh, the passion of rock-climbing! We forgot where we were. We strove to reach a goal just a few metres ahead, and once that was reached we fixed a new one a few metres higher. We had to take off the ice-coated goggles, as we could not see the little footholds on the smooth rock any more. And then we surmounted the very last steep step. What followed was a gentle slope with black gravel where the wind had swept off all the snow. Then a sharp crest of snow, and then we made out the aluminium tripod. The Chinese pyramid! I waited for Andrej and let him go first. A matter of friendship, nothing else. At that moment I felt tears rising to my eyes. On Gasherbrum I had been in front, and now it was Andrej's turn. At first he did not want to accept, but then he did and was the first to make the final step . . .

The summit!

We hugged and clapped each other on the shoulders. Tears . . . We had reached the highest point of our terrestrial globe.

We took off the oxygen sets along with the masks. A feeling of terrible freedom overwhelmed me, I felt like hovering in mid-air. It was a freedom acquired through hard work, won by myself, dependent on myself. We sat down together by the Chinese pyramid, with hardly any thought coming to our minds, but immensely happy because the strain was over. With the aim reached, I felt utterly empty. With a trembling hand I took the radio out of the rucksack.

'Hello, Camp I, hello, Tone, come in please.'
'I'm on the air.'
'Tone, we are on the top!'

The Yugoslavs accomplished some of the most testing climbing yet undertaken on Everest – Tone Skarja called the West Ridge 'the highest grade V in the world'. In Zaplotnik's picture (left), Stremfelj crosses somewhat easier ground on the Yellow Band, 1,600 feet below the summit.

'A DREAMLIKE SENSE
OF DISBELIEF'

1980–1993

The summit at 40° below

by *Andrzej Zawada*   Translation: Ingeborga Doubrawa-Cochlin and Peter Cochlin

As successive new routes on Everest were climbed, one alluring objective remained: a winter ascent. The challenge was taken up by the Poles, who already had a formidable reputation for winter climbing in the Himalayas, having made the first ascent of a 7,000 metre peak and narrowly failing to climb Lhotse. The expedition leader, Andrzej Zawada, who took part in both climbs, argued that it was time to 'open up new horizons' by making a winter attempt on Everest. The expedition faced difficulties from the start. The Nepalese authorities overcame their scepticism to grant permission with barely a month to go, forcing the expedition to send its equipment by air. Unable to afford more than five Sherpas, the climbers had to do all their own portering and faced plunging temperatures and recurring storms which wrecked their camps. Finally, in mid-January 1980, they set up a camp on the Lhotse Face, with just four weeks left to complete the climb.

The Polish winter expedition of 1979, pictured here in their Base Camp on the Khumbu Glacier, faced temperatures of minus 45°C and winds above 100mph. Illness and exhaustion took a constant toll and at times the expedition seemed doomed to fail. The British magazine Mountain *said that climbers were 'treading the borderline between will-power and insanity.'*

Pages 108/109: The Kangshung or East Face offered a new vision of Everest for the 1980s. In Stephen Venables's picture, Ed Webster from the 1988 Kangshung expedition is gazing at the face for the first time from a crest in the Kama Valley some ten miles away. The 'dreamlike sense of disbelief' was sensed by Venables upon completing a new route on the face.

On 15 January Camp III was erected on the wall of Lhotse by the group from Zakopane. Everyone was delighted with our progress – only 11 days of climbing and already three camps established. Then, over the radio we received the team's first impressions of conditions ahead: the wall of Lhotse was one large ice mountain! There was no pack snow in which it is so easy to hack out steps. The huge bergschrund below the ice-wall which drops down from the Geneva Spur was virtually impossible to climb. Now we would have to go up the right-hand side between the seracs. On this route there are two overhanging barriers of ice and we would have to use fixed ropes. Our elation at having set up Camp III so swiftly turned to depression.

From Camp III to the saddle of the South Col was a distance of 850 metres. Just 850 metres! At this height and in those wintry conditions, to climb these 850 metres was only just about in the realms of human possibility. We lost nearly one month trying to climb them, and during the many attempts half our team was out of action.

The first attempt was undertaken by Cichy, Heinrich, Holnicki and Wielicki on 23 January. They made a very brave attempt, using fixed ropes which had been left by other expeditions in the autumn and fixing new ones themselves. Wielicki reached the highest point, but even he, after depositing some gear, had to return to Camp III. Two days later another

attempt was made by Zurek and Pawlikowski, but hurricane-force winds made climbing impossible. During their retreat, Zurek was blown over by the wind and fell about 20 metres to the nearest piton. Although he was very badly bruised, he managed to reach Camp III unaided, and then, with the help of colleagues, made his way to Base Camp. On his way down he twice fell into crevasses. Unfortunately his injuries did not allow him to take any further part in the expedition and he had to go back to Poland.

All the time the bitter, raging winds made any movement arduous. Even getting to Camp III was a major problem. Several times Dmoch, Heinrich and Olech started out but, even with their great determination, they were unable to win the battle against the icy hurricanes. Week after nervous week went by. On 10 February we tried once more; but once again the weather defeated the indefatigable Heinrich, while his partner, Lwow, returned with frost-bite in his hands. More and more people were unable to take part in the climbs above Camp III, and our doctor, Robert Janik, had more and more work to do in Base Camp attending to the sick and injured.

During this phase of the expedition – the first ten days of February – only four members of the team were able to survive in these appalling conditions and to adjust to the high altitudes. They were Cichy, Fiut, Heinrich and Wielicki, and my plans and hopes were very much bound up with them. Which of them would reach the South Col? I was convinced it was only a psychological barrier preventing us from reaching it. If a person could climb to Camp III at 7,150 metres twice, three and even four times, I felt he could also climb to 8,000 metres, without any doubt. In my mind, I was nervously arranging the right combination of strengths and weaknesses to create the ideal partnership for the final assault. However, it turned out to be unnecessary, because at the critical moment the climbers with necessary qualities of mental and physical endurance were there. But before we could make the final assault, we still had to reach the South Col.

On 11 February, Cichy, Fiut, Holnicki and Wielicki set out. Each climbed at his own pace. A large sheet of solid, glassy ice made the climb very exacting. They reached the Yellow Rocks and climbed towards the Geneva Spur. From this point upwards there was the beginning of an exposed traverse in the rocks, slanting to the left of the ridge. In the middle of this, Holnicki retreated. The other three reached the South Col at 4 pm. There was a whirlwind raging and Cichy, who had helped to carry up some of the equipment, quickly withdrew to Camp III. Fiut and Wielicki tried unsuccessfully to erect a rather complicated American tent in these ferocious conditions, but gave up and took shelter in a small, one-pole bivouac tent. It saved their lives, but they had no chance to rest since they had to struggle all night to hold their small tent down in the savage storm. The oxygen they used revived their strength and warmed their bodies but they were not even able to make tea. Inside the tent the thermometer showed minus 40°C! Our earlier plan of placing the tent in a snow hole was unrealistic.

The constant winds driving through the saddle of the South Col had blown away all the snow, laying bare one gigantic rubbish tip containing multicoloured bottles of oxygen, butane canisters, and various assorted things, all discarded by previous expeditions. All night long we were in radio contact with the two climbers on the South Col. The appalling conditions they were in terrified all of us below. There was a great deal of discussion between camps, and when Cichy suggested that the two climbers on the South Col should go on and try and conquer Everest there were howls of protest. The whole success of the expedition was at a critical stage. If it was almost impossible to survive one night on the South Col, how could we even consider attempting the next 850 metres? There was no choice but to retreat.

In the morning of 13 February, the two men returned from the South Col to Camp III. Wielicki was complaining of frost-bite to his feet and decided to go down to Camp II. Fiut almost flew down directly

to Base Camp, so quickly did he reach it.

I was now convinced that the future of the expedition was out of my hands. How powerless is any leader at moments like these? How convenient is it, when an expedition breaks down in these circumstances, to blame the weather conditions? If I wanted to save the expedition there was only one thing to do, and that was to attempt the climb myself. My partner Szafirski agreed that this was the best way to get us out of the impasse. I was very worried as to how well I would be able to climb 1,500 metres in one attempt. I was in Camp III for the first time, yet I had to climb immediately to the South Col. We were climbing with oxygen, the weather was exceptionally mild, but despite this the climb took us the whole day. Shortly before sunset I reached the vast saddle of the South Col, just behind Szafirski. The dome of the summit of Everest was burning with an incredible purple glow. After removing our oxygen masks we were barely able to recognize one another, so bloated and livid were our distorted faces. Our movements in this thin atmosphere reminded us of scenes from the landing on the moon. We began to erect the Omnipotent Gore-Tex tent to establish Camp IV. We succeeded in bending only two of the fibre-glass supports, which proved sufficient to form the barrel-like shape of this new type of tent. We lit two butane heaters and immediately it became very warm inside. After placing ourselves comfortably in our sleeping-bags we asked our colleagues in Base Camp to put on some lively music for us.

Every evening we discussed our plans for the next day. That evening Cichy and Wielicki informed me that they would like to return to Camp III to attempt an assault on the summit. This was a pleasant surprise for me, particularly since Wielicki had suffered serious frost-bite in his toes and had not had much rest after climbing to the South Col. At the same time Heinrich informed us that he was going to climb from Camp III to Camp IV.

The following morning Szafirski started to climb, taking an extra oxygen bottle to leave as a reserve for the final assault team. He reached 8,100 metres but I was unable to climb with him since I had not acclimatized enough. Instead, I started to check the pressure in the oxygen bottles which had been discarded all over the South Col, and found six with a pressure higher than 230. After midday, Heinrich and Pasang reached Camp IV. They had climbed without any oxygen and were in excellent shape. We convinced Heinrich that he should go for the summit the following morning, provided the weather conditions were satisfactory. We left them our oxygen masks, and at about 4 pm started to go down.

I felt the lack of oxygen very much. Szafirski was in front of me – he was in a hurry to get down. After sunset, darkness came very quickly as usual. I was on a narrow ledge just before the Yellow Rocks, and could not find the piton with the next fixed rope. Szafirski had already descended through the rock band, and told me afterwards that he had no strength left to climb back up to guide me to the proper spot. I switched on my torch but still could not find the place. I decided to traverse out on to the icy wall, hoping to reach the fixed ropes. I managed to chip out two tiny footholds in the ice and stood on them tentatively with only the front spikes of my crampons. Below was a sheer drop of 1,000 metres of icy slab which ended in the open crevasse. Finally common sense prevailed and I made my way back to the rocks. The only thing to do was to wait for the dawn. I cut out a small platform and built a small wall of ice-blocks on the windward side. I took out all the clothes I had in my rucksack and put them on. Trembling with cold, I began the long wait. I was at 7,600 metres and it seemed as if the unusually bright stars were just above my head. Suddenly, down below, I saw lights moving in the vicinity of Camp III. It was Cichy and Wielicki. At great personal risk they were climbing up to come to my rescue. At about 2 am they reached me. They gave me some hot soup and rubbed me until I felt warm again. In the morning, I was back in Camp III.

The permission for this expedition was valid from 1 December till the end of February. The Nepalese Ministry, however, had asked me to agree that attempts to reach the summit would not continue after 15 February when we should start to raze our camps and withdraw to Base Camp. I asked if they would release us from these restrictions but by 14 February I had received no reply. On 15 February we sat by our radio telephones and waited with great anxiety for news from Heinrich on the South Col. If the reply was in the negative then his attempt on the summit of Everest would be our last chance. Climbing without oxygen, Heinrich and Pasang managed to reach 8,350 metres before returning. Meanwhile, the Ministry kept us waiting right up until the last moment, for it was 5 pm before they informed us that they had granted us two further days of climbing – our last two days! Now everything depended on the weather and strong nerves. On the morning of 16 February I said goodbye to Cichy and Wielicki as they left for the South Col.

They climbed with oxygen and reached the South Col after five hours whilst I made my own way down to Camp II where Wielicki, Heinrich and Pawlikowski were waiting. The rest of the expedition was at Base Camp. That evening we kept looking at the sky to see if the weather was going to change. During the

night we listened to the winds howling on the ridges above; but in the Western Cwm it was calm. The two climbers on the South Col told us they were in very good shape. They read the temperature outside their tent – it was minus 42°C.

On the morning of 17 February they reported to us over the radio at 6.30 am that they were about to start their climb, each taking one bottle of oxygen. From that moment it was impossible to sit still. The tension was unbearable. Hope and despair followed one another at each passing moment. As the hours passed and there was still no word over the radio, our anxiety was overwhelming. As a safety precaution Wielicki and Pawlikowski climbed up to Camp III. Then finally, at 2.25 pm the voice of Leszek Cichy resounded over the radio: 'Guess where we are!'

We were out of our minds with happiness. It was the most wonderful moment of our lives. Then we had to concern ourselves with their safe return from the summit. Wielicki had frost-bite in his toes, and they were both exhausted since their oxygen had run out on the South Summit. We spent another very tense night when Cichy reported his arrival at Camp IV but did not say Wielicki was with him; but everything turned out happily and on 19 February the whole team sat down to a celebration supper at Base Camp. We were the first to conquer Everest in winter! Each one of us had the right to feel the victor, including the absent Krzysztof Zurek, because each of us contributed to success and shared the common ideal.

Mountains only take on any meaning when humans are present among them. Humans experience the feelings of victories and defeats, and take with them something of these experiences when they return to the valley. Already our winter expedition of 1980 was behind us.

When the climbers reached the Lhotse Face (shown foreshortened above) they found it consisted almost entirely of sheer ice. Storms continued to drain the expedition's resources and with only four fit climbers it took a month to climb the face and reach the South Col.

A partner in myself

by Nena Holguin

Despite his success without oxygen equipment in 1978, Reinhold Messner remained convinced that the ultimate ascent had yet to be achieved. In 1978, he and Peter Habeler had been aided by an Austrian expedition climbing via the South Col; in 1980, Messner resolved to climb Everest without supplementary oxygen and entirely alone. He and his partner Nena Holguin, together with a Chinese liaison officer, set up Base Camp at one of the pre-war British sites. At first the heavy monsoon snowfall made climbing impossible but in mid-August the weather cleared. Messner began his attempt on 17 August, carrying a 44lb rucksack which included a tiny tent, sleeping-bag and mattress, a stove and food, and a camera. His account is related by Nena, who waited for him beneath the North Col.

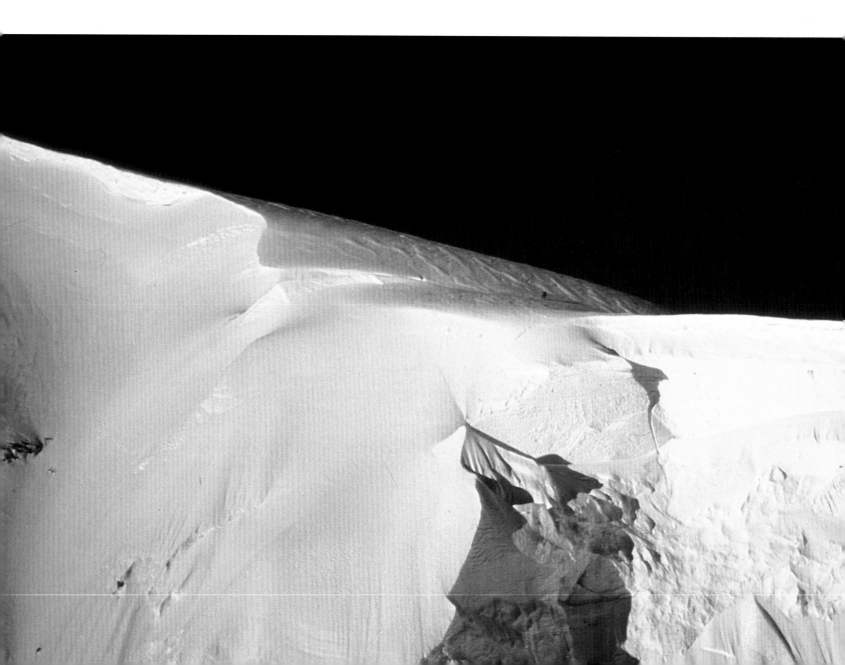

Being alone on a mountain does not guarantee you an experience of utter loneliness. Just in the same way that mingling in a crowd can never deprive you of solitude. It's merely that in one situation there's an accentuation of your fears and problems, while in the other you can easily become distracted or even encouraged to look away from them.

Well, there's nothing to distract me from my fears now. I'm 50 metres below the North Col and I've fallen down, down, down. It felt like eternity in slow motion, rebounding back and forth off the walls of ice, although it was in reality only eight metres deep.

And so I'm standing on a narrow platform. Is it thick or thin? I look up. I look down. It's all the same. It's black – everywhere. My headlamp's died. I see a twinkle from a lone star through a small hole somewhere up above.

All I can say is that despite all those fears I overcame on Nanga Parbat in '78 some new ones have been born. I fumble with the lamp. Ah ha! It works. I try

to make some sense of my situation. I know I shouldn't be down here. 'If I can climb out of here I'm going straight back down this crevasse-ridden snowfield and we're packing up and heading home.' 'But will I die down here instead?' 'Nena's not really so far away; there are only a few hundred metres between us. Down there at our camp along the glacier she's tucked away safely in a warm sleeping-bag.' 'There's a rope down there. Perhaps she could climb up this high alone and help me? But will she ever know where I am?' All the while these thoughts are racing through my mind, somehow I still don't feel all that uncomfortable. I'm actually quite relaxed, feeling peaceful and calm within.

Concentrating now on my next moves I find a small ramp leading diagonally across the ice, leaning inward but none the less taking me upward and out of this hole. I'm able to rationalize quickly once I step out into the crisp clear air. I must have been a little careless before, I tell myself. So, with great care, I span my body across the crevasse and using my ski sticks as an anchor step forward, arriving safely on the uphill side.

My natural instincts take over. It's not difficult now. As I reach the North Col the ridge extends above me up over gentle rolls, rising with only a gradually steepening gradient. The sun takes its time: centimetre by centimetre gold light floods the vastness beyond and the peaks reveal their summits one at a time according to their majestic height. I move on, my boots gripping the hard surface.

To say that the climbing goes on without incident can only mean that there's no particular interruption to one's smooth rhythm; there is always the sense of fascinating incidents going on inside. My whole being is taking part, witnessing this beautiful perfect day, perfect simply because I'm part of it, wide awake and aware with all my senses.

It's going quite well and I'm satisfied with myself. I'm in no rush. Time is mine to waste away. Time to think. Reflecting on my first solo attempts on a Himalayan giant, I'm able to realize a lot of things about myself and my approach to solo climbing. This time I'm here much more for the fun of it. In 1973 when I first headed off to solo Nanga Parbat my ideas were more vague, without direction. I was out to prove to the world, to prove to myself, that I could climb an 8,000-er alone. At the start I was determined but in the end I was heading nowhere. Perhaps then I was even stronger physically than I am now but psychologically I was unprepared.

In 1978 when I again set off for Nanga alone things had changed. I was much more in tune with my own body. I had not set off with the object of conquering

Almost lost in the white landscape, Messner (left) heads up the North Ridge, covered in heavy monsoon snow. Nena watched and photographed from their Advance Base on the Rongbuk Glacier. Messner bivouacked at 7,800 metres on the North-east Ridge but the next day was no longer visible from below.

Messner's bivouac tent, purpose-built for the attempt, consisted of a Gore-Tex cover stretched between two semi-circular aluminium poles. The total weight of his rucksack was 18 kilos and he photographed himself with an automatic camera mounted on his ice-axe.

a peak nor indeed of returning home a hero. What I wanted was to come to know and understand the fears of the world, my own fears. I wanted to feel new again. But it was a long struggle even then to accept myself completely. And for this reason it was perhaps my most important climb. There were still things I had to prove to myself – my self-sufficiency without dependence. During that climb my human side was awakened. It was a battle against my own body in which the will had to take control. It is difficult to say which stress is greater in such a situation, the physical or the psychological.

Here I am once more driving myself onward. I want to live out this dream, this feat of climbing Everest alone which before my solo ascent of Nanga seemed so far away, so impossible. Now for some reason it seems even easier than Nanga. There was no difficulty for me to leave the base at 6,500 metres and head on up here today.

I don't feel so far away from everything as I arrive at my first bivouac spot. There's a good flat surface on a snow-covered rock platform at 7,800 metres. Every preparation goes slowly and smoothly and I find it totally enjoyable to empty my rucksack and erect my small Gore-Tex home. The bright sun reflecting off the snow offers a great deal of warmth and comfort as I chew dried meat and sip this salty brew of Tibetan tea leaves. I don't feel alone. I instead sense a companionship. There's always that someone to keep me company when I reach these altitudes on my own. Perhaps it's that partner within myself.

I couldn't have asked for better circumstances. The daylight fades away leaving the glacier below in deep black shadow and this world of mountains surrounding me illuminated by spectacular orange then red rays.

Darkness falls and I'm at home inside.

I have to make the choice now of going on with less food and gas or going on painfully slower bogged down by the security of those extra rations. I lighten my load and with the tent rolled up loosely and fastened to my rucksack prepare to carry on. The night has been rewarding. My strength and energy levels are replenished after my sleep has been disturbed only by the powerful gusts of wind rather than by the ill effects of high altitude.

At 9 am the first sunlight gives a refreshing start. I'm feeling positive. But then as I begin to wade through snow over my knees my whole manner of thinking changes from this steady harmonious rhythm. What to do? I shall never get anywhere at this rate. I scan the slope of the North Face as it stretches across to the Norton Couloir. It certainly is a Great and Grand Couloir, I realize, as I think about its other names. It is impressive to think of the tons of snow that must through the years have thundered down that deep scar in the mountainside.

Obviously several avalanches have swept the face recently and it becomes apparent that my only chance of success lies in picking my way gingerly over a beaten-down snow surface to the couloir from where, with hopes of hard snow in the gully, I will be able to advance. So with a slow and cautious pace I move out across its wide dimension.

It is definitely not steep yet still it leaves me with an air of uncertainty. Anything falling from above will without a doubt sweep me from my feet. But then I allow these thoughts to become distracted occasionally as I look directly above my head and study the First and Second Steps, remembering the 1924 epic of Mallory and Irvine. How impossible it would have been for two climbers within that age of climbing technology and theory to surmount and overcome that great rock barrier, the protruding Second Step, not to mention at some unbelievable speed.

It seems too late in the afternoon as I arrive exhausted at an altitude of 8,200 metres. I'm not feeling as encouraged as yesterday. I've climbed the whole day but I'm only 400 metres higher.

On a mushroom of rock, ice and snow I feel safe enough to bivouac. It sits like a perch out above the entirety of all that's living – mountains, land and people. I haven't excluded myself from them. I'm in fact much more with them from here. I retire stretched out but the altitude is trying to take over. I'm no longer comfortable. Eating and drinking are an effort. 'It's too cramped in here.' 'There is simply not enough room.' 'Will I ever sleep?'

Already I'm feeling my power drifting away as I look out in the early morning at the puffy grey monsoon clouds swirling in all directions and rising quickly from the east. But I'm determined to go on. One litre of water takes too long to bring out of its icy cold nature to a warm satisfying temperature. So I drink the water lukewarm, take the camera around my neck and, wearing my crampons, grasp hold of my ice-axe and begin. I'm lightweight so perhaps there's a chance.

As I lose my orientation success is far from my mind. I'm thinking for the moment. The psychological burden of searching a way through the rock, clouds and ice up to the couloir, then a steep snow flank leading on to the rocky buttress extending down from the Summit Pyramid, weighs heavily on my spirit. Can I carry it?

Somehow and for some reason I go on. I'm nowhere in particular. I'm just climbing automatically, instinctively. I don't expect it but suddenly it's there – the tripod, the blessing of proof, the curse of destruction upon this perfect place of solitude.

While sitting on top of Nanga in '78 I felt as though I was born again, a witness to the whole creation. Now I've brought another dream into reality but there are no words to express this new feeling. The physical stress has reached its limit and the mind can't even react during that instant. I'm simply there.

At times I've searched out a face-to-face encounter with loneliness, searched for understanding and felt a loneliness that was no longer a handicap but a strength. But in no way could I ever claim to have found aloneness. I've merely opened a few doors, to have some slam behind and others lead to more. Slowly and carefully, step by step, I've learned to know something of myself, to love myself. Sometimes I took chances, I dared, and other times I held back too long. But along my way there's no turning back. I'm delighted on my voyage inward for there is always room to grow.

On the second day of his ascent, Messner found the North-east Ridge covered with thigh-deep soft snow and was compelled to traverse the North Face to the Norton Couloir. After bivouacking at 8,200 metres he left behind his tent and most of his equipment when going for the summit the next morning.

To spend eternity

by Maria Coffey

By the 1980s mountaineers were focussing on the 'last great problems' posed by Everest. Chief among these was the North-east Ridge, hideously long and posing formidable technical problems at high altitude, in particular the three gaunt Pinnacles which rise from the ridge between 26,000 and 27,500 feet. In 1982 Chris Bonington returned to Everest to attempt the ridge, leading a compact, lightweight expedition determined to climb without oxygen. The bid ended in disaster. Peter Boardman and Joe Tasker, two of the most respected climbers – and finest mountaineering writers – of their generation, embarked for the Pinnacles on 15 May. They were last glimpsed at dusk on 17 May, never to be seen alive again. That autumn Boardman's wife Hilary and Tasker's partner Maria Coffey travelled to Everest in a bid to come to terms with their deaths. By mid-September they had reached the Rongbuk Valley and were a short walk from the Langma La Pass, within sight of the mountain's Kangshung Face.

The expedition's first attempt reached the top of the First Pinnacle but had to turn back when Dick Renshaw suffered a mild stroke. Chris Bonington's photograph (left) taken from Camp II on 5 May, shows Tasker, Boardman and Renshaw at around 27,000 on the First Pinnacle. Above: Maria Coffey.

The rain fell relentlessly through the night and into the morning, turning to snow as we crested the valley and moved into a landscape of rock and sparse vegetation. I walked alone, locked into private thoughts and listening to the sounds of my own body moving through the silent surroundings.

Hilary's footprints were ahead of me in the snow, and I found her waiting in a small cave on the edge of a lake of the clearest blue which reflected the rocky slopes above it. A thermos flask and food stood ready: her sense of when my energy was about to flag was uncannily accurate, and she would always be there with supplies. Our trekking team was spread out as we moved along at individual paces, each reacting differently to the altitude. Hilary and I had been the first away that morning, carrying packs in case we reached the next camp site long before everyone else and wanted to put up our tents. The track was easy to follow, and Dong, our interpreter, had given Hilary careful instructions. It was good to feel so independent, and to realize that we had gained the trust of our Chinese guides.

We set off again after our snack and I hung back until Hilary was out of sight, reassured by her tracks but wanting to feel the solitude and remoteness of the place keenly around me once more. My pace settled into a regular plod and I moved slowly and easily, feeling warm and comfortable despite the low temperature. Wet snow fell around me, flakes landed on my face and immediately dissolved. The protective clothing was a cocoon, my breathing was amplified inside the jacket hood. A sense of peace settled over me. Suddenly, and totally unexpectedly, I felt Joe's presence. I have no explanation for this; my rejection of Catholicism in teenage years left me suspicious of the spiritual side of life. What happened on those high slopes in Tibet may have been generated by my own mind or may have been a manifestation of some form of energy from Joe. I really do not know, but I had experienced this awareness of him before. Shortly after hearing of his disappearance, I had asked my friend Sarah Richard to drive me to his house in Derbyshire where we had lived before he left for Everest. I wanted badly to be in the house and among all his things, yet it was a dreadful journey, knowing that I would not find him at home, not then or ever again. I sat in the car, distraught, unable to speak to Sarah, feeling sucked towards a horrible finality. And then, as we left the outskirts of Manchester and headed towards open country, I felt him there, all around me, comforting and reassuring. We reached Sarah's cabin first. She got out and I slid over into the driver's seat. I wanted to go to the house alone.

'Are you sure you're all right?'

She bent down to look through the open window. Her face was concerned.

'Yes, I'm fine now. It's not far. I'll see you in a while.'

Tasker (left) and Boardman rested for a week before making a new attempt on the Pinnacles. They returned to Advance Base (shown above) on 13 May. Before departing, Tasker wrote to Maria: 'There is a big job for Pete and me to do but hopefully it will go well.' Boardman told his wife Hilary: 'All is on our shoulders. It is a great committing adventure.'

I drove along a back lane, and experienced the same heightened awareness as when Dick Renshaw first told me Joe had disappeared. The afternoon was vibrant, trees reached out their branches towards the car and the leaves on them shimmered. Joe's presence was still there when I arrived and unlocked the house. I had been too preoccupied with work on my own place to visit it while he was away. It felt like minutes since the day we had left, even though it was three months before. I wandered around inside, soaking in the familiarity. On the bed I wrapped myself in the duvet, my nostrils filled with his smell, and I felt him about me then most powerfully. I cried, talked aloud like a child, and finally slept. A deep, dreamless, peaceful sleep. When I awoke the sun was still streaming through the window. Leaving the house was difficult. My impulse was to stay there, and wait. Only when I parked the car at the bottom of the track leading up to Sarah's cabin did the feeling of Joe gradually fade.

She was standing in the garden among long grasses, shading her eyes against the sun to watch my approach. The scene was uncannily still, as if she were a figure in a painting. I began to tell her.

'I know,' she said. 'He was in the car when I was driving. I felt him. It was really strong. I wasn't going to say anything in case it upset you.'

It has happened several times, only infrequently, but always intensely and without warning. And so, in Tibet, heading towards the Langma La Pass from where I hoped to glimpse the Kangshung Face, I did not try to block the feeling but allowed it to flow. Without knowing how or why, I felt infused by Joe as I plodded along. I listened to him talking to me, encouraging me. He was all around. I felt the gentle pressure of his hand on the back of my neck. This

was utter contentment, a sense of rightness as I headed up the wintry slopes.

Joe, or whatever the sensation had been, ebbed away, leaving me relaxed and smiling and still walking at a measured pace. The track became very narrow, cutting through a steep scree slope along a valley side. Far below me lay a long, densely grey lake with no reflection. Snow fell lightly, the air was damp and the cloud cover so low that mist swirled around me from time to time. My boots crunching on the loose rock broke the silence. In the distance, where the track curved and was swallowed by mist, some shapes took form. Several scrawny cattle swayed along the track until I had to scramble up the slope and make way for them. Behind the animals, carrying staffs and walking slowly and steadily, were an old man and a young boy. The man was slight, his face narrow, wrinkled and serene, and from his chin a long white beard fell in two strands. Their grey woollen blankets and felt boots seemed insubstantial against the snow and rocks. They stopped and regarded me seriously. 'Chomolungma?'

The old man pointed to where he had come from, towards the Langma La Pass. I nodded, and waited. All morning I had felt a stillness within me, a tenuous but undeniable link to a dimension outside the well-known and understood parameters of my world. Being high in the Himalayas, sensing the solidity, force and sheer permanence of the environment, was opening up my mind and allowing in a chink of awareness of the full scope and mystery of existence. This man and boy seemed creatures wholly connected to the mountain they stood upon. The child gazed up at me, unsmiling, with an air of wisdom and experience far beyond his years. His companion shook his head gravely. 'Chomolungma, Chomolungma,' he repeated, and taking my hands in his he intoned a prayer, perhaps a blessing. I welcomed this: I wanted to draw from the knowledge of ages that he surely possessed. He raised his hand in farewell and moved past me with the boy, towards their cattle. I watched until they went out of sight and imagined how we must have looked from high above, three tiny figures passing through a vast and unmoving landscape.

Beyond the prayer-flags of the Langma La Pass a bank of thick cloud lay over the Kangshung Face. Hilary sat very still, gazing towards it. I put my hand on her shoulder.

'The man and boy – did you meet them? Did he bless you?'

She nodded. We waited together, silently willing the mountain to reveal itself, until the three Swiss trekkers who made up our team arrived.

Jacques was in bad shape. We were now at 17,400

feet, he had pains in his chest and his pallor was a worrying grey. We divided up the contents of his small day-pack and his friend Denny stayed close and kept a watchful eye on him. Coming down the steep path from the pass, into the Kharma Valley, a yak driver and one of the porters prayed loudly at a high, sheer rock face and left offerings, small piles of food, on a ledge. At the head of this valley was Chomolungma, a sacred mountain, and they were showing respect.

On the valley floor the waters of a lake, startlingly blue from the copper salt, reflected our progress as we filed along its shores – heavily-laden yaks and porters, tired trekkers. A crowd of beaming girls appeared seemingly from nowhere and crowded round as the tents were erected. When they left I discovered that one of my gaiters and two stuff-sacks had gone with them, articles that had belonged to Joe. My fury was unreasonable, but I couldn't help feeling that they had taken away a tiny part of him. I drifted into a disgruntled sleep, woken near dawn by Hilary shaking snow from the tent roof and lighting candles to dry out the interior.

Chomolungma kept her Eastern Face shrouded for the next two days as we moved closer to the mountain across dramatically changing terrain. Moonlike landscapes on the high plains transmuted to muddy trails through lush vegetation in the valleys. We pressed on, crossing and recrossing rivers by rickety bridges or by precariously hopping from stone to stone, trudging through mud, willing the clouds to lift. I remembered Charlie Clarke and Chris Bonington predicting that there would be little chance of good weather on the east side of the mountain, but I was still convinced we would be lucky. The feeling of drawing so close was intense. Hilary was voluble in her grief: she talked and cried openly. I became increasingly withdrawn, conscious of tension building inside me. If Chris was right, if Joe and Pete had fallen down the Kangshung Face, then they were not far away, they were somewhere in the crevasses at the foot of Chomolungma. I immersed myself in an awareness of Joe's proximity, allowing it to override my loneliness and the reality of the loss. Asleep and awake I dreamed of somehow getting to his body, wrapping myself around his frozen form and breathing warmth and life back into him. It was an illusion born out of hopeless desperation.

Drying out round the stove at the end of the fourth

On 15 May, Boardman (ahead) and Tasker set off through flurries of wind-blown snow. They stayed at Camp II that night and the following day reached Camp III, a snow cave at 25,750 feet, just below the foot of the First Pinnacle.

day of trekking, we made a group decision to turn back. Going further towards the face meant crossing a glacial moraine that could be unstable after so much rain, and there was no indication of the weather clearing. Early the next morning Hilary and I walked up to a rocky knoll to make our private goodbyes. The Kangshung Face was ahead of us, hidden by the heavy mist that clung to it so resolutely, but I could feel its presence. Joe could be nearby, held somewhere within its folds. Perhaps this was as close to him as I would ever be again. With that thought the illusion snapped. There were no miracles to be had, the relationship was over, except for what I could cling to in memory. Chomolungma could not give him back to life. I sat down and began to weep, heaving sobs which bent me double as in the early days of grief. Hilary held me until I quietened and then I leaned on her and tried, brokenly, to express my thoughts. She looked over my head.

'Zhiang is coming.'

Our liaison officer walked slowly by, placed something on the cairn at the very top of the knoll, and then stood and looked towards the cloud-covered mountain. When he returned his face was set tight as if holding in feelings, and he did not glance in our direction. We went up to the cairn. Two cans of beer were set there, and a small posy of flowers lay between them. An offering to the mountain and a sign of respect to Joe and Pete.

We retraced our steps, back through the dense vegetation, up the muddy slopes and on to the windy plain. As night fell the mist rolled in around the camp site. In the big wigwam I chopped vegetables, drank whisky and tried to socialize, but I couldn't concentrate on conversation. My mind was outside, out in the mist and heading towards the mountain. After dinner I walked through the fog until I was out of earshot of the camp and away from its light. Squatting on my haunches, I felt the cloud close in and I imagined Joe walking towards me with his relaxed, loping stride, dressed in his usual garb of jeans, boots and sweater which varied little with the seasons. Had his ghost emerged from the mist I would hardly have been surprised, but nothing moved, there was no sound. I remembered an American girl I had met years before, in Patagonia. I had just arrived at Fitzroy National Park and she and her team of Italian climbers were preparing to leave. Her boyfriend had died on a nearby mountain the previous year, and she had travelled to South America to find his body and bury it. One of the climbers was a priest. They had reached the point on the glacier where her boyfriend and his companion had landed after the fall, said Mass and lowered the bodies into crevasses. She was young, in her twenties.

As we talked she was using an ice-axe to hammer nails into the wall of the wooden hut that was at the 'road head' of the park.

'This was his,' she said, waving the axe.

'You mean . . .'

'We found it beside him. I may as well use it. These nails will be good for hanging stuff on. And who knows, I might come back some time.'

'Are you glad you came?'

'Sure I am. Now I can believe he's really dead. Now I have a picture of him. Now . . .' She stopped for a second, her voice caught. 'It was good to at least be able to say goodbye.'

That girl . . . I couldn't remember her name, or what part of America she was from, or why she was with Italian climbers. But the feeling I had on that day came back clearly, my admiration of her composure and my wonder at her strength. I could never have foreseen it back then, but now I was envious of her, for her chance to say goodbye.

My legs had begun to cramp, and I was cold and damp. I stirred, stretched and returned to our tent, which was aglow with the light of several candles.

Crawling in, I discovered Hilary in the middle of a full-scale nose bleed. Her red thermal underwear was matched by the mounds of bloody tissues scattered around the sleeping-bags, and she was distraught with a mixture of grief and frustration at not being able to stop the flow of blood. I calmed her and the bleeding ceased, but her confusion carried through to her sleep. During the night her anguished cries woke me.

'No! No! Pete! *Pete!*'

She sat bolt upright, suddenly awake. In the dream she had relived the avalanche she had survived in Switzerland earlier that year, but I and her two nieces were with her and Pete was trying to dig us all out. For a while, then, we lay awake and she talked about the real avalanche, which had happened when Pete and Joe were on Everest, six weeks before they disappeared. She wrote to Pete about it and he replied: 'What is important is that you are alive and so am I.'

The sharp frost of the morning gave us hope that the mountain would appear. The clouds were playing a teasing game, allowing a glimpse of a peak and then covering it up again. Makalu appeared for a time and there was confusion over whether or not it was Chomolungma. We ran up a slope for a better view, our lungs heaving and burning in the thin, cold air. The face we saw was massive, spectacular and terrifying, but it was not the Kangshung.

Jacques was weak and despondent, so we took turns at walking with him and giving him encouragement. As I plodded up snow-covered slopes behind a yak, past tiny blue lakes, with the sun breaking through

and snow peaks appearing, the loveliness would send a shiver through me and I would be glad to be alive and to be there. Hilary and I hung back at the Langma La Pass, watching the clouds around Chomolungma, willing the curtain to open and show us the awesome vista behind. Three times the mists rolled back to reveal the summit, but the face stayed shrouded. Zhiang was hovering anxiously, wanting us to leave and follow the others, but we needed the steadying of those minutes, letting our thoughts settle before heading down from the mountain. It occurred to me that perhaps it was no coincidence that the Kangshung Face was not being revealed to us. Perhaps it was, after all, easier for us this way. I blew a kiss towards the east side of Everest and turned away.

Verdant hillsides pungent with juniper, and the gentle colours of irrigated fields and villages: after the landscapes of the high passes I felt I was seeing the lower Kharta Valley with new eyes. And as we began the drive to the northern side of Chomolungma I was calm, almost happy. Two eagles hovered high above us on the air currents. Joe and Pete, I thought, watching us leave. It was a fine place to spend eternity.

In May 1992, climbers from Kazakhstan found Boardman's body in a sitting position close to the Second Pinnacle, a short distance from where he and Tasker had last been seen. There was no sign of Tasker. It seemed likely that Tasker had fallen from the ridge and that Boardman had died, probably of exhaustion and the effects of altitude, while attempting a descent. The climber who found Boardman's body said that he was in a position of repose, 'looking like he was asleep'.

Above: the Pinnacles, wreathed in cloud, from 21,000 feet on the Rongbuk Glacier. The three Pinnacles can be seen through the cloud rising like fangs from the North-east Ridge. Boardman and Tasker crossed the snowy dip between the First and Second Pinnacles on 17 May, and were last seen approaching the Second Pinnacle as dusk fell.

The ice formations of the East Face were wrought into fantastical shapes, particularly in the claustrophobic gully named the Bowling Alley (right), between Snow and Pinsetter Camps on the lower part of the buttress. The climber is Dave Coombs.

A fine day for me

by Carlos Buhler

The Kangshung Face of Everest had long been considered unclimbable. In 1921 George Mallory dismissed it as impossible and the common verdict was that the avalanches which raked its flanks made it an unthinkable proposition. But in the early 1980s mountaineers began to reassess the risks. In 1981 an American expedition which included Ed Hillary and Kurt Diemberger climbed a giant buttress in the centre of the face before being stopped by the threat of avalanche. The Americans returned in 1983, bringing a rocket launcher and motor winch to fix an aerial ropeway for load-hauling. There were tensions over tactics and the composition of the summit party chopped and changed due to illness but the expedition built on the previous efforts. In extracts from his diary, Carlos Buhler describes the swings of mood and fortune as the team prepared for its summit push.

The 1983 US Kangshung Face expedition took on Everest's most awesome challenge – a 3,500 foot rock and ice buttress rising from the Kangshung Glacier, demanding the full range of modern climbing techniques. The expedition named it the Lowe Buttress, after their climber George Lowe, but it is now also known as the American Buttress. Right: Jay Cassell is shrouded by spindrift as he tackles a snow-covered crag near the top of the buttress. Above the buttress came a 7,700 foot climb up avalanche-prone snow slopes to the summit.

26 September

Camping at Pinsetter. Up and down and up and down. The radio's been going all morning! The people at Snow Camp told me not to come down – there were of course no loads to bring up. Then they told me to go up. Then to stay put. Then the whole day's carry was aborted – snowing too hard! So here I sit at Pinsetter, waiting to see what the weather will do. We're going to have to wait for October sun to settle those slopes. But I'm uncannily easy about time today. One month in base and it doesn't worry me a bit. Hey, I hope we don't lose anyone on that upper route by avalanche. Could be dicey up there.

27 September

I can't believe what just happened. I mentioned that I thought we should be sensitive to Geoff Tabin since he was feeling kind of left out and had a rough first experience on the mountain. One of the guys said I had no business saying such things and that it wasn't good for the team's chances if people worried about one member – natural selection was the thing. I just about felt like leaving there and then. Tears came to my eyes and I was embarrassed that someone might notice. But I don't really care. This whole episode reaffirms my thinking about going on a large trip

at 25,200 in Camp V. Kim is a gem up here, singing.

10 October

Well, George climbed Mount Everest yesterday. So did Dan and Jay. Lou, Kim and I did it the day before. Everest. Six on top. A dream comes true. First summit team. Kim, Lou and myself open the Kangshung Face to Everest's summit.

It's hard to keep a clear head through it all. Our move up to Camp VI on the 7th was uneventful. I moved up slowly and didn't race with Lou or Kim. That night we brewed up for four or five hours and then again at 1 am when we got up to go for the summit. Until 4 am we drank and drank. What followed was ten and three-quarter hours of gruelling trail breaking. It took us six hours to do the first 1,300 feet to 27,500, on the 'normal' ridge. Terrible, absolutely *terrible* snow conditions left us pretty wiped out. We ran into the seven Japanese trying to climb Everest without oxygen there and continued on.

I was amazed at the slope leading up to the South Summit – treacherous as hell. There was wind slab after we came up the Hillary Step and the thought of Mick Burke disappearing here in 1975 made me extremely wary. I tried to stay low on the left side of the ridge to avoid the huge cornices dropping over the East Face. I led it all with apprehension, but contentedly knowing that it was the final push to victory for the entire expedition. Kop had warned me that a few false summits would appear to be the top but when the true apex came it would be unmistakably clear. It was a good tip. When the top did come into view I waited for Kim and Lou to come up with me. The day was fantastic and the sun beat warmly on us even on those last few metres. Together the three of us cramponned up to the crest. It was all kind of a dream.

The air around us was very calm and it seemed as though we could have lit a candle on the summit. My small Olympus camera conveyed the truth of the temperature. It was hopelessly frozen. Kim took out a walkie-talkie and radioed down to Advance Base Camp. We could hear some Tibetan chanting – the local Yak herders who had stayed in Base Camp had begun to chant prayers for us at 5 am that morning and hadn't stopped all day long. I was pretty moved by their voices.

We took out a bunch of flags that needed to be photographed. As we'd removed our oxygen equipment, things went a bit slow. I was particularly interested in the way the Rongbuk

Some of the climbing on the buttress was the steepest and most testing ever achieved on Everest. In the photograph (left) Dave Cheesmond is using the technique known as jumaring or jugging to climb a rope on an overhanging section of rock near the tip of the buttress. The rope had previously been fixed in place by the lead climber. Right: Pinsetter Camp, located on an exiguous ledge halfway up the buttress. It was named Pinsetter because it was close to Bowling Alley Gully.

Glacier led out north to Tibet. Then came the gear photos – there was not much time to enjoy the view. I felt like we were a long way out on a fragile limb and the desire to start the descent burdened me. A strong sense of quiet satisfaction began to creep into my mind. In my oxygen-starved state, the dreamy realization that our goal was in our grasp began to take form. All we had to do was descend without an accident. I couldn't help thinking over and over of Mick Burke. I felt we had a long way to go that day.

We started down at 3.25 pm. I stopped to pick up a few stones and then Lou and Kim were out of view. It took a moment to realize I was alone at the top of the world – my moment to be the highest soul standing on earth. The descent was not so good. At the Hillary Step we bottlenecked with the five Japanese still going for the summit. Lou was moving like an old man – I only found out later he had stopped using oxygen because it was fogging up his glasses. I watched him go down the step ever so slowly, and when he and I reached the South Summit Kim was already far ahead. I could see him far down on the South-east Ridge. He must have been nervous about getting caught out after dark and was pouring on the speed. It was about 4.30, the sun was already low in the sky, and I too was feeling very pressed for time. Then we met a climber just coming up to the South Summit. I presumed he was another of the Japanese team we had met earlier in the day. Like them, he was climbing without an oxygen bottle.

'How much time to summit?' he asked me in

To ease the task of carrying their equipment up the buttress, the expedition used winches to ferry loads. The first (shown below), powered by a 5 hp engine and designed by expedition member John Boyle, could lift an 80lb pack almost 1,000 feet up the buttress. A second winch, using a counterweight of snow packed into a canvas bag, took the loads a further 700 feet. The expedition carried half a ton of equipment in this way. Right: The open slopes at last: after spending four weeks on the buttress, the expedition finally reached the snow slopes above. In Buhler's photograph, Dan Reid and Lou Reichardt are carrying loads to Camp IV; Chris Kopczynski is behind them, and another party of four can be seen, bottom left. The Kangshung Glacier is 5,000 feet below; the summit 6,000 feet above.

broken English. I didn't know what to say. It was so late now and with darkness coming the temperature would drop maybe 40 degrees. My throat was like dry ice and I could hardly speak. I pointed to my mask and said, 'With oxygen, maybe one hour. Without oxygen?' and just shrugged my shoulders.

'No time! No time!' he verbalized his thoughts as he looked up towards the Hillary Step where one of the Japanese was still working his way up the fixed ropes. He was absolutely right about the time. But someone trying Everest without oxygen is a motivated man and it was up to him to make his own decision, I thought. He told me he wasn't a Japanese climber but a Sherpa. He wanted to go down. It seemed the sensible thing to do, but again, I'd already made the top.

I took out a spare insulated mitten from my pack and my second water bottle which was inside it. I knew I wouldn't need it if we could get to the tent that night and set it down in the snow where I hoped the Japanese would find it. I carried on down the slope from the South Summit. It was hard packed snow and a fall would have been nearly impossible to arrest. I noticed that like me Lou was facing out as he descended. I was 40 or 50 feet ahead when I heard Lou's dry, raspy cry for help. I wheeled round and saw him splayed out on his back on the 35 degree slope with his head downhill. It didn't make sense! I sprinted up the slope on my front points and threw my body against his. The exertion made it feel that my air supply had been cut and I choked and gasped for air. For a few seconds we were a tangled mass of limbs and ice-axes. Lou had stepped into a small 10 or 12 inch crevasse, probably caused by the creep of the snow cover on the slope. He had his leg wedged in up to his knee and it was holding him in place on the slope as it curled over the lip of the crevasse.

After righting himself, Lou faced in for the remaining several hundred feet of steep slope. I wanted to catch Kim up before he dropped down on to the East Face and have him wait in case we had any more trouble getting down. I could see the Sherpa I had spoken to was also coming down. I descended as quickly as I could to Kim. By now he must have been quite cold and was insistent on going on. I felt there was nothing for me to do but wait for Lou to catch up.

After a few minutes, I again heard Lou shout. When he reached me, Lou explained what he had seen. A body had gone sliding by him on the slope and tumbled off the ridge on to the South-east Face and disappeared. It was the Sherpa I'd spoken to on the South Summit who had decided to turn back. We considered climbing into the South Col to tell the two Japanese who had stayed there, but then we met another Sherpa who was the first man's colleague. He seemed strangely impassive when we told him what had happened. With heavy hearts we started down on to the East Face. It was late and the sun dropped below the horizon before long. Kim was out of sight. We slid and plunged down the deep trough we had made on the way up. About 8 pm we reached the single tent of Camp VI.

Inside we found George, Kop, Jay and Dan. Kim had passed them and continued down to the next camp to make room for Lou and me. He was indeed incredibly fit. We six spent a terrible night in the three-man VE24 tent.

The next day Kop decided not to try for the summit after hearing about the Sherpa who had died. George reached the top ahead of Jay and Dan on 9 October. On his way up George crossed paths with the Japanese climber, Mr Endo, as he staggered down the mountain after a debilitating bivouac near the South Summit. Jay and Dan reached the top together several hours later in a whiteout. The weather was rapidly changing. As it turned out, only three of the five Japanese we had passed at the Hillary Step made it off the mountain alive. George brought down the ice-axe of one of the Japanese that he found stuck in the snow above the Hillary Step and sent it to his family in Japan.

11 October

I'm pretty wasted still today. Don't understand it really. But I'm going down after breakfast. Truly time to go home. I'm not getting stronger. I just lay in my bed all yesterday during a ten inch snow storm. This has foiled the attempt by the third summit team. We're clearing the mountain now. Everyone's coming off and when Dan and Jay are down the whole team will be safe.

13 October

These past days I have begun to realize that we actually opened a new route on Everest. That I was on top of that mighty peak and given the honour of breaking the way to the summit. I could never have imagined it. It is still sinking in.

14 October

For a long time I don't think I'll want to

The crowning moments: on 8 October, 38 days after starting the climb, Carlos Buhler, Kim Momb and Lou Reichardt went to the summit. They were followed by George Lowe, Daniel Reid and Jay Cassell on the next day. Lou Reichardt's photograph (far left) shows Buhler on the final stretch – very icy, Buhler found, and 'treacherous as hell'. It was from near here that three members of a Japanese expedition slipped to their deaths while the Americans were making their ascents. Left: Carlos Buhler, photographed by Reichardt, celebrates on the summit. In his diary Buhler wrote: 'It was all a kind of a dream.'

participate in another large expedition. But if I had to choose one major expedition over the last ten years from the USA to be a member of, this is the one. The folks have all returned healthy, successful and, amazingly enough, good friends. It doesn't mean there weren't differences. But on the whole everyone is on pretty damn good terms. That puts something very special into this trip.

18 October

My last view of Everest's East Face on this spectacular sunny day. Makalu, Chomo Lonzo, Lhotse and Everest. All in the most majestic of proportions. I still can't see myself on top. But knowing I was there makes me proud to have pushed myself to such a goal. Amazing activity, this mountain climbing. Right from the start I knew it was for me.

To reach the foot of their route, the Bulgarians had to make the steep ascent (below right) to the Lho La Pass. Higher up this section the climbing became more demanding and the Bulgarians installed a winch to ferry loads. The search for Prodanov after he reached the summit was led by Lyudmil Yankov, above.

childlike joy – or simply a long-restrained assertion of the spirit? On 21 April, people gathered in the streets and explained to each other the grandeur of the feat: not only as a sporting achievement, but as evidence of the Bulgarian national spirit. They were proud of Hristo Prodanov, happy that they were his brothers and sisters. That day was a marvellous one in Bulgaria: the sun shed its warmth on the greenery and the people walked about in a care-free mood. We Bulgarians know from where we started; we know how we have been held back in history; we know what anguish and misery are, and that is why we are thirsting for happiness. We had attained a lot in a short while: now the day had come when Hristo Prodanov lifted us up on Everest.

But Hristo was dying precisely in the hours of the most exalted enthusiasm. After leaving the summit, he was assailed by the darkness and by winds of increasing strength. That night he bivouacked somewhere around the Grey Towers at about 8,600 metres. His voice was clear but that was his only communication that night. In the morning he spoke again but by now he was suffering from the cold and altitude and his words were becoming muddled and

weak. He explained that he had lost his gloves and his hands were frost-bitten and that he could not move an inch from the place he had reached.

The other expedition members had spent an increasingly anxious night. In the morning, Sherpa Rindje tumbled through the door of Camp V, exhausted and suffering from the altitude. Then came Hristo's radio calls. From Base Camp, Avramov gave the order that all who had the strength and were the closest to Camp V were to give help immediately using oxygen apparatus. Without any delay, Lyudmil Yankov, Trifon Djambazov and even Sherpa Rindje set off for Camp V, while Ivan Vulchev headed up for Camp IV without oxygen. Thus a rescue bid, without precedent in the history of Bulgarian mountaineering, began in an attempt to save Hristo Prodanov.

New glorious names spring up: Ivan Vulchev, Lyudmil Yankov. Ivan Vulchev, aged 37, an associate professor of theoretical mechanics, with four 7,000 metre peaks and the Eiger wall behind him, forged ahead and by 6.30 that night had reached a height of 8,200 metres. By now total darkness had set in, the temperature was below minus 40°C, and the wind was

a hurricane. Avramov told him to return to Camp V but Ivan begged to go on. Avramov instructed him to obey and in about 30 minutes he arrived at Camp V.

Meanwhile Lyudmil Yankov was somewhere higher. Aged 30, an engineer in garden design, from a family of intellectuals and on his second Himalayan expedition, he became the favourite of all Bulgaria. At 10.45 that morning he and Trifon Djambazov had set off from Camp IV, equipped with three bottles of oxygen each and carrying a spare sleeping-bag, liquids and a primus stove. Djambazov could not go beyond Camp V but Yankov pressed on. This is his account:

'Above Camp V a steep ice couloir led to the Manfreda Chimney. I needed my utmost in strength and caution and climbed with great concentration, aware that I was all alone. Hristo was still making signals with the walkie-talkie switch but they were becoming less and less frequent. I had to hurry by whatever means I could, driven by despair and fear that I would not manage to reach Hristo before it was too late. Judging from the last words I had heard from him, he was somewhere above the Yellow Tower, more than six hours climbing above Camp V.

'Above 8,300 metres the old fixed ropes (left by the Russians) were torn down. Some were missing and none could be used. It was getting dark but happily I had my torch and so continued climbing. By now there was no way back to the camp for me – the only way was upwards. But I did not dwell

on my own predicament – all my thoughts were with Hristo. I tried to reassure him with my walkie-talkie but did not know if he could hear me.

'I carried on up until 9.30 pm. It was now pitch dark and I reached the end of the fixed ropes. All around me were black and voracious abysses, whose gaping eternity filled me with horror. I received orders from below to stop and bivouac there and then. My eyes were trying to pierce the darkness, looking up the interminable way to the summit. Hristo had to be somewhere up there and I could do nothing for him. A burning lump stuck in my throat. I did not want to believe that this was the end.

'I climbed down from 8,400 to 8,300 metres and spent a difficult, ice-cold night. At dawn I was barely able to extricate myself from the fresh snow which had piled on top of me. A gale was blowing, signifying the start of a storm, and I was compelled to carry on down. I had a fall of some 5 to 6 metres but luckily this had a happy end. At Camp V I found Trifon and Ivan together with Sherpa Rindje, who had barely survived. After a terrible struggle against the storm we reached Camp IV where the hurricane had swept everything away. Totally exhausted, we reached Camp II where we spent the night. The pain in my frost-bitten hands and in my heart did not let me sleep.

'It became clear later that after a night spent at 8,600 metres without oxygen and in temperatures of minus 40°C, Hristo could not have survived. He remained up there for good, with his peak, and became as one with his dream. I still regret that I could not have reached Hristo, at least for a proper farewell. But I would not have tried to close his eyes. He had to have them open, so that they could stare at that peak. For ever.'

Despite Prodanov's death, the Bulgarian expedition resumed its efforts. Eighteen days later, on 8 May, Ivan Vulchev and Metodi Savov – co-author of this account – reached the summit where they found Prodanov's rucksack and camera. Having run out of food and oxygen, and with no bivouac equipment, Vulchev and Savov were now in peril themselves. They spent the night at 8,700 metres and were found the next morning, suffering from exposure and frost-bite, by the next summit pair, Nikolai Petkov and Kiril Doskov. The four men descended by the South-east Ridge to the South Col, thereby completing the second traverse of Everest, following the Americans Hornbein and Unsoeld in 1963. At the South Col they were assisted by an Indian expedition who gave them shelter, food and oxygen. Vulchev recovered from his injuries but Savov had all his toes amputated after returning to Bulgaria.

Left: Prodanov, climbing without oxygen, prepares to set off from the West Shoulder on 20 April. The weather was windy but clear, but later turned against him. Below: expedition leader Avram Avramov. After the expedition Avramov declared: 'On the West Ridge you hold your fate in your own hands. Hristo did not lack the necessary fitness or skill. But luck turned its back on him.'

Sweet and sour

by *Andy Henderson*

Dwarfed by the North Face, five climbers inspect their route. The Australians were the only team on the face, in stark contrast to the half-dozen expeditions – including two from Australia – in the South Col that year. Henderson felt they were 'very privileged' to have the face to themselves.

The first Australian bid came in 1984. It was a bravura attempt: five young men who had never tackled an 8,000 metre peak before. They selected a new route, up the monumental snow-slopes of the North Face and into the Great (or Norton) Couloir, a giant, claustrophobic gully which had first deterred the British in the 1920s. After establishing a line of camps on the face, they prepared to enter the couloir. Andy Henderson's account describes two days during the expedition: 3 September, the day after an avalanche hit their route; and 3 October, when the team made its bid from Camp VI some 2,300 feet/700 metres below the summit. There were four in the summit group: Henderson, Tim Macartney-Snape, Greg Mortimer and Lincoln Hall, who turned back shortly after the start.

Everest's monumental North Face, rising 9,000 feet from the Rongbuk Glacier. The Great or Norton Couloir, which the Australians followed, is the angled gully, partly in shadow, to the left of the summit. The Hornbein Couloir is to the right.

September 3

With promptings from a lump of flesh at the base of my brain, chemicals begin flooding my system.

Increase heart rate.

Increase breathing.

Increase audio acuity.

'Andy dai, chia linos'. Loud, insistent but bearable.

Okay. Let's try a vision hookup. Eyes open and . . . nothing. Increase visual acuity . . . yes! There's a nose, about four inches away, framed by a beard and balaclava, sleeping-bag hood (his) and sleeping-bag hood (mine). Jim wallows slowly, like a harpooned whale on a gentle swell, his eyes firmly closed against the light which streams through the tent door. So far, so good. Let's try for a movement. More chemicals, boost tactile response, boost motor responses, boost vision, boost hearing, try and jack the level of consciousness up sufficiently to handle a search. My arm snakes out of my pit, towards the light, my hand loaded with info about a mug, possibly filled with tea. Such is my level of consciousness that 'I' know little or nothing of this.

My hand succeeds in its mission, and commences to close around the plastic mug of tea. Fractionally earlier temperature sensors in my fingers have sent their messages to the brain. As my fingers make first contact, the temperature data hits my brain like a bombshell. The air temperature is low. Very low. Life threateningly low. PANIC! More chemicals.

Clamp down on peripheral blood supply, boost consciousness, boost EVERYTHING. DO SOMETHING. Confusion reigns, my arm jerks, and tea courses down my face and sleeping bag, to the tent bilges where it joins the other frozen foulness.

I have now attained a sufficiently high level of consciousness to attempt the intricate task of speech.

'Shit', I mumble. Not bad for a first attempt, but the lips were not quite in the right position, the tongue was a bit slow off the mark, and there was a general lacklustre air about the whole effort. Again.

'Shit'. Better, much better. Tenzing, squatting in the darkness outside, chuckled quietly.

'Ako chia. Andy dai?'

'Uhn . . .', and I shove the mug out of the door again. It's 4 am and the stars are burning in a Guinness black sky. At this time of the day (night?) under the clear skies of Tibet it's mind bogglingly cold, and I'm forced to wipe a thin rime of ice off my glasses with a foetid pit liner. Jim was also fully awake now, propped up on one elbow and careful of his precariously balanced tea mug, as he rummaged through a chaos of medical equipment for his headtorch. If I have learned anything over the years it is that you should always know where your headtorch is when you hit the pit at night. Also your glasses, and piss-bottle. Especially your piss-bottle.

I was already dressed as I wriggled free of my pit. All I had to do was pull on my duvet booties, collect

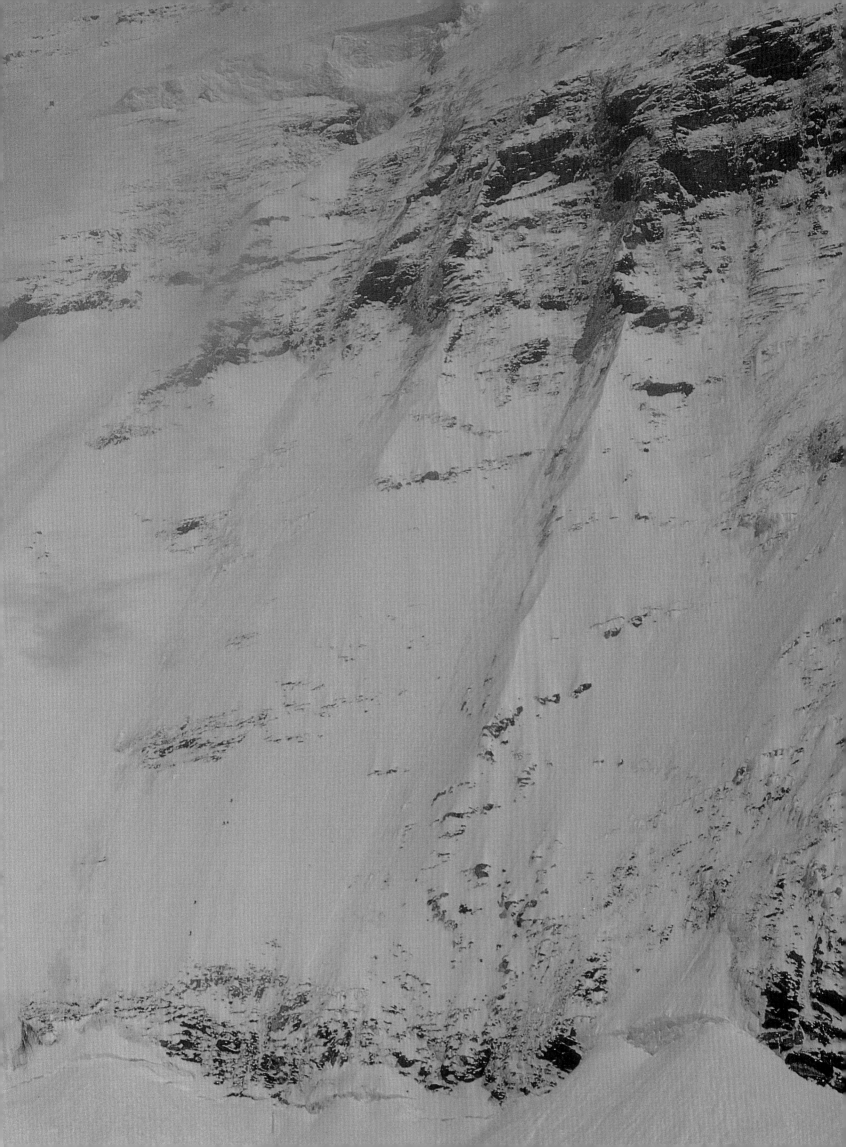

my mug and head for the mess tent. Around me the night was punctured by glowing domes and tunnels, the stillness by the quiet feral sounds of partner plotting with partner, by people worshipping the equipment they hope will keep them alive, by friend exhorting friend. As I shambled towards the four-person dome that serves as a mess tent for 12, my booties first crunch glacial ice and rubble, and then, briefly, biscuit pieces and other food detritus. Between the small stores tent and the mess and cooking tents the glacier is littered with the evidence of my carelessness. When we had retreated from Camp I several days before, in the face of continuing snow falls, I had been the last to leave, and so was responsible for securing the camp against storms and scavengers. The pikas [rodents] and goraks [crows] had outwitted me, and had eaten, or rendered inedible, an extraordinary quantity of freeze-dried chocolate and cheese. I could only hope the freeze-dried macaroni cheese would have the same effect on the little bastards as it had on humans, in which case they would have a short and constipated life.

In the cooking annexe to the mess tent candles flickered as Naryan and Tenzing laboured over the gas and shellite stoves to produce breakfast. It was their unenviable job to get the climbers and film crew out of bed in the morning, feed them, and then try to organize the shambles left in their wake. As well as these duties, they acted as managers for Advance Base Camp and Camp I. By comparison, Naryan and Tenzing regarded their stints carrying on the avalanche prone lower slopes of the face as light relief.

In the mess tent Jim and Colin wolfed down their porridge, knowing that, as members of the film crew, they would have to leave well before the climbers to get their several hundredweight of junk into position on time. Geof Bartram, Greg and myself were able to proceed at a more relaxed pace, slowly consuming our porridge before leisurely wandering through a plethora of vitamin pills, ginseng pills, pills for stress and pills for work. It was still dark when, full of pills, we rattled towards our dump of ski equipment, and arriving, called down curses of great potency upon those who had nicked our gear. Stocks in particular often went missing, and these soon became jealously guarded talismans, to be labelled, bound and stored near your tent for personal use only.

On the firm snows of pre-dawn it would take about two hours to reach our gear dump opposite the North Face. With the sun still below the North Col, the Northern Cwm was in shadow, although the upper section of the face was stippled with light.

One of the reasons I had taken to high altitude climbing was to avoid Alpine starts. I was yet to succeed, but it was hard to feel bitter in the pre-dawn stillness. Skis buzzed gently on the crusty snow, biting sweetly to climb. To the west, peaks blazed with the light of a new day. It would be a good one.

After the heavy snow, Geof, Greg and I were anxious to get back on the hill, whilst Tim and Lincoln had judged it to be still too dangerous. It was one of those minor disagreements which often arise during expeditions – you have to respect the other person's judgement – so Tim and Lincoln were back at Advance Base Camp.

Two and a half hours later Greg broke the silence. 'There seems to have been an avo down our route.'

Before the heavy snows we had fixed rope up the face to the mid-point of a rib on the western side of the Great Couloir, at an altitude of about 22,000 feet, and had dumped gear there for Camp II. Now a long tongue of debris stretched from the bottom of the route across the névé towards us. We continued exploring, and were soon forced to contact Advance Base Camp again.

'We've found the tent and one of the stoves we left behind,' I radioed. 'Camp II seems to have been relocated all over the glacier.' Greg repeated the conversation for the benefit of Geof's movie camera, and everyone was grateful that the avalanche hadn't wiped out an established, occupied camp.

'How's the gear dump?' asked Tim, referring to the stash of personal gear left in a 'schrund at the bottom of the face.

Avalanche! In Colin Monteath's dramatic photograph, a climber appears doomed as snow sweeps down towards him from the mouth of the Great Couloir (left). Although this avalanche passed him safely, it was close to this spot that the team's equipment was buried on 2 September. That avalanche also swept over the site of Camp II on the crest of the prominent rock rib directly above the climber. Below: Andy Henderson in the snow cave at 22,640 feet which served as Camp II. Even though the cave was hit by an avalanche, the climbers considered it 'bombproof'.

'OK, we think. We'll go up and check.'

Wimps like myself had left harnesses, crampons, etc at this site. The good skiers like Tim had also left their climbing boots, having changed into cross-country ski boots for the trip from the 'schrund to Camp I. For Tim it was three hours up, 20 minutes down.

The dump had been obliterated by the same avalanche that had taken out the Camp II site.

Two days later the gear still hadn't been recovered. Tim and Lincoln had come up from Advance Base Camp and at 21,000 feet the team had constructed a hole which seemed about the size of an Olympic pool, probed with avalanche probes, and had generally given the area a thorough going over. One of my most enduring memories of the expedition is of Tim solemnly tramping around on this vast cone of avalanche debris 'dousing' for gear with two pack stays lashed together. He had a few problems getting volunteers to work on his random pits, and soon even he had given up. Almost all those who had lost boots were able to replace them, either from camera crew gear, or in the case of the more obsessive, from their own stocks. Only Tim, with his huge feet, had no spares.

3 October

'Andy . . .'

'Uhn . . .'

'Not coming . . . too cold . . . too slow . . .'

'Uhn . . . OK.' On the day of the summit attempt Lincoln was dropping out.

The huddled figure in the shadows of the Great Couloir, bent double with the effort of conversation, looked small and very alone from my position high on the Yellow Band. Lincoln means many things to me, but I'm not used to thinking of him as either small, or alone – it was unsettling. I had had similar feelings two days before, as Geof, after giving me his share of the communal gear, disappeared down the fixed rope. Geof's decision to retreat in the face of overwhelming altitude problems was unavoidable, and had to be made before leaving the fixed ropes, which ended at about 25,000 feet, but I knew he would be bitterly disappointed. Never a peak bagger, Geof delighted in getting high just to see what he could see, and would have loved to have made it to 8,000 metres. I could feel his distress through the thin air.

I had my own problems now and was not able to give Lincoln the sympathy he deserved, and perhaps needed. The gentlest of people, he has a flair for disorganization which could make others weep with frustration. It never ceased to amaze me, then, how

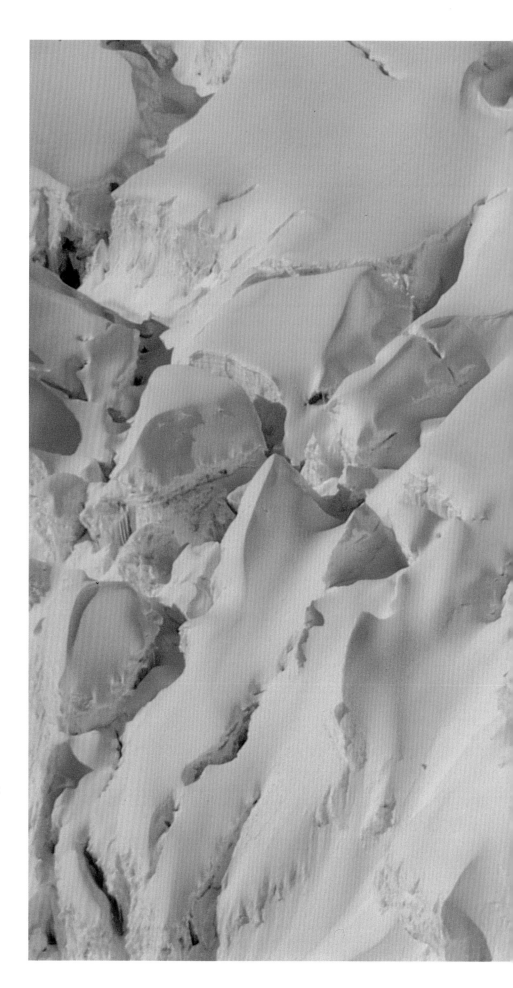

Geof Bartram approaches Camp II. He has just reached the crest of the rock rib shown on page 144, with the crevasses and seracs of the Rongbuk *Glacier below. Bartram was a mountain guide and trek leader, one of several in the team. But, says Henderson, 'we were not a picked national team of* *climbers, just mates from a variety of backgrounds and lifestyles – a disparate group who had developed respect and affection for each other over the years.'*

weakening all the time. They stopped for a rest but, as I caught up, started once again. I slumped in the snow and muttered, almost cried, 'I'll never make it'.

Odd heard me. 'You'll do it, Chris. Just get on your feet. I'll stay behind you.'

And on it went – broken rock, hard snow, then deep soft snow which Pertemba ploughed through, allowing me to keep up as I followed the well-formed steps made so laboriously by the people in front. The stars were beginning to vanish in the grey of the dawn and the mountains, most of them below us now, assumed dark silhouettes. The crest of the ridge, still above us, lightened and then the soaring peak of the South Summit was touched with gold from the east as the sun crept over the horizon.

By the time we reached the crest, the site of Hillary and Tenzing's top camp in 1953, all the peaks around us were lit by the sun's low-flung rays. The Kangshung Glacier, still in shadow, stretched far beneath us. The Kangshung Face itself was a great sweep of snow, set at what seemed an easy angle. Just below us some fixed rope protruded, a relic of the American expedition that climbed the face in the autumn of 1983. Across the face was the serrated crest of the North-east Ridge. I could pick out the shoulder where we had excavated our third snow cave in 1982 and, above it, the snow-plastered teeth of the Pinnacles where we had last seen Pete Boardman and Joe Tasker.

It was 5 in the morning. We were at 8,300 metres and it was time to change our cylinders. We set out again, plodding up the crest of the ridge, our shadows cast far into Nepal. Ever steepening, sometimes rock, mostly snow, it was much harder than I had imagined. It seemed to go on for ever. Glancing behind me, the black rocky summit of Lhotse, fourth highest mountain in the world, still appeared higher than us. A last swell of snow, with the wind gusting hard and threatening to blow us from our perch, and we were on the South Summit. We gathered on the corniced col just beneath it, the very place where Doug Scott and Dougal Haston had bivouacked on their way back in 1975.

There was a pause. Pertemba had broken trail all the way so far but the ridge between the South Summit and the final steepening of the Hillary Step looked formidable, a knife-edge of snow clinging to the rocky crest, with an intimidating drop on either side. Odd was worried about our oxygen supply. It had been three hours since we had changed bottles and he questioned whether we had enough to get back. The others had been climbing with a flow rate of three litres per minute, but I had found that this had not been enough. I had been turning mine on to four and so would have even less. But at this stage

I was prepared to risk anything to get to the top.

Pertemba said decisively: 'We go on'.

Bjorn took the initiative and pushed to the front. Ang Lhakpa got out the rope, 20 metres between the six of us, and Bjorn tied one end round his waist so that it trailed behind him, more of a token than anything else, as we followed. The going to the foot of the Hillary Step was more spectacular than difficult, but the step itself was dauntingly steep.

Odd took a belay and Bjorn started up, wallowing in the unconsolidated snow, getting an occasional foothold on the rock wall to the left. Pertemba followed, digging out an old fixed rope abandoned by a previous expedition. The step was about 20 metres high and Bjorn anchored the rope around a rock bollard near its top. The others followed, using the rope as a handrail.

I was last, but Dawa Nuru waved me past. I gathered he had run out of oxygen – he and Ang Lhakpa had been climbing on just one bottle while carrying our spare bottles to the crest of the ridge. As I struggled up the step, panting, breathless, apprehensive, I felt what was almost the physical presence of Doug Scott beside me. It was as if I could see his long straggly hair and wire-rimmed glasses and could sense his reassurance and encouragement, pushing me on. Then Les, my father-in-law, appeared too. A man of quiet wisdom and great passion, he had thrown the I Ching just before I left home and predicted my success. This was something that had given me renewed confidence whenever I doubted my ability to make it.

Doug and Les got me to the top of the Hillary Step and disappeared. I seemed to have the mountain to myself, for the others had vanished round the corner ahead. I felt as if I had to squeeze out my last bit of will power to join them. Push one foot in front of the other, pant hard to capture what little air and oxygen was flowing into my mask, and then take another careful step along the corniced ridge that led to the summit.

A break in the cornice and there, framed below me to the right, was the North-east Ridge, with its crazy ice towers and snow flutings, seeming to go on and on. I thought again of Pete and Joe – perhaps their bodies were still down there. Another step, and the ridge was hidden by a curl of snow. Now I was at the spot where Pete Boardman had last seen Mick Burke in 1975. Pete and Pertemba had been on their way back down; Mick – that cocky, aggressive, very funny figure I remembered so well – was going for the summit on his own. He never came back. Thoughts of other lost friends from Everest came flooding in: Nick Estcourt who forced the route through the Rock Band in 1975 and died on K2; and

Despite using supplementary oxygen, Bonington found the section of the South-east Ridge below the South Summit *exhausting work. 'Ever steepening, sometimes rock, mostly snow, it was much harder than I had imagined.' Lower down he* *collapsed in the snow but the Norwegian Odd Eliassen urged him to go on.*

'Ya gotta want it!'

by Sharon Wood

By 1986 five women – compared to 182 men – had reached the summit. None were from North America, and none had done so by a new route. In April an 18-strong Canadian expedition began an attempt on the West Ridge, aiming to become the first team to reach the ridge by the North Spur of the West Shoulder and continue from there to the summit. Sharon Wood was a mountain guide from Alberta with big-mountain experience in the Andes. By mid-May exhaustion and stress had reduced the team to half a dozen active climbers, with Wood and her climbing partner Dwayne Congdon chosen to make the summit bid.

19 May, morning, Camp V, 25,000 feet
I wriggled my body through the snow tunnel entrance until my head came up level with the platform and I could look inside. My first sight was disappointing: Barry Blanchard and Kevin Doyle huddled together looking tired and beaten. No one had slept well that night. We were all spent from running the race for the last two months against the encroaching monsoon. At best we had another week before the bad weather shut us down; at worst it had already arrived.

Some time ago we had entered a second race, our wasting bodies against time. Here we breathed a quarter of the oxygen that one breathes at sea-level. For our bodies to continue to get fuel in this atmosphere our muscle is metabolized for energy. We looked like we had spent the last year in a refugee camp.

We had a hard day ahead of us, the hardest yet, but this felt like our last chance. If we succeeded in getting this camp in place today two of us would push on for the summit tomorrow. We had made the decision to start using supplementary oxygen. Each tank weighed 20lbs; by the time we strapped on two bottles each, on top of the supplies for Camp VI, our packs came to 70lbs per person. The oxygen we had thought would help instead hindered us. At the oxygen flow-rate we set, it was just enough to compensate for the weight difference.

We followed the last stretches of rope out across the face. Six hours of maintaining a painfully slow pace against the ever increasing winds got us approximately a kilometre across on to the face. At 26,500 feet we came to the end of the ropes. This is where the climbing begins by entering a gash that

splits the formidable North Face right to the summit, a snow-and-ice gully of 40 to 60 degrees in angle, sometimes narrowing to shoulder-width and broken by the occasional steep rocky step. Only 2,500 feet to go but over the most difficult terrain and without the aid of ropes. The ropes were our umbilical cord to home, to safety, the last connection to security. We would soon leave them behind. I was the first to arrive. I scratched out a perch on the 45 degree slope and busied myself with untangling and dividing up a 600 foot section of small diameter rope that we planned to use on the difficult sections higher up. Barry arrived and settled in to wait for the others. I gratefully continued to occupy all thought and energy in my struggle with the rope.

Barry let out a muffled cry from under his mask, pointed upwards and dove for the anchor at my feet. Helpless, trapped in my sluggishness, I looked up to see a cascade of rocks ricocheting off the walls of the gully, crashing and bouncing straight for us. There was no time for me to do anything but watch in fear.

By some miracle the rocks missed us. In those few moments of terror, it seemed like hours of heart-beats and thoughts had rushed by, precious, irretrievable energy lost. Barry and I went no further than to exchange glances. It was just last year on another climb that I had been torn off my feet and had my shoulder broken when I was struck by a much smaller rock. Now this message from the mountain: commit or go home, but do not hesitate.

Minutes later Dwayne and Kevin arrived. Unaware of the previous excitement, Dwayne asked, 'What are we waiting for?'

The departure from the ropes was an experience I had anticipated for years. It was time to enter that icy gauntlet. I looked up and strained my eyes to focus on some trailings of old rope dangling high on the walls, left there from past attempts. They had been beaten by the wind, and were now barely recognizable, just ghostly tattered shreds. The relentless wind, our

The Canadians' route took them from the Rongbuk Glacier on the Tibetan side of Everest up the 5000-foot North Spur on to Everest's West Shoulder. From there a 1½-mile climb took them to the foot of the West Ridge proper. In the picture (left) Sharon Wood is crossing easy-angled snow between Camps IV and V at around 24,000 feet. The expedition fixed ropes on these sections as protection against the intense wind.

Above: Two climbers at 22,000 feet on the rising series of snow crests on the North Spur, providing a route from the Rongbuk Glacier to the West Ridge. The steepest sections of the spur reached an angle of 60 degrees.

Pages 160/161: The view from the ridge – an expedition member looks out over Tibet from 24,000 feet.

constant adversary, tore rocks and snow from the face thousands of feet above and funnelled it into the narrow chasm we were climbing. We hugged the walls, hoping the larger debris would miss us. If the person leading faltered, someone else would step in front to keep us moving.

Climbing up through that gauntlet was like crossing thin ice; the only things supporting me were my hopes. All the words of advice and support given to me by friends came pouring back as clearly as the day they were said.

Just a few days ago our leader, Jim Elzinga, pulled Dwayne and me aside. He said, 'Just treat that place up there like any other mountain. Don't die for it. No mountain is worth that cost.' Later the four of us were fighting our way back up the mountain through a bad part of a storm. I repeated Jim's argu-

ment to Kevin. 'The hell it is,' he replied. 'It's a one-shot deal. We can't come back tomorrow!' He promptly turned and continued with his teeth to the wind.

That day and the next we rode mostly on Kevin's and Barry's resolve. Their commitment became a great source of inspiration and drive. They clearly made it their goal to get Dwayne and me to that high point, Camp VI, in spite of the difficult and dangerous conditions, and in spite of the fact that they would climb no higher unless Dwayne or I fell sick. This concept of 'treat it like any other mountain' has its place, but if the truth be known, one's bearing on limits – the margin one leaves – is altered significantly in a place like this. Mount Everest is the grand arena. Here performance takes precedence over all else. It was this element in combination with people like

Kevin Doyle who possessed an overpowering, infectious sense of commitment that drove me on.

20 May, mid-morning, above Camp VI, 27,000 feet

Summit day – Dwayne and I cowered against the wind-ravaged cliffs. We had been climbing for hours but making little progress. Jim Elzinga's raspy voice crackled over the radio: 'Ya gotta want it!' They could see us. Those words echoed down the caverns of my memory, taking me back one year to a dismal day in Toronto. I was attempting to follow Jim through his regular training regime of running up the 1,000 feet of stairs of the CN Tower – not once but three times in the same go. No one else possesses the power to motivate and inspire me to such a masochistic act. I could hear his feet pattering up the metal stairs many flights above me. The same words had echoed down the grey cold stairwell, down through the depths of my fatigue: 'Ya gotta want it!' Simple but highly effective. Dwayne and I began to solo up through the Rock Band trailing out a rope and securing it to use later as a handrail to find our way back down. We knew it would be dark the next time we groped for it. Each step higher involved more and more concentration until we reached a level where the involvement was so intense it prevailed over all else and the fears and doubts faded. It was this state of ultimate commitment and performance which proved to be the most exhilarating experience of the trip.

20 May, evening, 30 feet below the summit

At 29,000 feet, in slow motion, at times reduced to all fours, we made the last few steps. I regretted leaving my ice-axe two hours ago. Back there, I had assumed we were only 20 feet from the summit. I had perched myself on a rock, unzipped four layers of zippers and dug into the depths of my clothing to where the radio had been warmly nestled all day. I knew that in just a few feet we would step on to the wind-exposed ridge where the temperature would drop drastically.

I had kept the radio on and turned up to full volume all day, but we had only spoken into it once. To talk we had to bare our fingers and at those temperatures we would risk frost-bite in seconds. When I pressed the transmit button I surprised myself with the sound of my own voice. I then realized how little Dwayne and I had spoken that day. We were so well synchronized in thought, determination and decision that we had not found it necessary to exchange many words.

When I finally spoke over the radio I sounded as though we were out for a day hike; I think I wanted to alleviate all the concern I sensed from our anxious onlookers and team-mates. After all, it was 8 pm in the evening, darkness would surely intercept before

we got down, forcing a night on the mountain without shelter. I explained that we were doing well and just 20 feet from the top. Cheers of joy and congratulations crackled through the receiver, then came the news that for some reason they could no longer spot us. The reason was to become clear just around the corner. Dwayne came up and led through towards the top. But what we thought would take us minutes took us another hour as we surmounted one false summit after another. Finally there was no more up. We came together for the final steps to the highest point on earth.

At 9 in the evening on top of Mount Everest the sun can be seen setting over an awesome curving horizon. I am sure it was beautiful but to us it meant something very different. We took our masks off and kneeled down, succumbing to the wind, our relief and our fatigue. We were aware we had made it, but there was nothing more. The radio was silent, long forgotten; there was nothing anyone could do for us now.

One nagging concern dominated: here we were on the highest point on earth and the sun was setting; when it set we would be left behind. Encumbered in our multiple layers of insulation and our oxygen apparatus, we managed an awkward embrace.

We stole a brief and knowing glance down upon a peak 1,200 feet below and just 30 miles away: Makalu, the fifth highest mountain in the world, a mountain we had failed on two years before. We had come so close. To have that experience behind us was comforting. We had learned some valuable lessons there; we had paid our dues. We belonged here.

There was no time to entertain any philosophical revelations; we simply had a job to finish. Dwayne got out his camera; I got out the flags and we began clicking off the frames one by one. Just as I had unfurled a huge yellow flag, the wind tore it from my grip. I followed its chaotic course down across the knife-edge ridge and out over the giants of the Himalayas until it finally disappeared. I felt so small. It could have been a dream.

Above: Sharon Wood photographed on the summit by Dwayne Congdon; after Wood unfurled her flag the wind tore it from her grip.

Plaudits and Brickbats

The Japanese have an impressive record on Everest, occupying third place in the list of ascents. They have specialised in large-scale media-sponsored expeditions, counter to the latterday fashion of light-weight teams. Their tactics have sometimes proved controversial and they figure sadly high in the statistics of Everest fatalities. But they have also provided examples of individual courage and audacity to rank with any others in the Everest story.

The Japanese played a prominent role in the early attempts on the South-west Face. Their first visits to Everest came in 1969, and that autumn Naomi Uemura, their foremost Himalayan mountaineer, led a group who reached around 26,500 feet.

The Japanese were back in strength in 1970, making a dual attempt on the South-west Face and the South Col route. Like the Americans in 1963, they suffered from the dilemma of which route to make their priority and in the end concentrated on an ascent via the South Col. On 11 May Uemura and his partner Teruo Matsuura became the first Japanese to reach the summit, followed by a second pair the next day.

Uemura was back on Everest the following year as a member of the ill-starred International Expedition which reached 27,400 feet on the South-west Face. The Japanese fared no better on the face during a post-monsoon attempt in 1973 but two of their climbers, Yasuo Kato and Hisahi Ishiguro, scored a notable double first by going to the summit from the South Col. No one had succeeded in the post-monsoon period before and no one had done so without an intermediary camp on the South-east Ridge.

Following the British ascent of the South-west Face in 1975 – and Junko Tabei's feat in becoming the first woman to reach the summit, via the South Col, in the same year – the Japanese switched their attention to the North Face and North Ridge. After a reconnaissance in 1979, they achieved multiple success in 1980. First Yasuo Kato embarked on an attempt on the North Col and North-east Ridge route previously climbed only by the Chinese. His partner was compelled to give up after leaving their last camp but Kato pressed on alone – also becoming the first climber, other than Sherpas, to make a second ascent.

Above, top: Naomi Uemura, the foremost Japanese mountaineer of his generation and a member of the first Japanese team to climb Everest, in 1970. Bottom: Yasuo Kato, who achieved three notable ascents in ten years, including the first in the post-monsoon season; the photograph is a self-portrait after he reached the summit alone via the North-east Ridge in 1980. Kato disappeared on Everest after making a winter ascent the following year. Right: a scene at the North Face Base Camp during the Asian Friendship Expedition – comprising climbers from Japan, China and Nepal – in 1988.

A week later Tsuneoh Shigehiro and Takashi Ozaki made the first full ascent of the North Face, climbing from the Rongbuk Glacier into the Hornbein Couloir – a true 'direct' route. They too overcame several setbacks, for one member of their team was killed by an avalanche and the summit pair ran out of oxygen several hundred feet below the summit.

Kato returned to Everest in 1982, this time bidding to make the second winter ascent. This time his luck ran out. He reached the summit from the South Col on 27 December, while his partner, Toshiaki Kobayashi, gave up 200 feet below the top. They were forced to bivouac at the South Summit and that night the mountain was hit by a storm. They were never seen again and their colleagues believe they were blown off the mountain.

In 1983 came a multiple tragedy which brought strong international criticism. Five Japanese climbers reached the summit from the South-east Ridge on 8 October, shortly after the US Kangshung team. Two slipped to their deaths during the descent and Pasang Temba fell after retreating from the South Summit. The *American Alpine Journal* accused the Japanese of 'inexcusable tactics' by climbing individually and not accepting responsibility for their colleagues.

That criticism could emphatically not be levelled at Kazunari Murakami when two of his colleagues were forced to bivouac after a South Col ascent in October 1985, one snowblind, the other with severe frost-bite. Murakami carried fresh oxygen to them from the South Col early the next morning, almost certainly saving their lives.

In 1988 the Japanese took part in the Asian Friendship Expedition, with no fewer than 254 members from China, Nepal and Japan, including 36 from Japanese television. It was divided into two teams, making bids via the North and South Cols respectively. Right on schedule, nine climbers and a three man TV crew reached the summit via both routes on 5 May and the resultant TV pictures were beamed to an estimated 280 million viewers.

'Whatever one may think of the motives for such an expedition,' commented Walt Unsworth in the authoritative history of the mountain, *Everest* 'it was an outstanding feat of organization and technology'.

Get down or die

by Stephen Venables

One of the most remarkable ascents was made by the British mountaineer Stephen Venables in 1988. He and three Americans, climbing without porters or supplementary oxygen, set a new route on the Kangshung Face, following a buttress south of the line taken by the US expedition of 1983. After brilliant technical climbing followed by a battle through heavy snow, the team reached the South Col on 10 May. Two days later, Venables and the Americans Robert Anderson and Ed Webster made their attempt. With his colleagues falling behind from exhaustion, only Venables reached the top. He was now in an appalling predicament, hours behind schedule, with bad weather brewing and darkness imminent, facing the perilous solo descent to the South Col. At 3.50 pm, having spent just ten minutes on the summit, Venables started down.

The expedition began its summit push on 8 May. In Venables's photograph, right, Paul Teare (ahead) and Ed Webster are at 6,600 metres, having just left Camp I on 9 May. Ahead lies the long trudge through unconsolidated snow to Camp II at 7,450 metres, which took an exhausting 14 hours. In the background (right) is the triple summit of Chomo Lonzo, 7,790 metres.

The wind was mounting now, starting to blow spindrift in my face. I hurried on, using gravity to speed myself back towards the Hillary Step. As I came over the last hump the clouds enveloped me completely. Suddenly I realized that I was heading too far to the right, down towards the South-west Face. I headed back up to the left, peering through my iced-up sunglasses at the swirling greyness. I was utterly alone in the cloud and there was no sign of the South Summit. I felt disorientated and frightened, remembering the tragedy of 1975 when Mick Burke, the last person to complete the South-west Face, went alone to the summit and never came back. Somewhere up here, in conditions like this, blinded behind iced glasses, even more myopic than me, he had made an unlucky mistake, probably falling through one of those fragile cornices overhanging the Kangshung Face. I suddenly noticed the dim outline of one of those bulbous overhangs just in front of me and veered back right. For God's sake don't do a Mick Burke. Just concentrate. You've gone too far left now. Head for that rock – must be solid ground there. Now I could pick out some tracks – my tracks almost filled with spindrift already, but tracks nonetheless. This is right. But it's so difficult. Must have a rest. I sank down and sat in the snow. Then I continued wearily, too slowly, legs sagging, head bowed. I stopped after only a few paces but forced myself not to sit down, leaning instead on my ice-axe. I took a few steps again, willing my legs not to sag and crumple.

It was snowing now, stinging my face and encrusting my glasses. I had to wipe them with a clumsy mitten, clearing a hole to peer through, searching for landmarks. I recognised clumps of rock and followed them to the pinnacle above the Hillary Step. Then came the hard part, taking off mittens, pulling up some slack in the fixed rope and clipping it into my waist belt karabiner with an Italian hitch. I pulled my mittens back on and started to abseil down the cliff. Even though I was moving downhill it was exhausting. Possibly the waist belt was pulling up and constricting my diaphragm, for I had to slump and rest during the 20 metre abseil, gasping for breath. I continued in a frantic blind struggle to the bottom of the step where I fell over and collapsed on the side of the ridge, hyperventilating furiously.

It had never happened before and I was terrified. This was quite new – this ultra-rapid panting, like a fish out of water incapable of getting oxygen into its gills. I panted harder and harder, clutching at the air, frantic to refill my lungs. But nothing seemed to get beyond my throat and for a ghastly moment I thought that I was going to suffocate. Then the air started to get through, and I gasped great sobs of relief as my breathing slowed to normal again.

I had to move. Get off that rope and continue. Take mittens off and unclip from the rope. Now, quickly get those mittens back on again. The first one is always easy but the second one won't go. I can't grip it – can't make those useless numb fingers work. It's all

Records and tragedies

by Geoff Tabin

In September 1992 Pierre Tardivel, a 29-year-old mountain guide from the French Alps, made the highest ski run in the world. Starting at Everest's South Summit, he descended 10,500 feet in three hours; the snow, he wrote, was 'paradise'. In the picture (right) he is at 23,750 feet, with Lhotse behind.

By the end of the 1980s, Everest was threatening to become a circus. Climbers were competing to make speed ascents and to dream up the latest stunt – to parapente or ski from the summit. Ascents multiplied as the Nepalese eased restrictions on the numbers permitted on the mountain. New route variants were attempted and the first commercial expeditions arrived. The death rate climbed. In 1988 Geoff Tabin, a member of the 1981 and 1983 US Kangshung teams, witnessed all this at first hand when he took part in an American expedition which put seven climbers – including two women – on the summit.

Geoff Tabin, a doctor from Rhode Island, USA, reached the summit on 2 October 1988. It was his third attempt and Everest's 248th ascent. In the same week, 22 climbers went to the top – and there were 215 more ascents in the next four years. Activity became the most frenzied in May 1992, with 58 ascents within six days, including 32 on a single day, 12 May.

The ridge I am climbing is barely two feet wide. To the east is a sheer drop of 11,000 feet into Tibet. Westward it is 7,000 feet down into Nepal. The angle increases from 70 degrees to vertical at the Hillary Step. Climbing unroped, I delicately balance the crampons on my right foot on an edge of rock. I swing my left foot, with all my remaining strength, into the adjoining ice, and I gasp for breath. Forty feet higher the angle eases. Adrenalin mixed with joy surges through me. After eight hours of intense concentration, I know I will make it.

The 70 mile an hour wind threatens to blow me off the ridge. The ambient temperature is far below zero. Yet I feel flushed with warmth. Ahead stretches a five foot wide pathway leading gently upward. Thirty minutes later, just after 10 am, the path ends in a platform of ice the size of a small desk. Everything is below me. I am the 223rd person to stand on the summit of Mount Everest.

The sky is deep blue and cloudless. The cliché is true, the vistas do seem to stretch infinitely in all directions. I look down over Lhotse on to the endless chain of mountains in Nepal. The Tibetan plateau on the other side extends to the horizon, where I can see the curve of the world dropping away. For 15 minutes I savour the view as the highest person on earth. Then the crowds start to arrive.

Within less than an hour climbers from three countries are taking turns being photographed on the summit of Everest. An American woman arrives on top. A Korean makes the climb solo to commemorate the closing ceremony of the Seoul Olympics. On the way down the woman, Peggy Luce, takes a near fatal fall. And this is one of the dullest days of the season. Thirteen teams from ten countries made at least one attempt on every face and ridge on Mount Everest during the post monsoon season of 1988. Everyone was out to set a record or do something new.

I was with the North-west American Everest expedition. Our team of 11 climbers, led by Seattle attorney Jim Frush, included three women bidding to become the first American women to climb Mount Everest. As a physician, my first priority was a safe and healthy expedition. As a climber who had attempted Everest twice before, my second goal was getting myself up the mountain. Having been there before also gave me a realistic perspective on the task ahead. Any success would have to be a team effort. Peggy Luce, Diana Dailey and Stacy Allison were all selected for their climbing ability, strength and personal qualities. On the mountain we would all be equal. Chomolungma treats everyone equally. The Sherpas

and Tibetans who live in her shadow call her the Goddess Mother of the Earth – Chomolungma. They believe she resides in the mountain bearing her name. The Sherpas know the suffering Chomolungma can cause. Before going to Everest we must go to the Thyangboche Monastery for a *Pujah*, or blessing ceremony, for safety on the climb. Twenty monks chanted continuously for 24 hours, six monks created an intricate sand painting beseeching Chomolungma to be kind, and we had personal blessings from the Rimpoche Lama. He said prayers for my safety and tied a blessed red 'protection cord' around my neck.

Finally, on 24 August we walked out of the rain into the snow of Base Camp at 17,500 feet on the Khumbu Glacier, which would be our home for two months. Garbage from past expeditions was strewn about and had to be cleaned up. Ironically, much of the debris had 'Everest Clean-up Expedition' stamped on it.

A large Korean team moved in next to us. They had a permit for the South Pillar route, so we worked together to fix the route. Among our neighbours was the 'most dangerous man in Korea', Hong Gil Om, who has a fifth degree black belt in Tae Kwon Do, a second degree black belt in Ju Jitsu, and is a member of Korea's elite anti-terrorist squad. We were paired together on the ascent on the Khumbu Icefall. Or rather, Om pulled me up the Icefall to fix the rope trail. When the Czechoslovakian, New Zealand and French Mount Everest expeditions arrived, the French

without supplemental oxygen, in under 24 hours, live on radio back to France. He was also rushing to get up before his countrymen Michel Parmentier and Benoît Chamoux made an ascent from the north side. At 8 pm, he turned on his headlamp and began dashing up the mountain.

Batard stumbled back to camp at 6 pm the next evening. He claimed to have reached 26,000 feet before he was stopped by bad snow conditions and exhaustion. He told me in his heavily accented English, 'I don't eat two days, I come Pheriche, I anger and think bad, is no good. Now I eat, then summit maybe.'

Batard rested six days before learning via the radio that Chamoux and Parmentier were making their bid. He suited up, fortified himself with black coffee, and sprinted again, this time leaving at 6 pm. Late the next afternoon I met him descending to Camp III. His thin face had the skin drawn tight over prominent cheekbones. Only his bulging eyes differentiated his face from a skull. He seemed to have aged ten years. I gave him tea as he muttered, 'I make 100 vertical below top. I can make summit, but I die. I am so sick, every breath vomit, vomit, so I think maybe I go down now or else I die.'

Batard's decision was a wise one. We later learned that Parmentier died of exhaustion and exposure on the North Face, having persisted in his attempt after his companions gave up. On the same day a small avalanche hit one of the Spanish tents on the West Ridge killing Narayan Shresta, a high altitude porter who had summitted in 1985.

Meanwhile, Chomolungma revealed a gentler side to her personality. The daily monsoon storms stopped. Her flanks basked in the glow of bright sunshine. My lungs burned as I climbed the vertical mile of ice to our high camp on the South Col. Three or four gasping breaths between steps did little to ease the pain. My mind, dulled by a lack of oxygen, felt as clear and light as it would the morning after drinking a fifth of Jack Daniels, six shots of tequila and a bottle of red wine. I reached the col at 2.30 pm. All things considered, I was moving pretty well.

I reflected on the craziness of risking my life for an endeavour so reliant on luck. Five years ago I had been at this altitude ready to try for the top when a storm nearly took my life. Now, I dared to think I might make it, while silently beseeching Chomolungma to remain kind for a few more days. I thought about my Karma and fingered the red string around my neck as I gazed towards the Summit Ridge.

Regaining my breath on the South Col, I was actually pleased by how strong I felt. I wished I could continue up. But we still had to establish our assault camp and stock it with food, fuel and oxygen before attempting

On 26 September 1988, while Tabin watched from below, Jean Marc Boivin, another guide from the French Alps, made a parapente jump from the summit (left). He descended 8,000 feet in eleven minutes and made a perfect landing in the Western Cwm. On the same day Marc Batard (top) made his third attempt to climb Everest, solo and without supplementary oxygen, in 24 hours. He did it in 22 and a half hours, comfortably beating the previous record of 39 hours set by two Swiss climbers in 1986. Benoît Chamoux (below) led a group attempt, known as 'esprit d'équipe' or 'team spirit', on the North Face. After it retreated from 650 feet below the summit, one team member, Michel Parmentier, stayed on the face to make a second attempt. He reached 27,500 feet but died of exposure during his descent.

were already riven into factions. They were backed by French television, who had paid $6 million to ensure live pictures from the summit. The newcomers were told they must pay a share of the cost of establishing the route through the Icefall. The New Zealanders and French settled but the Slovak leader, Jozef Just, was adamant that they would not give in to capitalism on a mountain. 'Ziss Iss Bullsheeet!' he growled. 'You climber, we climber, must share, no pay! Zis Iss Bullsheet!'

In the midst of the debate a diminutive Frenchman approached the crowd. 'I go tonight.' He turned and walked quickly away with his 'Marc Batard 24-Hour Everest' support team scurrying after him.

Marc Batard was going to race up Everest, solo and

the summit. Securing the ropes, I descended.

The weather remained perfect. Every team, except the Spanish who were delayed by their Sherpa's funeral, made rapid progress. The Slovaks claimed the first success. Jozef Just and Duson Becik powered to the 27,890 foot summit of Lhotse via a new route after an all night push from Camp III on Everest. They, along with team-mates Peter Bozik and Jaraslov Jasko, were merely preparing to attack the most difficult climb ever attempted, an Alpine-style ascent, without oxygen, of Everest's South-west Face.

The Slovaks were not the only ones with outrageous plans. Jean-Marc Boivin, a 36 year old mountain guide, from Chamonix, France, came to Everest with his newest toy, a light steerable parachute called a parapente. Boivin was also going to carry skis to the top. Depending on wind and snow conditions he would ski or fly, whichever was more fun.

Marc Batard no longer saw Everest as fun. He wanted to go home. 'I must make top, you know. I no want go up more, but is not possible to make sponsors if no success here.'

At 6 on the evening of 25 September Marc left Base Camp for his third and final charge. Five hours later, the 'mighty' Om left his tent at 27,000 feet on the South Pillar along with another Korean and two Sherpas. At midnight Boivin and the French 'extreme dream' team set out from the South Col. The two groups met at the South Summit, continuing the last hour up the final ridge together. At 3.30 pm on 26 September, 11 climbers from four different countries embraced on the summit of Mount Everest. An hour later, 22 hours after leaving Base Camp, a 'very much exhausted' Marc Batard joined them. His phenomenal solo speed ascent was soon to be matched by an equally prodigious speed descent.

I was at Camp II at 21,600 feet when I heard from the French radio that Boivin was going to jump. Taking off from the absolute summit he plummeted like a stone. Then the parapente caught air and he began to soar. He was still just a dot, a mile above me, as he slowly began to lap Everest, Lhotse and Nuptse. He added one more loop for good measure before touching down at Camp II as lightly as a feather, on his feet, with Everest in the background, the sun at a 45 degree angle on his face and his hat and glasses off – six feet from his camera crew. The crowd of 20 Sherpas, climbers and cameramen who witnessed the landing began screaming and applauding. Boivin responded with a shy smile. He had descended 8,000 feet in 11 minutes.

Three days later Stacy Allison, Steve Ruoss and Jim Frush left camp for the summit. They expected three Sherpas to come with them, each carrying an extra

In February 1990, 17 months after his parapente descent from the summit of Everest, Jean-Marc Boivin (above) went to Angel Falls in Venezuela to make a film for French television about base jumping – the hazardous sport of making short-distance parachute jumps from buildings, cliffs and other fixed points. After several successful jumps, Boivin died when an unexpected gust of wind drove him into the rock face.

cylinder of oxygen. Only one, Pasang Gyalzen, arrived. None of them was willing to risk going to the top without extra oxygen. Frush decided on a lottery. He told Pasang to think of a number between one and ten. Then whichever American was closest would get the gas. Everyone picked a number and the slightly-built Sherpa was terrified. He later confided to me, 'I think "Why they ask me this? Why they make me choose? How to choose?" Then I think, "Who is nice to give big tip?" I think maybe Stacy give best bonus. So, I say, "Stacy most close".' Cursing their bad luck, Jim and Steve turned back while Stacy climbed into history as the first American woman to reach the summit of Mount Everest.

Two days later, on 1 October, I returned to the South Col along with Peggy Luce and three Sherpas. At midnight, when we planned to leave, it was impossible to stand outside the tents. We finally left at 2 am, leaning into the 80 mile per hour gusts.

Climbing by moonlight, we made good progress up the icy slopes. 'One slip and you are dead, concentrate!' I kept commanding myself, as I tried to ignore the rapid pounding in my chest. Once above the Hillary Step, unadulterated joy welled up inside of me. I knew that I was going to reach the summit of Mount Everest. The peak seemed to be just ahead.

The New Zealanders could not find a route to climb.

Lydia Bradey, a smiling, sleek, 27 year old free spirit with long blonde dreadlocks from Christchurch, New Zealand, was not happy. Lydia, one of the most experienced female mountaineers in the world, had her sights firmly fixed on Everest. She told me she was going to be the first woman to climb Everest without oxygen even if she had to go solo and without a permit.

My team-mates Don Goodman, Johnny Petroske, Dave Hambly, Diana Dailey, as well as Ruoss and Frush, still had summit aspirations. French television was now broadcasting live and needed to reach the top with a camera.

By now a plume of snow was blowing off the summit, indicating that the jet stream had lowered. The crowd gathered at Camp II to wait for a break in the wind. It annihilated two or three tents daily and made radio communication to Base Camp difficult. Its roar was slightly less on 12 October, and the next day French cameraman Serge Koenig and two Sherpas, the brothers Lhakpa Sonam and Pasang Temba, went for the top. Koenig and Lhakpa Sonam made it but the cable connecting the camera to the transmitter broke and there was no live broadcast. In the French tent the director walked in circles declaring 'c'est une tragedie!'

Chomolungma quickly reminded everyone what is really tragic. A frost-bitten Koenig reached the South Col but both his Sherpas fell to their deaths during the descent. Then, as if to mock the day's efforts, the winds suddenly abated. At midnight four Spaniards and two Sherpas prepared for a summit try. Leaving the tent they encountered Lydia. 'D'ya mind if I tag along, mate?' The Spanish shrugged and they headed up.

An hour from camp the Spanish came upon the bodies of the Sherpas. They continued up to the South Summit where Sergi Martinez became very weak. The Spaniards left Martinez all their remaining oxygen and pushed to the top. Sherpa Ang Rita made it too, without supplementary oxygen – a record fifth ascent.

Meanwhile, in an effort to take advantage of the lull in the wind, Steve Ruoss and Johnny Petroske headed for the South Col. The four Slovaks also prepared to leave, taking with them two sleeping-bags, two days' worth of food and a small stove to melt snow. Even if they completed the ascent according to schedule, they would be climbing for three days without supplementary oxygen in the so-called 'death zone' above 8,000 metres.

Meanwhile the Spanish summit team returned to find Martinez lapsing in and out of consciousness. They used rope to make a stretcher to drag and lower him down. They met Lydia at the South Summit crawling

Rubbish dump on the South Col: Chris Bonington's photograph (far left), taken during his ascent in 1985, shows discarded oxygen cylinders and other detritus abandoned by the spiralling number of Everest expeditions. In 1988 the British mountaineer John Barry helped organise the first 'Everest clean up' expedition which took 47 young men and women to the Nepal Base Camp where they burned or buried hundreds of sacks of rubbish (left). Now enlightened expeditions budget to collect and dispose of their litter. In a controversial move, however, the Nepal Government attempted to limit expeditions to Everest by imposing charges of $10,000 per climber, to apply from the autumn of 1993.

But when I reached the ridge crest, another, higher point rose above me. Chomolungma teased me with several more false summits before the ridge dropped sharply away. Everything was below me.

The summit of Mount Everest was everything I had fantasized it to be and more. Then the Korean, Mr Nam, came along, followed by our three Sherpas and Peggy Luce, becoming the second American female to stand atop the world. After 45 minutes I renewed my concentration and started down. I returned to Camp II before dark. I did not learn until later that Peggy fell on the descent, arresting herself inches from an 8,000 foot drop. She lost her sunglasses and quickly became snow-blind. Fortunately, Sherpa Dawa Tsering had stayed behind and guided her down safely.

Chomolungma had now allowed a record 23 of us on her crest, but a two-day storm signalled her mood had changed. Back at Base Camp I celebrated success with Om and Duson Becik. Having no language in common mattered little. Our communication was perfect.

Not everyone was celebrating. Three groups had not been able to capitalize on the good weather. The Spanish failed on the West Ridge. French television could not begin its live broadcasts until 4 October because its satellite was being used for the Olympics.

*In one of the most
audacious feats linked to
Everest, the British
climber/photographer Leo
Dickinson led a dual
balloon flight over the
mountain in October
1991. In Dickinson's
photograph (right), taken
after he has passed
eastward over Everest into
Tibet, the second balloon
can be discerned in the
clear sky in the top left of
the picture. Dickinson
obtained a superb view of
the Kangshung Face, with
the American Buttress
rising from the Kangshung
Glacier in the centre, and
the buttress followed by the
British/American 1988
team to the left. Above is
the dip of the South Col,
with Lhotse to the left and
the South and main
summit of Everest
prominent to the right.*

upward on all fours. It was already 4.30 in the after-noon. They told her to descend but she refused. Already extended and fearing that Martinez would die, they did not argue. Ang Rita looked her in the eye and said, 'You are going to die!'

The exhausted Spanish dragged Martinez back to the South Col at 8.30 pm. My team radioed permission to use our oxygen. When they went to fetch the mask they found Lydia crawling around outside. She said she had made the summit, but couldn't find her tent. They pointed her in the right direction and watched her crawl away.

In the morning, even with the oxygen, Martinez was blind and unable to walk. The Spaniards began lowering him down the Lhotse Face. Steve and Johnny had tried to summit again but when they saw the condition Martinez was in they turned around to help. It took 12 hours to get him to Camp III. Steve, a physician, diagnosed severe cerebral oedema and gave him little chance of survival. The next day he was lowered to Camp II. Finally, 20 climbers, representing every team, carried him down through the Khumbu Icefall to Base Camp. The French television helicopter then evacuated him and another Spaniard with severe frost-bite to Kathmandu.

As that drama resolved, a more intense one started. The four Slovaks called on the radio to say that they had completed their ascent of the South-west Face, reaching the South Summit at 8.30 pm on 16 October. Having taken one day longer than expected, they were out of food and fuel and were about to spend their third night without oxygen or a tent. They said that they were tired and dehydrated but otherwise fine. They planned to summit the next morning and descend via the South Col.

On 17 October Jozef Just pushed on to the top alone and then joined his companions on the descent. In their last radio transmission, at four o'clock, they said that three were blind and all were exhausted, but they were on their way down to the South Col. Don Goodman, Diana Dailey and Dave Hambly went to the South Col. Nothing.

The next morning the jet stream winds returned with a vengeance. No further trace of the Slovaks was found.

In all, an amazing 51 people reached the summit of Mount Everest in 1988. Ten died trying. Leaving the mountain in the wake of tragedy it was hard to find meaning in my accomplishment. On the other side of the planet Bobby McFerrin was rising to the top of the popular music charts preaching, 'Don't worry, be happy.'

The Sherpas have a similar philosophy, 'Kay Guarnay.' Literally, it translates into 'What to do when there is nothing to do?' In practical terms, they don't worry about what they can't control, and are very happy. Here I was, and there was nothing more that I could do. Touching the red string around my neck, I repeated 'Kay Guarnay' and began the long walk back to Kathmandu.

ALL TOES ARE NUMB
by Sue Cobb

Feet. All toes on both feet are completely numb. Some have frost-nip (frozen exterior tissue), but not frost-bite, so they will revive over time. I will lose some toenails. **Legs.** One of my knees, twisted on the moraine below Advance Base Camp, is sore, but except when bridgecrawling, it seems to be stable. **Trunk and central body.** My tummy complained vehemently for the first time today. Diarrhoea, which almost everybody has had at some point, attacked unmercifully. (Not pleasant. Especially if it's below minus 30°C with blowing snow. I won't try to describe the problems.) My ribs are still acutely painful. My cough has graduated to a blood-letting exercise, as well as an interrupter of breathing. Almost everybody gets some kind of vaginitis or crotch itch. I've got that, too (the former). No piles, though – which I know others have. **Neck and head.** A sore throat is a constant companion because of the cold, dry air. Many people have had severe headaches. I have had one or two minor ones. Retinal haemorrhaging is not uncommon. My vision is blurred. Mental confusion, lethargy, lassitude, inability to lift a crampon – these have plagued us all. Everything I've read about the effects of oxygen deprivation is true.

This is by far my worst day physically. I'm not strong enough to try a summit attempt. I peaked many days ago. I might not have made the summit, but I felt great and I could have given it an all-out try. Now I am a basket case. Great timing, Cobb. Great timing.

What is it that causes us to want to go higher? How does it make sense to fight minus 50°C temperatures and winds over 100 miles per hour and face death to stand on the highest spot on earth? How did this common desire and will come to be in this widely diverse, pitifully drained, last remaining handful of climbers sleeping tonight on the edge of Everest?

Advance Base Camp, East Rongbuk Glacier, spring 1991: John English's photograph (left) shows typically inhospitable weather, with spindrift blown from the foot of the ridge swirling around the tents. Pitched on the site of the old Camp III of the pre-war expeditions, Advance Base is an hour's walk from the start of the route. While most expeditions attempting the Pinnacles Ridge had to contend with savage weather, Roger Mear's photograph (right) shows surprisingly benign conditions. Taken in 1989, it shows two climbers approaching the foot of Bill's Buttress – one of two possible starts to the route. While Barker reached 27,700 feet in 1991, two Sherpas subsequently went to the summit.

the North Col again, but this was going to be the last time.

Next day we set off up the ridge towards Camp II. We had two Sherpa lads with us and also a large team of Americans from one of the mechanized expeditions. As we got higher up the ridge the wind got worse and worse. It must have been blowing about 50 miles per hour and as we came out on to the shoulder it was very difficult to stand up.

When we got to Camp II we found that one of our tents had been shredded by the wind and this meant that the four of us had to spend the night in one small two-man tent. It was impossible to cook with four of us sitting up in the tent and we had a bad night with the wind trying to blow the tent off the mountainside.

In the morning the wind was still very strong and so we spent the day pitching another tent and trying to rest, if that is possible at that sort of altitude. The following day, the wind having dropped somewhat, we were happy to go on. We thought of going down, but to return would be so wearying that we decided to hang on to what we had. It is also true that the average person has only so many days at such a height in them, and we used up a lot of ours.

We had to carry a tent and food up to Camp III which had not been established. By this time even the Sherpas were getting picky about what they carried and we had to leave some of the kit behind. The climbing is over slabs and very steep scree slopes covered in powder snow – delightful. After we had been going a couple of hours, Olaf decided that he had had enough and turned back. We finally got to the camp and pitched our tent half on and half off a small ledge. The two Sherpas went down leaving me on my own. There were some Americans about 100 metres away but even so it was a bit spooky as the sun went down.

The next day the American team were going for the top at 3 in the morning and I hoped to be able to keep up with them although they were all on the magic gas. When the morning came my boots were so brittle with the cold that I could not get them on and when I tried to heat them over the stove they caught fire. Then my torch went out due to the cold and I began to get somewhat agitated. I finally had to wait until dawn before I set off far behind the other team.

It was very cold – maybe minus 35°C – and when I got towards the top of the Yellow Band the wind began to rise again. My hands and feet were very cold, on the edge of frost-bite, and I had long icicles hanging from my beard; away at the back of my mind a little red light began to blink. By now I was right on the edge of the ridge. I could see the summit of Lhotse just across the way on the right-hand side and on the left I looked down on Pumori, way, way, below. This is one of the very special places of the earth.

I turned up the side of a little tower and realized that this must be the First Step. I was catching up with the American lads and this cheered me up quite considerably. To be fair to them, they were re-fixing some of the fixed ropes in readiness for the waiting hordes below. It would be a great service to mountaineering if some public benefactor could clear all the ropes and ladders and other rubbish from the mountain, and while I am on the subject, let's ban oxygen and we can all go back to real climbing.

Enough of that, possibly because I've just noticed that I am clipped into some old fixed line anyway.

There was a narrow snow arête in front of me and what I suppose was the Second Step just beyond. That bloody wind was getting to me and I sat down in the snow halfway along the arête and had a little think and a look around.

The camera was frozen, but then I am not a great clicker, you spend your time to better avail by looking properly and remembering. Okay, so I'm chicken-shit, I laughed to myself, and turned round. Just going back was not going to be a total breeze.

On the way down you have to work even harder to keep your mind on the job in hand and I began to feel incredibly tired. I stopped off at Camp III to tidy it up for the next team who would be coming through. I thought of stopping there but then realized that was not good thinking. My toes wanted to get down as fast as possible and so I went on down, seemingly for ever.

So there you are, nice try. I count my fingers and toes and it still gives me a nice even number, and I will remember that ten-minute rest on the ridge for quite a while.

EVEREST - THE THIRTEEN ROUTES

In the 40 years since its first ascent, Everest was climbed by 13 principal different routes. The dates show when expeditions on a new route reached the summit. The numbers are keyed to the routes shown on the two diagrams.

1 29 MAY 1953. The first ascent, following seven failures by the British and two by the Swiss, by Edmund Hillary and Tenzing Norgay. Their route, via the Western Cwm to the South Col and up the South-east Ridge (part hidden and shown by dotted line in diagram), became the standard means of ascent: of 485 ascents by 31 December 1992, 338 went this way. Although the 1953 expedition was British,

Hillary was from New Zealand, Tenzing from India; no British climber reached the summit until 1975 (see route 4). See page 60.

2 25 MAY 1960. The controversial Chinese ascent, once disputed but now widely accepted. The Chinese made much of the fact that they succeeded on the route where the pre-war British failed, climbing from the North Col to the crest of the North-east Ridge. The two Chinese summit climbers, Wang Fu-chou and Chu Yin-hua – the third, Konbu, was Tibetan – attributed their success to the superiority of the Chinese system. Total ascents: 48. See page 66.

3 22 MAY 1963. The US West Ridge ascent by Tom Hornbein and Willi Unsoeld,

who also completed the first traverse of the mountain – ascending by one route, descending by another (in this case, the South-east Ridge/South Col). Although described as a West Ridge route, it is now regarded as a West Ridge/North Face ascent, since the climbers traversed from the ridge to the couloir which now bears Hornbein's name. It also remains one of the rarest routes on Everest, for no one else had climbed it by December 1992. See page 71.

4 24 SEPTEMBER 1975. The British ascent of the South-west Face – one of the most important climbs of the post-war years, helping to open up the great faces of the Himalayas. Above the Great Central Gully

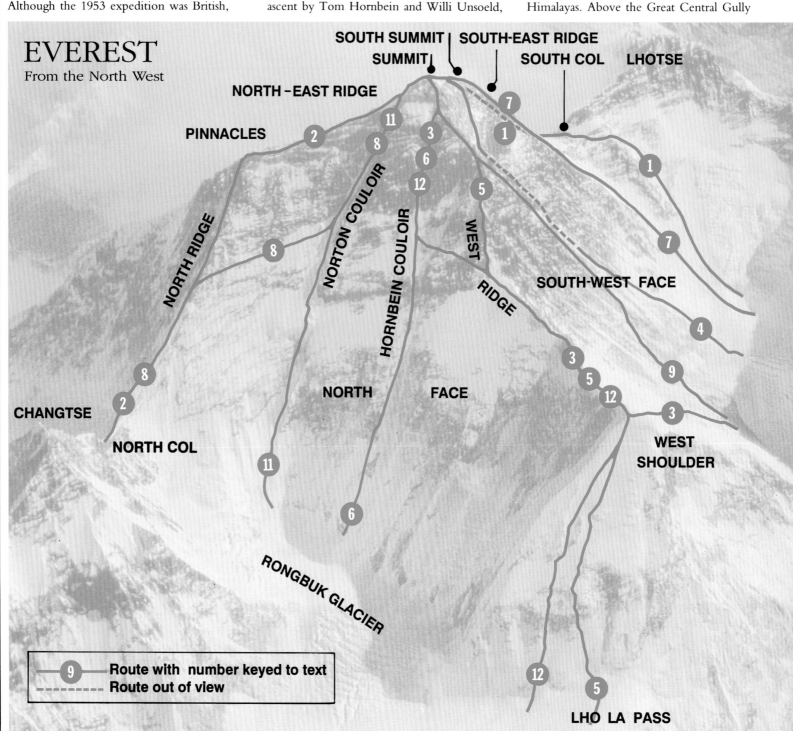

EVEREST
From the North West

SOUTH SUMMIT | SOUTH-EAST RIDGE
SUMMIT | SOUTH COL   LHOTSE
NORTH-EAST RIDGE
PINNACLES
NORTH RIDGE
NORTON COULOIR
HORNBEIN COULOIR
WEST RIDGE
SOUTH-WEST FACE
NORTH   FACE
CHANGTSE
NORTH COL
RONGBUK GLACIER
WEST SHOULDER
LHO LA PASS

— Route with number keyed to text
- - - - Route out of view

(part-hidden on diagram), the key lay in a gully at 26,000 feet at the left-hand end of the Rock Band. Dougal Haston and Doug Scott had stunning summit views but the weather deteriorated for Peter Boardman and Pertemba the next day. Mick Burke, who disappeared after meeting Boardman and Pertemba, is widely believed to have reached the summit. Total ascents: 5. See page 86.

5 13 MAY 1979. The Yugoslav ascent which 'straightened out' the West Ridge – instead of veering on to the North Face, the Yugoslavs followed the ridge all the way, accomplishing the hardest sustained rock climbing on Everest to that date. The summit climbers – headed by Andrej Stremfelj and Nejc Zaplotnik, followed by three the next day – descended via the Hornbein Couloir,

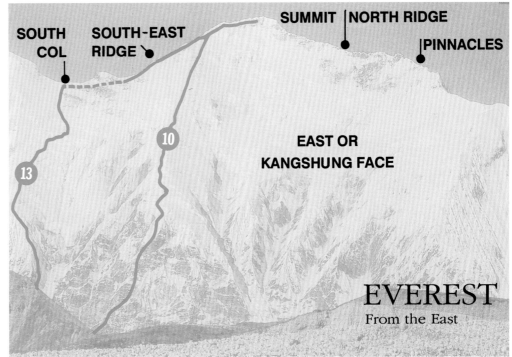

EVEREST
From the East

although Ang Phu fell to his death. Total ascents: 10. See page 104.

6 10 MAY 1980. The first full ascent of the North Face, by the Japanese Tsuneoh Shigehiro and Takashi Ozaki. Starting from the Rongbuk Glacier, they took a direct line up a gully – now known as the Japanese Couloir – which led into the Hornbein Couloir. Total ascents: 7. See page 164.

7 19 MAY 1980. A notable Polish success, following their first winter ascent (see page 111) three months before. The Poles followed the South Pillar at the right-hand edge of the South-west Face. The Rock Band took 16 days to climb and Jerzy Kukuczka and Andrzej Czok reached the summit in a gale. There had been 5 ascents by the end of 1992, while another 20 summit climbers followed the pillar to mid-height before traversing to the South Col.

8 20 AUGUST 1980. The most formidable climb of all – Reinhold Messner's ascent, solo and without oxygen, from the north. Messner had hoped to follow the Chinese route on to the North-east Ridge but soft snow forced him to traverse on to the face. After reaching the Norton (or Great) Couloir he climbed it almost directly to the summit. Total ascents: 18. See page 114.

9 4 MAY 1982. The Russian ascent, made on the first Everest attempt by Soviet climbers, of the South-west Pillar, left of the Great Central Gully on the South-west Face. Including the leading pair, Eduard Myslovski and Volodya Balyberdin, 11 Soviet climbers reached the summit – the highest number on a new route. Total ascents: 11. See page 124.

10 8 OCTOBER 1983. The audacious US ascent of the East or Kangshung Face, following a reconnaissance in 1980 and an

attempt to 22,800 feet in 1981. The route ascended a 3,500 foot buttress followed by 7,500 foot snow slopes to just below the South Summit. The summit trio of Lou Reichardt, Kim Momb and Carlos Buhler was followed by three climbers the next day. Total ascents: 6. See page 128.

11 3 OCTOBER 1984. The bravura ascent, by an unheralded Australian team, of the North Face via the Great or Norton Couloir. The summit pair, Tim Macartney-Snape and Greg Mortimer, became the second climbers (after Reinhold Messner) to set up a new route without using supplementary oxygen; Andy Henderson turned back 150 feet below the summit. Total ascents: 4. See page 142.

12 20 MAY 1986. An impressive 'double' for Canadian Sharon Wood, the first North American woman to climb Everest and the first woman to do so by a new route. The expedition climbed to the West Shoulder from the Rongbuk Glacier; although two previous expeditions had done this, neither had continued to the summit. Wood and summit partner Dwayne Congdon followed the US 1963 line by traversing to the Hornbein Couloir. They remained the only climbers to have taken this route, although in May 1989 a Polish expedition established a variant by going to the Lho La Pass from the Khumbu Glacier and then following the Canadian line. See page 158.

13 12 MAY 1988. The second ascent of the Kangshung Face, taking a line to the left of the 1983 route, by a US team plus the British Stephen Venables; of the three who went for the summit from the South Col, only Venables reached the top. This was the second new route completed solo and the third by a party without supplementary oxygen. Total ascents: 4. See page 166.

NUPTSE

STERN CWM

FALL

KHUMBU GLACIER

The geology of Everest

by *Leni Gillman*

The Himalayan mountains were born of a cataclysmic collision between India and Asia which began about 50 million years ago and continues today. Although you would scarcely notice it, Everest is getting higher each year.

To comprehend how this can be, it is necessary to understand the theory of tectonic plates. The earth comprises an inner core, an intermediary mantle and an outer crust. The crust consists of what geologists call tectonic plates, of which there are two kinds: continental plates, which are relatively light, and heavier oceanic plates. The plates are constantly moving and the crust is unstable where the two kinds of plates meet, crushing against one another to produce earthquakes and volcanoes as violent reminders of the earth's latent power. In the Himalayas the rocks continue to rupture under the massive compression caused by India's impact with Asia.

Geologists estimate that this titanic process began 200 million years ago. Previously, they believe, there was a single vast continent called Pangaea – and they find evidence for this in similarities in geological structures across now widely-separated continents, as well as in the distribution of plants and animals. Then Pangaea began to fragment, with the land masses drifting apart on their plates. In the south the area that consisted of Antarctica, Australia and India broke up, with the Indian plate moving north-east.

About 80 million years ago India had become an island continent separated from Asia by an ocean known as the Tethys Sea. India continued to migrate for another 30 million years, gradually closing the Tethys Sea and finally crashing into Asia. This impact created the Tibetan plateau and Himalayan mountains.

India's arrival unleashed massive waves of pressure and heat. The heavy rocks of the oceanic plate beneath the Tethys Sea were subducted or pushed down into the earth's mantle, eventually to be recycled. (The Indus Valley now forms the visible edge of the subduction zone where the Tethys Sea vanished.) The Tethys sea-bed was thrust up and as the sea closed, India was forced upward into a complex fold system – the Himalayas. This process is not over yet. Having already driven Asia some 900 miles north, India is still buckling and pushing northward and anti-clockwise into Asia by about three centimetres a year.

Visitors to the Himalayas see a breathtaking and awesome landscape. To connect this vision with the primeval forces that created it, and to understand how the rocks which climbers cling to were formed, requires a leap of the imagination. Under the massive heat and pressure resulting from the collision of continents, the rocks changed – metamorphosed – sometimes repeatedly.

The consequences are visible in the Chomolungma massif, as the four peaks of Everest, Lhotse, Nuptse and Changtse are termed. The lower levels are composed mainly of the metamorphic rocks which intruded into the base of the massif from the earth's mantle. They are schists, which are coarse-grained and crystalline and split easily into thin layers. Among the schists are gneisses and migmatites, all strongly metamorphic, bearing witness to having been wrought under profound heat and stress.

Higher up we find a huge intrusion of granite, called the Makalu granite formation, which is strikingly evident on the lower part of the Nuptse-Lhotse wall. It is light coloured and erodes characteristically in blocks. Above this are sedimentary rocks, which were laid down under the Tethys Sea and were only weakly metamorphosed. The clays, silts and chalky remains of marine animals were transformed into pelites, shale, sandstone, and limestone. Everest climbers know them as the famous 'Yellow Band'.

The Yellow Band is in two formations. The first, on Everest's South-west Face and Lhotse's South Wall, is the lower of the two. Some 1,640 feet/500 metres higher up on the north side of Everest is the Upper Yellow Band, which is about 390 feet/120 metres thick.

The Summit Pyramid of Everest, sometimes called the Sagarmatha, is a purer limestone, greyish with sandy layers and other debris. It is curious to contemplate that the highest peak of the world was formed 325 million years ago on an ancient sea bed, now extinct.

The Himalayas are young mountains; they have been through their adolescence, and still have some growing to do. The weather will always chip away at them. But as climbers gather at Base Camp they might pause to wonder whether Everest's yearly growth of three centimetres might be undone by the erosion they cause.

The three great faces of Everest are revealed simultaneously in this breath-taking aerial photograph, taken from over the summit at 35,000 feet. Above the summit are the sunlit snows of the Kangshung Face; below right, the South-west Face; in shadow, left, the North Face. The photograph was taken on 22 December 1984 by Swissair Photo+Surveys, based in Zurich, and was part of a sequence used by Bradford Washburn to help compile his map of Everest, reproduced on page 14.

Mother goddess of the earth: in a second photograph by Kurt Keller of Swissair Photo+Surveys, the great ridges of Everest appear to embrace the landscape. The central feature of the mountain is the North Face, with the West Ridge descending to the right and North-east and North Ridges to the left. To the right of Everest, beyond the Western Cwm, is the Lhotse-Nuptse Ridge. The foreground is dominated by the confluence of the main Rongbuk Glacier, descending from the North Face, and the West Rongbuk Glacier, entering from the right.

THE MOUNT EVEREST FOUNDATION

EVEREST
40th ANNIVERSARY
1953 - 1993

In the aftermath of the triumphant first ascent, the Himalayan Committee of the Alpine Club and the Royal Geographical Society had a pleasing problem on its hands. It had funds left over from financing the 1953 venture; and royalties were beginning to flow in from John Hunt's expedition book, *The Ascent of Everest*, and Tom Stobart's film, *The Conquest of Everest*. What should it do with the money?

Its answer was imaginative and far-sighted. It decided to invest the proceeds to set up a fund which would be administered by the Mount Everest Foundation to assist and encourage climbing and exploration in less-frequented mountain regions, together with research into their 'geology, ethnology and similar sciences'. The Duke of Edinburgh agreed to become its patron.

Since that time the Foundation has dispensed almost £500,000 in grants to a total of over 900 expeditions from Britain and New Zealand. It assisted the first ascents of Kangchenjunga, Nuptse, the Annapurna South-west Face, the Ogre, Kongur, and the 1988 Kangshung Face route on Everest. Today it concentrates its help on ascents of new routes on high peaks, often by small Alpine-style teams avoiding the use of supplementary oxygen, and it encourages expeditions of an exploratory and innovative nature. In 1992 it backed 43 expeditions to 11 different countries, including Greenland, Mongolia and Ecuador.

At the same time the Foundation has maintained its goal of supporting scientific work, such as the Royal Geographical Society expedition to Mulu in Sarawak, the RGS International Karakoram project, and high-altitude studies during the first ascent of Kongur. Its aims include protection of mountains, their peoples, culture and wild life, and it lays down a strict environmental policy for the teams it supports.

The Foundation is run by members drawn equally from the Alpine Club and the RGS, together with a representative from the British Mountaineering Council. To ensure that the bulk of its funds are devoted to its principal aims, all the members are unpaid. As part of the 40th anniversary celebrations in 1993 it launched an appeal for fresh funds to maintain the value of its grants. Its address is the Royal Geographical Society, 1 Kensington Gore, London SW7 2AR.

Everest – the first forty years

by Xavier Eguskitza

Between May 1953 and December 1992, Everest was climbed 485 times by 428 people. The list shows the name and nationality of the climbers, the date and the route, and the nationality and leaders of their expeditions. Where climbers have made more than one ascent – and 39 have done so – the ordinal number of each of their ascents is shown; the highest number achieved is seven, by Ang Rita. The 16 women to have climbed Everest (none have done so more than once) are indicated with the letter f. For further explanations, see footnote on page 197.

No.	Name	Nationality	Date	Route	Exp	Leader
				ASCENTS OF EVEREST (29 May 1953-31 December 1992)		
1	Edmund Hillary	New Zealander	29 May 1953	South-east Ridge	British	John Hunt
2	Tenzing Norgay	Indian Sherpa	29 May 1953	South-east Ridge	British	John Hunt
3	Jürg Marmet	Swiss	23 May 1956	South-east Ridge	Swiss	Albert Eggler
4	Ernst Schmied	Swiss	23 May 1956	South-east Ridge	Swiss	Albert Eggler
5	Hans-Rudolf von Gunten	Swiss	24 May 1956	South-east Ridge	Swiss	Albert Eggler
6	Adolf Reist	Swiss	24 May 1956	South-east Ridge	Swiss	Albert Eggler
7	Wang Fu-chou	Chinese	25 May 1960	North Col to North-east Ridge	Chinese	Shih Chan-chun
8	Chu Ying-hua	Chinese	25 May 1960	North Col to North-east Ridge	Chinese	Shih Chan-chun
9	Konbu	Tibetan	25 May 1960	North Col to North-east Ridge	Chinese	Shih Chan-chun
10	James Whittaker	American	1 May 1963	South-east Ridge	American	Norman Dyhrenfurth
11	Nawang Gombu (1)	Indian Sherpa	1 May 1963	South-east Ridge	American	Norman Dyhrenfurth
12	Luther Jerstad	American	22 May 1963	South-east Ridge	American	Norman Dyhrenfurth
13	Barry Bishop	American	22 May 1963	South-east Ridge	American	Norman Dyhrenfurth
14	William Unsoeld	American	22 May 1963	West Ridge from Western Cwm	American	Norman Dyhrenfurth
15	Thomas Hornbein	American	22 May 1963	West Ridge from Western Cwm	American	Norman Dyhrenfurth
16	A.S. Cheema	Indian	20 May 1965	South-east Ridge	Indian	Mohan S. Kohli
17	Nawang Gombu (2)	Indian Sherpa	20 May 1965	South-east Ridge	Indian	Mohan S. Kohli
18	Sonam Gyatso	Indian Sikkimese	22 May 1965	South-east Ridge	Indian	Mohan S. Kohli
19	Sonam Wangyal	Indian Ladakhi	22 May 1965	South-east Ridge	Indian	Mohan S. Kohli
20	C.P. Vohra	Indian	24 May 1965	South-east Ridge	Indian	Mohan S. Kohli
21	Ang Kami	Indian Sherpa	24 May 1965	South-east Ridge	Indian	Mohan S. Kohli
22	Hari Pal Singh Ahluwalia	Indian	29 May 1965	South-east Ridge	Indian	Mohan S. Kohli
23	Harish Chandra S. Rawat	Indian	29 May 1965	South-east Ridge	Indian	Mohan S. Kohli
24	Phu Dorji	Nepalese Sherpa	29 May 1965	South-east Ridge	Indian	Mohan S. Kohli
25	Teruo Matsuura	Japanese	11 May 1970	South-east Ridge	Japanese	Saburo Matsukata
26	Naomi Uemura	Japanese	11 May 1970	South-east Ridge	Japanese	Saburo Matsukata
27	Katsutoshi Hirabayashi	Japanese	12 May 1970	South-east Ridge	Japanese	Saburo Matsukata
28	Chotare	Nepalese Sherpa	12 May 1970	South-east Ridge	Japanese	Saburo Matsukata
29	Rinaldo Carrel	Italian	5 May 1973	South-east Ridge	Italian	Guido Monzino
30	Mirko Minuzzo	Italian	5 May 1973	South-east Ridge	Italian	Guido Monzino
31	Shambu Tamang (1)	Nepalese Tamang	5 May 1973	South-east Ridge	Italian	Guido Monzino
32	Lhakpa Tenzing	Nepalese Sherpa	5 May 1973	South-east Ridge	Italian	Guido Monzino
33	Claudio Benedetti	Italian	7 May 1973	South-east Ridge	Italian	Guido Monzino
34	Virginio Epis	Italian	7 May 1973	South-east Ridge	Italian	Guido Monzino
35	Fabrizio Innamorati	Italian	7 May 1973	South-east Ridge	Italian	Guido Monzino
36	Sonam Gyalzen	Nepalese Sherpa	7 May 1973	South-east Ridge	Italian	Guido Monzino
37	Hisashi Ishiguro	Japanese	26 Oct 1973	South-east Ridge	Japanese	Michio Yuasa
38	Yasuo Kato (1)	Japanese	26 Oct 1973	South-east Ridge	Japanese	Michio Yuasa
39	Junko Tabei (f)	Japanese	16 May 1975	South-east Ridge	Japanese	Eiko Hisano (f)
40	Ang Tsering	Nepalese Sherpa	16 May 1975	South-east Ridge	Japanese	Eiko Hisano (f)
41	Phantog (f)	Tibetan	27 May 1975	North Col to North-east Ridge	Chinese	Shih Chan-chun
42	Sonam Norbu	Tibetan	27 May 1975	North Col to North-east Ridge	Chinese	Shih Chan-chun
43	Lotse	Tibetan	27 May 1975	North Col to North-east Ridge	Chinese	Shih Chan-chun
44	Samdrub	Tibetan	27 May 1975	North Col to North-east Ridge	Chinese	Shih Chan-chun
45	Darphuntso	Tibetan	27 May 1975	North Col to North-east Ridge	Chinese	Shih Chan-chun
46	Kunga Pasang	Tibetan	27 May 1975	North Col to North-east Ridge	Chinese	Shih Chan-chun
47	Tsering Tobgyal	Tibetan	27 May 1975	North Col to North-east Ridge	Chinese	Shih Chan-chun
48	Ngapo Khyen	Tibetan	27 May 1975	North Col to North-east Ridge	Chinese	Shih Chan-chun
49	Hou Sheng-fu	Chinese	27 May 1975	North Col to North-east Ridge	Chinese	Shih Chan-chun
50	Dougal Haston	Scottish	24 Sep 1975	South-west Face	British	Chris Bonington
51	Doug Scott	English	24 Sep 1975	South-west Face	British	Chris Bonington
52	Peter Boardman	English	26 Sep 1975	South-west Face	British	Chris Bonington
53	Pertemba (1)	Nepalese Sherpa	26 Sep 1975	South-west Face	British	Chris Bonington
?	Mick Burke	English	26 Sep 1975	South-west Face	British	Chris Bonington
54	Michael (Bronco) Lane	English	16 May 1976	South-east Ridge	British	Tony Streather

No.	Name	Nationality	Date	Route	Exp	Leader
55	John (Brummy) Stokes	English	16 May 1976	South-east Ridge	British	Tony Streather
56	Chris Chandler	American	8 Oct 1976	South-east Ridge	USA	Phillip Trimble
57	Robert Cormack	American	8 Oct 1976	South-east Ridge	USA	Phillip Trimble
58	Ko Sang-Don	South Korean	15 Sep 1977	South-east Ridge	S Korean	Kim Young-Do
59	Pemba Norbu	Nepalese Sherpa	15 Sep 1977	South-east Ridge	S Korean	Kim Young-Do
60	Wolfgang Nairz	Austrian	3 May 1978	South-east Ridge	Austrian	Wolfgang Nairz
61	Robert Schauer	Austrian	3 May 1978	South-east Ridge	Austrian	Wolfgang Nairz
62	Horst Bergmann	Austrian	3 May 1978	South-east Ridge	Austrian	Wolfgang Nairz
63	Ang Phu *(1)*	Nepalese Sherpa	3 May 1978	South-east Ridge	Austrian	Wolfgang Nairz
64	Reinhold Messner *(1)*	Italian Tyrolean	8 May 1978	South-east Ridge	Austrian	Wolfgang Nairz
65	Peter Habeler	Austrian	8 May 1978	South-east Ridge	Austrian	Wolfgang Nairz
66	Reinhard Karl	West German	11 May 1978	South-east Ridge	Austrian	Wolfgang Nairz
67	Oswald Ölz	Austrian	14 May 1978	South-east Ridge	Austrian	Wolfgang Nairz
68	Franz Oppurg	Austrian	14 May 1978	South-east Ridge	Austrian	Wolfgang Nairz
69	Sepp Mack	West German	14 Oct 1978	South-east Ridge	W German	Karl Herrligkoffer
70	Hubert Hillmaier	West German	14 Oct 1978	South-east Ridge	W German	Karl Herrligkoffer
71	Hans Engl	West German	14 Oct 1978	South-east Ridge	W German	Karl Herrligkoffer
72	Jean Afanassieff	French	15 Oct 1978	South-east Ridge	French	Pierre Mazeaud
73	Nicolas Jaeger	French	15 Oct 1978	South-east Ridge	French	Pierre Mazeaud
74	Pierre Mazeaud	French	15 Oct 1978	South-east Ridge	French	Pierre Mazeaud
75	Kurt Diemberger	Austrian	15 Oct 1978	South-east Ridge	French	Pierre Mazeaud
76	Wanda Rutkiewicz *(f)*	Polish	16 Oct 1978	South-east Ridge	W German	Karl Herrligkoffer
77	Robert Allenbach	Swiss	16 Oct 1978	South-east Ridge	W German	Karl Herrligkoffer
78	Sigi Hupfauer	West German	16 Oct 1978	South-east Ridge	W German	Karl Herrligkoffer
79	Willi Klimek	West German	16 Oct 1978	South-east Ridge	W German	Karl Herrligkoffer
80	Mingma Nuru	Nepalese Sherpa	16 Oct 1978	South-east Ridge	W German	Karl Herrligkoffer
81	Ang Dorje *(1)*	Nepalese Sherpa	16 Oct 1978	South-east Ridge	W German	Karl Herrligkoffer
82	Ang Kami *(1)*	Nepalese Sherpa	16 Oct 1978	South-east Ridge	W German	Karl Herrligkoffer
83	Georg Ritter	West German	17 Oct 1978	South-east Ridge	W German	Karl Herrligkoffer
84	Bernd Kullmann	West German	17 Oct 1978	South-east Ridge	W German	Karl Herrligkoffer
85	Jernej Zaplotnik	Yug. Slovenian	13 May 1979	West Ridge Integrale	Slovenian	Tone Skarja
86	Andrej Stremfelj *(1)*	Yug. Slovenian	13 May 1979	West Ridge Integrale	Slovenian	Tone Skarja
87	Stane Belak	Yug. Slovenian	15 May 1979	West Ridge Integrale	Slovenian	Tone Skarja
88	Stipe Bozic *(1)*	Yug. Croatian	15 May 1979	West Ridge Integrale	Slovenian	Tone Skarja
89	Ang Phu *(2)*	Nepalese Sherpa	15 May 1979	West Ridge Integrale	Slovenian	Tone Skarja
90	Gerhard Schmatz	West German	1 Oct 1979	South-east Ridge	W German	Gerhard Schmatz
91	Hermann Warth	West German	1 Oct 1979	South-east Ridge	W German	Gerhard Schmatz
92	Hans von Känel	Swiss	1 Oct 1979	South-east Ridge	W German	Gerhard Schmatz
93	Pertemba *(2)*	Nepalese Sherpa	1 Oct 1979	South-east Ridge	W German	Gerhard Schmatz
94	Lhakpa Gyalzo	Nepalese Sherpa	1 Oct 1979	South-east Ridge	W German	Gerhard Schmatz
95	Ray Genet	American	2 Oct 1979	South-east Ridge	W German	Gerhard Schmatz
96	Hannelore Schmatz *(f)*	West German	2 Oct 1979	South-east Ridge	W German	Gerhard Schmatz
97	Sungdare *(1)*	Nepalese Sherpa	2 Oct 1979	South-east Ridge	W German	Gerhard Schmatz
98	Tilman Fischbach	West German	2 Oct 1979	South-east Ridge	W German	Gerhard Schmatz
99	Günter Kämpfe	West German	2 Oct 1979	South-east Ridge	W German	Gerhard Schmatz
100	Nick Banks	New Zealander	2 Oct 1979	South-east Ridge	W German	Gerhard Schmatz
101	Ang Phurba	Nepalese Sherpa	2 Oct 1979	South-east Ridge	W German	Gerhard Schmatz
102	Ang Jangbo	Nepalese Sherpa	2 Oct 1979	South-east Ridge	W German	Gerhard Schmatz
103	Leszek Cichy	Polish	17 Feb 1980	South-east Ridge	Polish	Andrzej Zawada
104	Krzysztof Wielicki	Polish	17 Feb 1980	South-east Ridge	Polish	Andrzej Zawada
105	Yasuo Kato *(2)*	Japanese	3 May 1980	North Col to North-east Ridge	Japanese	Hyoriko Watanabe
106	Tsuneoh Shigehiro	Japanese	10 May 1980	North Face (Hornbein Couloir)	Japanese	Hyoriko Watanabe
107	Takashi Ozaki *(1)*	Japanese	10 May 1980	North Face (Hornbein Couloir)	Japanese	Hyoriko Watanabe
108	Martín Zabaleta	Spanish Basque	14 May 1980	South-east Ridge	Basque	Juan-Ignacio Lorente
109	Pasang Temba	Nepalese Sherpa	14 May 1980	South-east Ridge	Basque	Juan-Ignacio Lorente
110	Andrzej Czok	Polish	19 May 1980	South Pillar	Polish	Andrzej Zawada
111	Jerzy Kukuczka	Polish	19 May 1980	South Pillar	Polish	Andrzej Zawada
112	Reinhold Messner *(2)*	Italian Tyrolean	20 Aug 1980	North Col to North Face	Solo	Reinhold Messner
113	Chris Kopczynski	American	21 Oct 1981	South Pillar to South-east Ridge	American	John West
114	Sungdare *(2)*	Nepalese Sherpa	21 Oct 1981	South Pillar to South-east Ridge	American	John West
115	Chris Pizzo	American	24 Oct 1981	South Pillar to South-east Ridge	American	John West
116	Yong Tenzing	Nepalese Sherpa	24 Oct 1981	South Pillar to South-east Ridge	American	John West
117	Peter Hackett	American	24 Oct 1981	South Pillar to South-east Ridge	American	John West
118	Volodya Balyberdin *(1)*	Soviet Russian	4 May 1982	South-west Pillar	Russian	Yevgeni Tamm
119	Eduard Myslovski	Soviet Russian	4 May 1982	South-west Pillar	Russian	Yevgeni Tamm
120	Sergei Bershov	Soviet Ukrainian	4 May 1982	South-west Pillar	Russian	Yevgeni Tamm
121	Mikhail Turkevich	Soviet Ukrainian	4 May 1982	South-west Pillar	Russian	Yevgeni Tamm
122	Valentin Ivanov	Soviet Russian	5 May 1982	South-west Pillar	Russian	Yevgeni Tamm
123	Sergei Yefimov	Soviet Russian	5 May 1982	South-west Pillar	Russian	Yevgeni Tamm
124	Valeri Khrishchaty	Soviet Kazakh	8 May 1982	South-west Pillar	Russian	Yevgeni Tamm
125	Kazbek Valiev	Soviet Kazakh	8 May 1982	South-west Pillar	Russian	Yevgeni Tamm
126	Valeri Khomutov	Soviet Russian	9 May 1982	South-west Pillar	Russian	Yevgeni Tamm
127	Vladimir Puchkov	Soviet Russian	9 May 1982	South-west Pillar	Russian	Yevgeni Tamm
128	Yuri Golodov	Soviet Kazakh	9 May 1982	South-west Pillar	Russian	Yevgeni Tamm
129	Laurie Skreslet	Canadian	5 Oct 1982	South-east Ridge	Canadian	William March
130	Sungdare *(3)*	Nepalese Sherpa	5 Oct 1982	South-east Ridge	Canadian	William March

No.	Name	Nationality	Date	Route	Exp	Leader
131	Lhakpa Dorje *(1)*	Nepalese Sherpa	5 Oct 1982	South-east Ridge	Canadian	William March
132	Pat Morrow	Canadian	7 Oct 1982	South-east Ridge	Canadian	William March
133	Pema Dorje *(1)*	Nepalese Sherpa	7 Oct 1982	South-east Ridge	Canadian	William March
134	Lhakpa Tshering	Nepalese Sherpa	7 Oct 1982	South-east Ridge	Canadian	William March
135	Yasuo Kato *(3)*	Japanese	27 Dec 1982	South-east Ridge	Japanese	Yasuo Kato
136	Peter Jamieson	American	7 May 1983	South-east Ridge	American	Gerhard Lenser (W.G.)
137	Gerald Roach	American	7 May 1983	South-east Ridge	American	Gerhard Lenser (W.G.)
138	David Breashears *(1)*	American	7 May 1983	South-east Ridge	American	Gerhard Lenser (W.G.)
139	Ang Rita *(1)*	Nepalese Sherpa	7 May 1983	South-east Ridge	American	Gerhard Lenser (W.G.)
140	Larry Nielson	American	7 May 1983	South-east Ridge	American	Gerhard Lenser (W.G.)
141	Gary Neptune	American	14 May 1983	South-east Ridge	American	Gerhard Lenser (W.G.)
142	Jim States	American	14 May 1983	South-east Ridge	American	Gerhard Lenser (W.G.)
143	Lhakpa Dorje II	Nepalese Sherpa	14 May 1983	South-east Ridge	American	Gerhard Lenser (W.G.)
144	Kim Momb	American	8 Oct 1983	East Face to South-east Ridge	American	James Morrissey
145	Louis Reichardt	American	8 Oct 1983	East Face to South-east Ridge	American	James Morrissey
146	Carlos Buhler	American	8 Oct 1983	East Face to South-east Ridge	American	James Morrissey
147	Haruichi Kawamura	Japanese	8 Oct 1983	South Pillar to South-east Ridge	Japanese	Haruichi Kawamura
148	Shomi Suzuki	Japanese	8 Oct 1983	South Pillar to South-east Ridge	Japanese	Haruichi Kawamura
149	Haruyuki Endo	Japanese	8 Oct 1983	South-east Ridge	Japanese	Hiroshi Yoshino
150	Hiroshi Yoshino	Japanese	8 Oct 1983	South-east Ridge	Japanese	Hiroshi Yoshino
151	Hironobu Kamuro	Japanese	8 Oct 1983	South-east Ridge	Japanese	Hiroshi Yoshino
152	George Lowe	American	9 Oct 1983	East Face to South-east Ridge	American	James Morrissey
153	Dan Reid	American	9 Oct 1983	East Face to South-east Ridge	American	James Morrissey
154	Jay Cassell	American	9 Oct 1983	East Face to South-east Ridge	American	James Morrissey
155	Takashi Ozaki *(2)*	Japanese	16 Dec 1983	South-east Ridge	Japanese	Kazuyuki Takahashi
156	Noboru Yamada *(1)*	Japanese	16 Dec 1983	South-east Ridge	Japanese	Kazuyuki Takahashi
157	Kazunari Murakami	Japanese	16 Dec 1983	South-east Ridge	Japanese	Kazuyuki Takahashi
158	Nawang Yonden	Nepalese Sherpa	16 Dec 1983	South-east Ridge	Japanese	Kazuyuki Takahashi
159	Hristo Ivanov Prodanov	Bulgarian	20 Apr 1984	West Ridge	Bulgarian	Avram Iliev Avramov
160	Ivan G. Vulchev	Bulgarian	8 May 1984	West Ridge, South-east Ridge down	Bulgarian	Avram Iliev Avramov
161	Metodi Stefanov Savov	Bulgarian	8 May 1984	West Ridge, South-east Ridge down	Bulgarian	Avram Iliev Avramov
162	Nikolay Petkov	Bulgarian	9 May 1984	West Ridge, South-east Ridge down	Bulgarian	Avram Iliev Avramov
163	Kiril Doskov	Bulgarian	9 May 1984	West Ridge, South-east Ridge down	Bulgarian	Avram Iliev Avramov
164	Phu Dorjee	Indian Sherpa	9 May 1984	South-east Ridge	Indian	Darshan Kumar Khullar
165	Bachendri Pal *(f)*	Indian	23 May 1984	South-east Ridge	Indian	Darshan Kumar Khullar
166	Dorjee Lhatoo	Indian Sherpa	23 May 1984	South-east Ridge	Indian	Darshan Kumar Khullar
167	Ang Dorje *(2)*	Nepalese Sherpa	23 May 1984	South-east Ridge	Indian	Darshan Kumar Khullar
168	Sonam Palzor	Indian Ladakhi	23 May 1984	South-east Ridge	Indian	Darshan Kumar Khullar
169	Tim Macartney-Snape *(1)*	Australian	3 Oct 1984	North Face (Norton Couloir)	Australian	Geoffrey Bartram
170	Greg Mortimer	Australian	3 Oct 1984	North Face (Norton Couloir)	Australian	Geoffrey Bartram
171	Bart Vos	Dutch	8 Oct 1984	South-east Ridge	Dutch	Herman Plugge
172	Jozef Psotka	Slovak	15 Oct 1984	South Pillar, South-east Ridge down	Slovak	Frantisek Kele
173	Zoltan Demjan	Slovak	15 Oct 1984	South Pillar, South-east Ridge down	Slovak	Frantisek Kele
174	Ang Rita *(2)*	Nepalese Sherpa	15 Oct 1984	South Pillar, South-east Ridge down	Slovak	Frantisek Kele
175	Philip Ershler	American	20 Oct 1984	North Col to North Face	American	Louis W. Whittaker
176	Bjorn Myrer-Lund	Norwegian	21 Apr 1985	South-east Ridge	Norwegian	Arne Naess
177	Odd Eliassen	Norwegian	21 Apr 1985	South-east Ridge	Norwegian	Arne Naess
178	Pertemba *(3)*	Nepalese Sherpa	21 Apr 1985	South-east Ridge	Norwegian	Arne Naess
179	Ang Lhakpa Dorje	Nepalese Sherpa	21 Apr 1985	South-east Ridge	Norwegian	Arne Naess
180	Chris Bonington	English	21 Apr 1985	South-east Ridge	Norwegian	Arne Naess
181	Dawa Norbu	Nepalese Sherpa	21 Apr 1985	South-east Ridge	Norwegian	Arne Naess
182	Arne Naess	Norwegian	29 Apr 1985	South-east Ridge	Norwegian	Arne Naess
183	Stein Aasheim	Norwegian	29 Apr 1985	South-east Ridge	Norwegian	Arne Naess
184	Haavard Nesheim	Norwegian	29 Apr 1985	South-east Ridge	Norwegian	Arne Naess
185	Ralph Höibakk	Norwegian	29 Apr 1985	South-east Ridge	Norwegian	Arne Naess
186	Sungdare *(4)*	Nepalese Sherpa	29 Apr 1985	South-east Ridge	Norwegian	Arne Naess
187	Ang Rita *(3)*	Nepalese Sherpa	29 Apr 1985	South-east Ridge	Norwegian	Arne Naess
188	Pema Dorje *(2)*	Nepalese Sherpa	29 Apr 1985	South-east Ridge	Norwegian	Arne Naess
189	Chowang Rinzing	Nepalese Sherpa	29 Apr 1985	South-east Ridge	Norwegian	Arne Naess
190	Richard Bass	American	30 Apr 1985	South-east Ridge	Norwegian	Arne Naess
191	David Breashears *(2)*	American	30 Apr 1985	South-east Ridge	Norwegian	Arne Naess
192	Ang Phurba II *(1)*	Nepalese Sherpa	30 Apr 1985	South-east Ridge	Norwegian	Arne Naess
193	Oscar Cadiach	Spanish Catalan	28 Aug 1985	North Col to North-east Ridge	Catalan	Conrad Blanch
194	Toni Sors	Spanish Catalan	28 Aug 1985	North Col to North-east Ridge	Catalan	Conrad Blanch
195	Carles Vallés	Spanish Catalan	28 Aug 1985	North Col to North-east Ridge	Catalan	Conrad Blanch
196	Ang Karma	Nepalese Sherpa	28 Aug 1985	North Col to North-east Ridge	Catalan	Conrad Blanch
197	Shambu Tamang *(2)*	Nepalese Tamang	28 Aug 1985	North Col to North-east Ridge	Catalan	Conrad Blanch
198	Narayan Shrestha	Nepalese Newari	28 Aug 1985	North Col to North-east Ridge	Catalan	Conrad Blanch
199	Etsuo Akutsu	Japanese	30 Oct 1985	South-east Ridge	Japanese	Kuniaki Yagihara
200	Satoshi Kimoto	Japanese	30 Oct 1985	South-east Ridge	Japanese	Kuniaki Yagihara
201	Hideji Nazuka	Japanese	30 Oct 1985	South-east Ridge	Japanese	Kuniaki Yagihara
202	Teruo Saegusa *(1)*	Japanese	30 Oct 1985	South-east Ridge	Japanese	Kuniaki Yagihara
203	Mitsuyoshi Sato	Japanese	30 Oct 1985	South-east Ridge	Japanese	Kuniaki Yagihara
204	Kuniaki Yagihara	Japanese	30 Oct 1985	South-east Ridge	Japanese	Kuniaki Yagihara
205	Noboru Yamada *(2)*	Japanese	30 Oct 1985	South-east Ridge	Japanese	Kuniaki Yagihara
206	Sharon Wood *(f)*	Canadian	20 May 1986	West Ridge (from Tibet)	Canadian	Jim Elzinga

No.	Name	Nationality	Date	Route	Exp	Leader
207	Dwayne Congdon	Canadian	20 May 1986	West Ridge (from Tibet)	Canadian	Jim Elzinga
208	Erhard Loretan	Swiss	30 Aug 1986	North Face (Hornbein Couloir)	French/Swiss	Pierre Béghin
209	Jean Troillet	Swiss	30 Aug 1986	North Face (Hornbein Couloir)	French/Swiss	Pierre Béghin
210	Huh Young-Ho	South Korean	22 Dec 1987	South-east Ridge	S Korean	Hahm Tak-Young
211	Ang Rita (4)	Nepalese Sherpa	22 Dec 1987	South-east Ridge	S Korean	Hahm Tak-Young
212	Noboru Yamada (3)	Japanese	5 May 1988	North Col-South Col Traverse	Asian	Tsuneoh Shigehiro
213	Ang Lhakpa Nuru (1)	Nepalese Sherpa	5 May 1988	North Col-South Col Traverse	Asian	Tsuneoh Shigehiro
214	Cerin Doji	Tibetan	5 May 1988	North Col-South Col Traverse	Asian	Tsuneoh Shigehiro
215	Ang Phurba II (2)	Nepalese Sherpa	5 May 1988	South Col-North Col Traverse	Asian	Kunga Sherpa
216	Ringen Puncog	Tibetan	5 May 1988	South Col-North Col Traverse	Asian	Kunga Sherpa
217	Da Cering	Tibetan	5 May 1988	South Col-North Col Traverse	Asian	Kunga Sherpa
218	Susuma Nakamura	Japanese	5 May 1988	North Col to North-east Ridge	Asian	Tsuneoh Shigehiro
219	Shoji Nakamura	Japanese	5 May 1988	North Col to North-east Ridge	Asian	Tsuneoh Shigehiro
220	Teruo Saegusa (2)	Japanese	5 May 1988	North Col to North-east Ridge	Asian	Tsuneoh Shigehiro
221	Munehiko Yamamoto	Japanese	5 May 1988	North Col to North-east Ridge	Asian	Tsuneoh Shigehiro
222	Li Zhixin	Chinese	5 May 1988	North Col to North-east Ridge	Asian	Tsuneoh Shigehiro
223	Lhakpa Sona	Nepalese Sherpa	5 May 1988	North Col to North-east Ridge	Asian	Tsuneoh Shigehiro
224	Sungdare (5)	Nepalese Sherpa	10 May 1988	South-east Ridge	Asian	Kunga Sherpa
225	Padma Bahadur	Nepalese Tamang	10 May 1988	South-east Ridge	Asian	Kunga Sherpa
226	Stephen Venables	English	12 May 1988	East Face to South Col	American	Robert Anderson
227	Paul Bayne	Australian	25 May 1988	South-east Ridge	Australian	Austin Brookes
228	Patrick Cullinan	Australian	25 May 1988	South-east Ridge	Australian	Austin Brookes
229	John Muir	Australian	28 May 1988	South-east Ridge	Australian	Austin Brookes
230	Jean-Marc Boivin	French	26 Sep 1988	South-east Ridge	French	François Poissonnier
231	Michel Metzger	French	26 Sep 1988	South-east Ridge	French	François Poissonnier
232	Jean-Pierre Frachon	French	26 Sep 1988	South-east Ridge	French	François Poissonnier
233	Gérard Vionnet-Fuasset	French	26 Sep 1988	South-east Ridge	French	François Poissonnier
234	André Georges	Swiss	26 Sep 1988	South-east Ridge	French	François Poissonnier
235	Pasang Tshering	Nepalese Sherpa	26 Sep 1988	South-east Ridge	French	François Poissonnier
236	Sonam Tshering (1)	Nepalese Sherpa	26 Sep 1988	South-east Ridge	French	François Poissonnier
237	Ajiwa (1)	Nepalese Sherpa	26 Sep 1988	South-east Ridge	French	François Poissonnier
238	Kim Chang-Sun	South Korean	26 Sep 1988	South Pillar to South-east Ridge	S Korean	Choi Chang-Min
239	Pema Dorje (3)	Nepalese Sherpa	26 Sep 1988	South Pillar to South-east Ridge	S Korean	Choi Chang-Min
240	Uhm Hong-Gil	South Korean	26 Sep 1988	South Pillar to South-east Ridge	S Korean	Choi Chang-Min
241	Marc Batard (1)	French	26 Sep 1988	South-east Ridge	Solo	Marc Batard
242	Jang Bong-Wan	South Korean	29 Sep 1988	South Pillar to South-east Ridge	S Korean	Choi Chang-Min
243	Chang Byong-Ho	South Korean	29 Sep 1988	South Pillar to South-east Ridge	S Korean	Choi Chang-Min
244	Chung Seung-Kwon	South Korean	29 Sep 1988	South Pillar to South-east Ridge	S Korean	Choi Chang-Min
245	Stacy Allison (f)	American	29 Sep 1988	South-east Ridge	American	James Frush
246	Pasang Gyalzen	Nepalese Sherpa	29 Sep 1988	South-east Ridge	American	James Frush
247	Peggy Luce (f)	American	2 Oct 1988	South-east Ridge	American	James Frush
248	Geoffrey Tabin	American	2 Oct 1988	South-east Ridge	American	James Frush
249	Nima Tashi (1)	Nepalese Sherpa	2 Oct 1988	South-east Ridge	American	James Frush
250	Phu Dorje (1)	Nepalese Sherpa	2 Oct 1988	South-east Ridge	American	James Frush
251	Dawa Tshering	Nepalese Sherpa	2 Oct 1988	South-east Ridge	American	James Frush
252	Nam Sun-Woo	South Korean	2 Oct 1988	South Pillar to South-east Ridge	S Korean	Choi Chang-Min
253	Serge Koenig	French	13 Oct 1988	South-east Ridge	French	Serge Koenig
254	Lhakpa Sonam	Nepalese Sherpa	13 Oct 1988	South-east Ridge	French	Serge Koenig
?	Pasang Temba	Nepalese Sherpa	13 Oct 1988	South-east Ridge	French	Serge Koenig
255	Jerónimo López	Spanish Galician	14 Oct 1988	South-east Ridge	Catalan	Lluis Belvis
256	Nil Bohigas	Spanish Catalan	14 Oct 1988	South-east Ridge	Catalan	Lluis Belvis
257	Lluis Giner	Spanish Catalan	14 Oct 1988	South-east Ridge	Catalan	Lluis Belvis
258	Ang Rita (5)	Nepalese Sherpa	14 Oct 1988	South-east Ridge	Catalan	Lluis Belvis
259	Nima Rita (1)	Nepalese Sherpa	14 Oct 1988	South-east Ridge	Calalan	Lluis Belvis
260	Lydia Bradey (f)	New Zealander	14 Oct 1988	South-east Ridge	N Zealand	Rob Hall
261	Jozef Just	Slovak	17 Oct 1988	South-west Face	Slovak	Ivan Fiala
262	Stipe Bozic (2)	Yug. Croatian	10 May 1989	South-east Ridge	Macedonian	Jovan Poposki
263	Dimitar Ilijevski	Yug. Macedonian	10 May 1989	South-east Ridge	Macedonian	Jovan Poposki
264	Ajiwa (2)	Nepalese Sherpa	10 May 1989	South-east Ridge	Macedonian	Jovan Poposki
265	Sonam Tshering (2)	Nepalese Sherpa	10 May 1989	South-east Ridge	Macedonian	Jovan Poposki
266	Viktor Groselj	Yug. Slovenian	10 May 1989	South-east Ridge	Macedonian	Jovan Poposki
267	Ricardo Torres	Mexican	16 May 1989	South-east Ridge	American	Walt McConnell
268	Phu Dorje (2)	Nepalese Sherpa	16 May 1989	South-east Ridge	American	Walt McConnell
269	Ang Dannu	Nepalese Sherpa	16 May 1989	South-east Ridge	American	Walt McConnell
270	Adrian Burgess	English	24 May 1989	South-east Ridge	American	Karen Fellerhoff
271	Ang Lhakpa Nuru (2)	Nepalese Sherpa	24 May 1989	South-east Ridge	American	Karen Fellerhoff
272	Sonam Dendu (1)	Nepalese Sherpa	24 May 1989	South-east Ridge	American	Karen Fellerhoff
273	Roddy Mackenzie	Australian	24 May 1989	South-east Ridge	American	Karen Fellerhoff
274	Eugeniusz Chrobak	Polish	24 May 1989	West Ridge (Hornbein Couloir)	Polish	Eugeniusz Chrobak
275	Andrzej Marciniak	Polish	24 May 1989	West Ridge (Hornbein Couloir)	Polish	Eugeniusz Chrobak
276	Toichiro Mitani	Japanese	13 Oct 1989	South-east Ridge	Japanese	Ken Kanazawa
277	Hiroshi Ohnishi	Japanese	13 Oct 1989	South-east Ridge	Japanese	Ken Kanazawa
278	Atsushi Yamamoto	Japanese	13 Oct 1989	South-east Ridge	Japanese	Ken Kanazawa
279	Tchiring Thebe Lama	Nepalese Khas	13 Oct 1989	South-east Ridge	Japanese	Ken Kanazawa
280	Chuldin Dorje	Nepalese Sherpa	13 Oct 1989	South-east Ridge	Japanese	Ken Kanazawa
281	Cho Kwang-Je	South Korean	13 Oct 1989	South Pillar to South-east Ridge	S Korean	Kim In-Tae

No.	Name	Nationality	Date	Route	Exp	Leader
282	Carlos Carsolio	Mexican	13 Oct 1989	South-east Ridge	Mexican	Carlos Carsolio
283	Chung Sang-Yong	South Korean	23 Oct 1989	West Ridge from Nepal	S Korean	Lee Suk-Woo
284	Nima Rita (2)	Nepalese Sherpa	23 Oct 1989	West Ridge from Nepal	S Korean	Lee Suk-Woo
285	Nuru Jangbu	Nepalese Sherpa	23 Oct 1989	West Ridge from Nepal	S Korean	Lee Suk-Woo
286	Ang Rita (6)	Nepalese Sherpa	23 Apr 1990	South-east Ridge	Nepalese	Chitra Bahadur Gurung
287	Ang Kami (2)	Nepalese Sherpa	23 Apr 1990	South-east Ridge	Nepalese	Chitra Bahadur Gurung
288	Pasang Norbu	Nepalese Sherpa	23 Apr 1990	South-east Ridge	Nepalese	Chitra Bahadur Gurung
289	Top Bahadur Khatri	Nepalese (Army)	23 Apr 1990	South-east Ridge	Nepalese	Chitra Bahadur Gurung
290	Robert Link	American	7 May 1990	North Col to North-east Ridge	Internat.	Jim Whittaker
291	Steve Gall	American	7 May 1990	North Col to North-east Ridge	Internat.	Jim Whittaker
292	Sergei Arsentiev	Soviet Russian	7 May 1990	North Col to North-east Ridge	Internat.	Jim Whittaker
293	Grigori Lunyakov	Soviet Kazakh	7 May 1990	North Col to North-east Ridge	Internat.	Jim Whittaker
294	Da Cheme	Tibetan	7 May 1990	North Col to North-east Ridge	Internat.	Jim Whittaker
295	Gyal Bu	Tibetan	7 May 1990	North Col to North-east Ridge	Internat.	Jim Whittaker
296	Ed Viesturs (1)	American	8 May 1990	North Col to North-east Ridge	Internat.	Jim Whittaker
297	Mistislav Gorbenko	Soviet Ukrainian	8 May 1990	North Col to North-east Ridge	Internat.	Jim Whittaker
298	Andrei Tselishchev	Soviet Kazakh	8 May 1990	North Col to North-east Ridge	Internat.	Jim Whittaker
299	Ian Wade	American	9 May 1990	North Col to North-east Ridge	Internat.	Jim Whittaker
300	Da Qiong	Tibetan	9 May 1990	North Col to North-east Ridge	Internat.	Jim Whittaker
301	Luo Tse	Tibetan	9 May 1990	North Col to North-east Ridge	Internat.	Jim Whittaker
302	Ren Na	Tibetan	9 May 1990	North Col to North-east Ridge	Internat.	Jim Whittaker
303	Gui Sang (f)	Tibetan	9 May 1990	North Col to North-east Ridge	Internat.	Jim Whittaker
304	Yekaterina Ivanova (f)	Soviet Russian	10 May 1990	North Col to North-east Ridge	Internat.	Jim Whittaker
305	Anatoli Moshnikov	Soviet Russian	10 May 1990	North Col to North-east Ridge	Internat.	Jim Whittaker
306	Yervand Ilyinski	Soviet Kazakh	10 May 1990	North Col to North-east Ridge	Internat.	Jim Whittaker
307	Aleksandr Tokarev	Soviet Russian	10 May 1990	North Col to North-east Ridge	Internat.	Jim Whittaker
308	Mark Tucker	American	10 May 1990	North Col to North-east Ridge	Internat.	Jim Whittaker
309	Wang Ja	Tibetan	10 May 1990	North Col to North-east Ridge	Internat.	Jim Whittaker
310	Peter Athans (1)	American	10 May 1990	South-east Ridge	American	Glenn Porzak
311	Glenn Porzak	American	10 May 1990	South-east Ridge	American	Glenn Porzak
312	Ang Jangbu	Nepalese Sherpa	10 May 1990	South-east Ridge	American	Glenn Porzak
313	Nima Tashi (2)	Nepalese Sherpa	10 May 1990	South-east Ridge	American	Glenn Porzak
314	Dana Coffield	American	10 May 1990	South-east Ridge	American	Glenn Porzak
315	Brent Manning	American	10 May 1990	South-east Ridge	American	Glenn Porzak
316	Michael Browning	American	10 May 1990	South-east Ridge	American	Glenn Porzak
317	Dawa Nuru	Nepalese Sherpa	10 May 1990	South-east Ridge	American	Glenn Porzak
318	Peter Hillary	New Zealander	10 May 1990	South-east Ridge	N Zealand	Robert Hall
319	Robert Hall (1)	New Zealander	10 May 1990	South-east Ridge	N Zealand	Robert Hall
320	Gary Ball (1)	New Zealander	10 May 1990	South-east Ridge	N Zealand	Robert Hall
321	Rudy Van Snick	Belgian	10 May 1990	South-east Ridge	N Zealand	Robert Hall
322	Apa (1)	Nepalese Sherpa	10 May 1990	South-east Ridge	N Zealand	Robert Hall
323	Andrew Lapkass	American	11 May 1990	South-east Ridge	American	Glenn Porzak
324	Tim Macartney-Snape (2)	Australian	11 May 1990	South-east Ridge	Australian	Tim Macartney-Snape
325	Mikael Reuterswäld	Swedish	11 May 1990	South-east Ridge	N Zealand	Robert Hall
326	Öskar Kihlbörg	Swedish	11 May 1990	South-east Ridge	N Zealand	Robert Hall
327	Alex Lowe	American	4 Oct 1990	South-east Ridge	American	Hooman Aprin
328	Dan Culver	Canadian	4 Oct 1990	South-east Ridge	American	Hooman Aprin
329	Yves Salino	French	4 Oct 1990	South-east Ridge	French	Laurence de la Ferrière
330	Hooman Aprin	American	5 Oct 1990	South-east Ridge	American	Hooman Aprin
331	Ang Temba	Nepalese Sherpa	5 Oct 1990	South-east Ridge	American	Hooman Aprin
332	Erik Decamp	French	5 Oct 1990	South-east Ridge	French	Marc Batard
333	Nawang Thile	Nepalese Sherpa	5 Oct 1990	South-east Ridge	French	Marc Batard
334	Sonam Dendu (2)	Nepalese Sherpa	5 Oct 1990	South-east Ridge	French	Marc Batard
335	Marc Batard (2)	French	5 Oct 1990	South-east Ridge	French	Marc Batard
336	Christine Janin (f)	French	5 Oct 1990	South-east Ridge	French	Marc Batard
337	Pascal Tournaire	French	5 Oct 1990	South-east Ridge	French	Marc Batard
338	Bok Jin-Young	South Korean	6 Oct 1990	South-east Ridge	Japan/S Kor	Nobuo Kuwahara
339	Kim Jae-Soo	South Korean	6 Oct 1990	South-east Ridge	Japan/S Kor	Nobuo Kuwahara
340	Park Chang-Woo	South Korean	6 Oct 1990	South-east Ridge	Japan/S Kor	Nobuo Kuwahara
341	Dawa Sange	Nepalese Sherpa	6 Oct 1990	South-east Ridge	Japan/S Kor	Nobuo Kuwahara
342	Pemba Dorje	Nepalese Sherpa	6 Oct 1990	South-east Ridge	Japan/S Kor	Nobuo Kuwahara
343	Babu Tshering (1)	Nepalese Sherpa	6 Oct 1990	South-east Ridge	French	Marc Batard
344	Andrej Stremfelj (2)	Yug. Slovenian	7 Oct 1990	South-east Ridge	Slovenian	Tomaz Jamnik
345	Marija Stremfelj (f)	Yug. Slovenian	7 Oct 1990	South-east Ridge	Slovenian	Tomaz Jamnik
346	Janez Jeglic	Yug. Slovenian	7 Oct 1990	South-east Ridge	Slovenian	Tomaz Jamnik
347	Lhakpa Rita (1)	Nepalese Sherpa	7 Oct 1990	South-east Ridge	Slovenian	Tomaz Jamnik
348	Cathy Gibson (f)	American	7 Oct 1990	South-east-Ridge	American	Hooman Aprin
349	Aleksei Krasnokutsky	Soviet Russian	7 Oct 1990	South-east Ridge	American	Hooman Aprin
350	Phinzo	Nepalese Sherpa	7 Oct 1990	South-east Ridge	American	Hooman Aprin
351	Jean-Noël Roche	French	7 Oct 1990	South-east Ridge	French	Laurence de la Ferrière
352	Bertrand 'Zébulon' Roche	French	7 Oct 1990	South-east Ridge	French	Laurence de la Ferrière
353	Denis Pivot	French	7 Oct 1990	South-east Ridge	French	Laurence de la Ferrière
354	Alain Desez	French	7 Oct 1990	South-east Ridge	French	Laurence de la Ferrière
355	René De Bos	Dutch	7 Oct 1990	South-east Ridge	French	Laurence de la Ferrière
356	Ang Phurba III	Nepalese Sherpa	7 Oct 1990	South-east Ridge	French	Laurence de la Ferrière
357	Nima Dorje (1)	Nepalese Sherpa	7 Oct 1990	South-east Ridge	French	Laurence de la Ferrière

No.	Name	Nationality	Date	Route	Exp	Leader
358	Ang Temba II	Nepalese Sherpa	8 May 1991	South-east Ridge	Nepalese	Lobsang (Sherpa)
359	Sonam Dendu (3)	Nepalese Sherpa	8 May 1991	South-east Ridge	Nepalese	Lobsang (Sherpa)
360	Apa (2)	Nepalese Sherpa	8 May 1991	South-east Ridge	Nepalese	Lobsang (Sherpa)
361	Peter Athans (2)	American	8 May 1991	South-east Ridge	American	Peter Athans
362	Mark Richey	American	15 May 1991	South-east Ridge	American	Rick Wilcox
363	Yves La Forest	Canadian	15 May 1991	South-east Ridge	American	Rick Wilcox
364	Rick Wilcox	American	15 May 1991	South-east Ridge	American	Rick Wilcox
365	Barry Rugo	American	15 May 1991	South-east Ridge	American	Rick Wilcox
366	Eric Simonson	American	15 May 1991	North Col to North Face	American	Eric Simonson
367	Bob Sloezen	American	15 May 1991	North Col to North Face	American	Eric Simonson
368	George Dunn	American	15 May 1991	North Col to North Face	American	Eric Simonson
369	Andy Politz	American	15 May 1991	North Col to North Face	American	Eric Simonson
370	Lhakpa Dorje (2)	Nepalese Sherpa	15 May 1991	North Col to North Face	American	Eric Simonson
371	Ang Dawa (1)	Nepalese Sherpa	15 May 1991	North Col to North Face	American	Eric Simonson
372	Ed Viesturs (2)	American	15 May 1991	South-east Ridge	American	Ed Viesturs/R. Link
373	Mingma Norbu	Nepalese Sherpa	15 May 1991	North Face (Hornbein Couloir)	Swedish	Jack Berg
374	Gyalbu	Nepalese Sherpa	15 May 1991	North Face (Hornbein Couloir)	Swedish	Jack Berg
375	Mike Perry	New Zealander	17 May 1991	North Col to North Face	American	Eric Simonson
376	Battista Bonali	Italian	17 May 1991	North Face (Norton Couloir)	Italian	Oreste Forno
377	Leopold Sulovsky	Czech	17 May 1991	North Face (Norton Couloir)	Italian	Oreste Forno
378	Lars Cronlund	Swedish	20 May 1991	North Face (Hornbein Couloir)	Swedish	Jack Berg
379	Mark Whetu	New Zealand Maori	21 May 1991	North Col to North Face	American	Eric Simonson
380	Brent Okida	American	21 May 1991	North Col to North Face	American	Eric Simonson
381	Babu Tshering (2)	Nepalese Sherpa	22 May 1991	North Col to North Face	British	Harry Taylor
382	Chuldin	Nepalese Sherpa	22 May 1991	North Col to North Face	British	Harry Taylor
383	Greg Wilson	American	24 May 1991	North Col to North Face	American	Eric Simonson
384	Muneo Nukita	Japanese	27 May 1991	North Col to North Face	Japanese	Muneo Nukita
385	Junichi Futagami	Japanese	27 May 1991	North Col to North Face	Japanese	Muneo Nukita
386	Nima Dorje (2)	Nepalese Sherpa	27 May 1991	North Col to North Face	Japanese	Muneo Nukita
387	Phinzo Norbu	Nepalese Sherpa	27 May 1991	North Col to North Face	Japanese	Muneo Nukita
388	Fco. José 'Coque' Pérez	Spanish Valencian	6 Oct 1991	South-east Ridge	Spanish	Juan-Carlos Gómez
389	Rafael Vidaurre	Spanish Valencian	6 Oct 1991	South-east Ridge	Spanish	Juan-Carlos Gómez
390	José-Antonio Garcés	Spanish Aragonese	6 Oct 1991	South-east Ridge	Spanish	Juan-Carlos Gómez
391	Antonio Ubieto	Spanish Aragonese	6 Oct 1991	South-east Ridge	Spanish	Juan-Carlos Gómez
392	Volodya Balyberdin (2)	Soviet Russian	7 Oct 1991	South-east Ridge	Russian	Volodya Balyberdin
393	Anatoli Bukreev	Soviet Kazakh	7 Oct 1991	South-east Ridge	Russian	Volodya Balyberdin
394	Roman Giutashvili	Soviet Georgian	10 Oct 1991	South-east Ridge	Russian	Volodya Balyberdin
395	Dan Mazur	American	10 Oct 1991	South-east Ridge	Russian	Volodya Balyberdin
396	Prem Singh	Indian	10 May 1992	South-east Ridge	Indian	Hukam Singh
397	Sunil Dutt Sharma	Indian	10 May 1992	South-east Ridge	Indian	Hukam Singh
398	Kanhaiya Lal (Pokhriyal)	Indian	10 May 1992	South-east Ridge	Indian	Hukam Singh
399	Ned Gillette	American	12 May 1992	South-east Ridge	N Zealand	Rob Hall
400	Doron Erel	Israeli	12 May 1992	South-east Ridge	N Zealand	Rob Hall
401	Cham Yick-Kai	Hong Kong (Chinese)	12 May 1992	South-east Ridge	N Zealand	Rob Hall
402	Gary Ball (2)	New Zealander	12 May 1992	South-east Ridge	N Zealand	Rob Hall
403	Douglas Mantle	American	12 May 1992	South-east Ridge	N Zealand	Rob Hall
404	Rob Hall (2)	New Zealander	12 May 1992	South-east Ridge	N Zealand	Rob Hall
405	Randall Danta	American	12 May 1992	South-east Ridge	N Zealand	Rob Hall
406	Guy Cotter	New Zealander	12 May 1992	South-east Ridge	N Zealand	Rob Hall
407	Sonam Tshering (3)	Nepalese Sherpa	12 May 1992	South-east Ridge	N Zealand	Rob Hall
408	Ang Dorje II	Nepalese Sherpa	12 May 1992	South-east Ridge	N Zealand	Rob Hall
409	Tashi Tshering	Nepalese Sherpa	12 May 1992	South-east Ridge	N Zealand	Rob Hall
410	Apa (3)	Nepalese Sherpa	12 May 1992	South-east Ridge	N Zealand	Rob Hall
411	Ang Dawa (2)	Nepalese Sherpa	12 May 1992	South-east Ridge	N Zealand	Rob Hall
412	Ingrid Baeyens (f)	Belgian	12 May 1992	South-east Ridge	N Zealand	Rob Hall
413	Ronald Naar	Dutch	12 May 1992	South-east Ridge	Dutch	Ronald Naar
414	Edmond Oefner	Dutch	12 May 1992	South-east Ridge	Dutch	Ronald Naar
415	Dawa Tashi	Nepalese Sherpa	12 May 1992	South-east Ridge	Dutch	Ronald Naar
416	Nima Temba	Nepalese Sherpa	12 May 1992	South-east Ridge	Dutch	Ronald Naar
417	Aleksandr Gerasimov	Russian	12 May 1992	South-east Ridge	Russian	Vyacheslav Volkov
418	Andrei Volkov	Russian	12 May 1992	South-east Ridge	Russian	Vyacheslav Volkov
419	Ilia Sabelnikov	Russian	12 May 1992	South-east Ridge	Russian	Vyacheslav Volkov
420	Ivan Dusharin	Russian	12 May 1992	South-east Ridge	Russian	Vyacheslav Volkov
421	Skip Horner	American	12 May 1992	South-east Ridge	American	Todd Burleson
422	Louis Bowen	American	12 May 1992	South-east Ridge	American	Todd Burleson
423	Vernon Tejas	American	12 May 1992	South-east Ridge	American	Todd Burleson
424	Dawa Temba	Nepalese Sherpa	12 May 1992	South-east Ridge	American	Todd Burleson
425	Ang Gyalzen	Nepalese Sherpa	12 May 1992	South-east Ridge	American	Todd Burleson
426	Lobsang	Indian Sherpa	12 May 1992	South-east Ridge	Indian	Hukam Singh
427	Santosh Yadav (f)	Indian	12 May 1992	South-east Ridge	Indian	Hukam Singh
428	Mohan Singh (Gunjyal)	Indian	12 May 1992	South-east Ridge	Indian	Hukam Singh
429	Sange Mudok	Nepalese Sherpa	12 May 1992	South-east Ridge	Indian	Hukam Singh
430	Wangchuk	Nepalese Sherpa	12 May 1992	South-east Ridge	Indian	Hukam Singh
431	Sergei Penzov	Russian	14 May 1992	South-east Ridge	Russian	Vyacheslav Volkov
432	Vladimir Zakharov	Russian	14 May 1992	South-east Ridge	Russian	Vyacheslav Volkov
433	Yevgeni Vinogradsky	Russian	14 May 1992	South-east Ridge	Russian	Vyacheslav Volkov

No.	Name	Nationality	Date	Route	Exp	Leader
434	Fedor Konyukhov	Russian	14 May 1992	South-east Ridge	Russian	Vyacheslav Volkov
435	Cristián García-Huidobro	Chilean	15 May 1992	East Face to South Col	Chilean	Rodrigo Jordán
436	Rodrigo Jordán	Chilean	15 May 1992	East Face to South Col	Chilean	Rodrigo Jordán
437	Juan-Sebastián Montes	Chilean	15 May 1992	East Face to South Col	Chilean	Rodrigo Jordán
438	Peter Athans (3)	American	15 May 1992	South-east Ridge	American	Todd Burleson
439	Keith Kerr	British	15 May 1992	South-east Ridge	American	Todd Burleson
440	Todd Burleson	American	15 May 1992	South-east Ridge	American	Todd Burleson
441	Hugh Morton	American	15 May 1992	South-east Ridge	American	Todd Burleson
442	Lhakpa Rita (2)	Nepalese Sherpa	15 May 1992	South-east Ridge	American	Todd Burleson
443	Man Bahadur Tamang	Nepalese Tamang	15 May 1992	South-east Ridge	American	Todd Burleson
444	Dorje	Nepalese Sherpa	15 May 1992	South-east Ridge	American	Todd Burleson
445	Francisco Gan	Spanish Catalan	15 May 1992	South Pillar to South-east Ridge	Spanish	Francisco Soria
446	Alfonso Juez	Spanish Castilian	15 May 1992	South Pillar to South-east Ridge	Spanish	Francisco Soria
447	Ramón Portilla	Spanish Madrilian	15 May 1992	South Pillar to South-east Ridge	Spanish	Francisco Soria
448	Lhakpa Nuru	Nepalese Sherpa	15 May 1992	South Pillar to South-east Ridge	Spanish	Francisco Soria
449	Pemba Norbu II	Nepalese Sherpa	15 May 1992	South Pillar to South-east Ridge	Spanish	Francisco Soria
450	Mauricio Purto	Chilean	15 May 1992	South-east Ridge	Chilean	Mauricio Purto
451	Ang Rita (7)	Nepalese Sherpa	15 May 1992	South-east Ridge	Chilean	Mauricio Purto
452	Ang Phuri	Nepalese Sherpa	15 May 1992	South-east Ridge	Chilean	Mauricio Purto
453	Jonathan Pratt	British	15 May 1992	South-east Ridge	Czech	Miroslav Smid
454	Juan-Mari Eguillor	Spanish Basque	25 Sep 1992	South-east Ridge	Basque	Pedro Tous
455	Patxi Fernández	Spanish Basque	25 Sep 1992	South-east Ridge	Basque	Pedro Tous
456	Alberto Iñurrategi	Spanish Basque	25 Sep 1992	South-east Ridge	Basque	Pedro Tous
457	Félix Iñurrategi	Spanish Basque	25 Sep 1992	South-east Ridge	Basque	Pedro Tous
458	Giuseppe Petigax	Italian	28 Sep 1992	South-east Ridge	Italian	Agostino Da Polenza
459	Lorenzo Mazzoleni	Italian	28 Sep 1992	South-east Ridge	Italian	Agostino Da Polenza
460	Mario Panzeri	Italian	28 Sep 1992	South-east Ridge	Italian	Agostino Da Polenza
461	Pierre Royer	French	28 Sep 1992	South-east Ridge	Italian	Agostino Da Polenza
462	Lhakpa Nuru (2)	Nepalese Sherpa	28 Sep 1992	South-east Ridge	Italian	Agostino Da Polenza
463	Benoit Chamoux	French	29 Sep 1992	South-east Ridge	Italian	Agostino Da Polenza
464	Oswald Santin	Italian	29 Sep 1992	South-east Ridge	Italian	Agostino Da Polenza
465	Abele Blanc	Italian	30 Sep 1992	South-east Ridge	Italian	Agostino Da Polenza
466	Giampietro Verza	Italian	30 Sep 1992	South-east Ridge	Italian	Agostino Da Polenza
467	Josu Bereziartua	Spanish Basque	1 Oct 1992	South-east Ridge	Basque	Pedro Tous
468	Eugène Berger	Luxemburgian	1 Oct 1992	South-east Ridge	French	Bernard Muller
469	Mikel Reparáz	Spanish Basque	3 Oct 1992	South-east Ridge	Basque	Pedro Tous
470	Pedro Tous	Spanish Basque	3 Oct 1992	South-east Ridge	Basque	Pedro Tous
471	Juan Tomás	Spanish Catalan	3 Oct 1992	South-east Ridge	Basque	Pedro Tous
472	Ralf Dujmovits	German	4 Oct 1992	South-east Ridge	German	Ralf Dujmovits
473	Sonam Tshering (4)	Nepalese Sherpa	4 Oct 1992	South-east Ridge	German	Ralf Dujmovits
474	Michel Vincent	French	7 Oct 1992	South-east Ridge	French	Michel Vincent
475	Wally Berg	American	9 Oct 1992	South-east Ridge	American	Wally Berg
476	Augusto Ortega	Peruvian	9 Oct 1992	South-east Ridge	American	Wally Berg
477	Alfonso de la Parra	Mexican	9 Oct 1992	South-east Ridge	American	Wally Berg
478	Apa (4)	Nepalese Sherpa	9 Oct 1992	South-east Ridge	American	Wally Berg
479	Pasang Kami	Nepalese Sherpa	9 Oct 1992	South-east Ridge	American	Wally Berg
480	Philippe Grenier	French	9 Oct 1992	South-east Ridge	French	Michel Pellé
481	Michel Pellé	French	9 Oct 1992	South-east Ridge	French	Michel Pellé
482	Thierry Defrance	French	9 Oct 1992	South-east Ridge	French	Michel Pellé
483	Alain Roussey	French	9 Oct 1992	South-east Ridge	French	Michel Pellé
484	Pierre Aubertin	French	9 Oct 1992	South-east Ridge	French	Michel Pellé
485	Scott Darsney	American	9 Oct 1992	South-east Ridge	French	Michel Pellé

For individual ascents, Nepali climbers stand at the top of the list with 119. US climbers are second with 66, Japanese third with 35. In view of Britain's prominent role in the history of Everest, readers may be surprised to learn that climbers from the United Kingdom figure in only 13th place, with 10 ascents. The full tally of the remaining 34 nationalities (listed according to 1993 boundaries) is: France 26; China 23; Spain 22; India, Russia 20; Germany, Italy 14; South Korea 13; New Zealand 11; United Kingdom 10; Switzerland 9; Austria, Poland, Kazakhstan, Australia, Slovenia 7; Canada, Norway 6; Bulgaria 5; Netherlands, Chile 4; Slovakia, Ukraine, Sweden, Mexico 3; Belgium, Croatia 2; Macedonia, Georgia, Czech Republic, Israel, Hong Kong, Luxembourg, Peru 1.

The list contains four controversial entries. The first two are those of Mick Burke (26 September 1975) and Pasang Temba (13 October 1988), both of whom died on the mountain. In each case there is no absolute proof that they reached the summit, although their colleagues are convinced that they did. In the strict accounting of Everest statistics, their presumed ascents have not been included in the final total of 485. In two other cases, Bart Vos (8 October 1984) and Lydia Bradey (14 October 1988), other climbers expressed doubts as to whether they had succeeded, although in Bradey's case these were largely withdrawn. In accordance with the convention of accepting climbers at their word, both ascents have been included in the list.

As for the number of expeditions, the last to appear in the list, led by the Frenchman Michel Pellé, was appropriately the 100th to succeed. Of those 100, 19 were organized in the US, 13 in Japan and the remainder in 26 other countries. The total number of expeditions since 1921 – including illegal ones – is 280, giving a failure rate of 64 per cent.

EVEREST – THE DEATHS

With 115 fatalities over 70 years, there has been an inescapable death-toll on Everest. It is a sombre comment on the Sherpas' contribution to the history of Everest that by far the highest number of deaths – 42 – occurred to climbers from Nepal. (See footnote for further details.)

No.	Name	Nationality	Date	Exp	Location	Cause
					VERIFIED DEATHS ON EVEREST ON OR ABOVE BASE CAMPS (to 31 December 1992)	
1	Norbu	Indian Sherpa	7 Jun 1922	British	Below North Col	Avalanche
2	Lhakpa	Indian Sherpa	7 Jun 1922	British	Below North Col	Avalanche
3	Pasang	Indian Sherpa	7 Jun 1922	British	Below North Col	Avalanche
4	Pema	Indian Sherpa	7 Jun 1922	British	Below North Col	Avalanche
5	Sange	Indian Sherpa	7 Jun 1922	British	Below North Col	Avalanche
6	Dorje	Indian Sherpa	7 Jun 1922	British	Below North Col	Avalanche
7	Temba	Indian Sherpa	7 Jun 1922	British	Below North Col	Avalanche
8	Shamsherpun	Nepalese Gurkha	13 May 1924	British	Above Rongbuk Base Camp	Frostbite, brain haemorrhage
9	Manbahadur	Indian Gurkha	17 May 1924	British	At Rongbuk Base Camp	Frostbite, pneumonia
10	George Leigh Mallory	British	8 Jun 1924	British	North-east Ridge	Disappeared
11	Andrew Irvine	British	8 Jun 1924	British	North-east Ridge	Disappeared
12	Maurice Wilson	British	Jun 1934	Solo	East Rongbuk Glacier	Exhaustion
13	Mingma Dorje	Sherpa	31 Oct 1952	Swiss	Lhotse Face	Falling ice
14	Shao Si-ching	Chinese	May 1960	Chinese	North-east Ridge	Not known
15	Liu Lien-man	Chinese	25 May 1960	Chinese	North-east Ridge, 8700 metres	Cold, exhaustion
16	Nawang Tsering	Sherpa	28 Apr 1962	Indian	Lhotse Face	Falling rocks
17	John Breitenbach	American	23 Mar 1963	American	Icefall	Falling serac
18	Phu Dorje	Sherpa	18 Oct 1969	Japanese	Icefall	Collapsed snow bridge
19	Mima Norbu	Sherpa	5 Apr 1970	Japanese	Icefall	Avalanche
20	Nima Dorje	Sherpa	5 Apr 1970	Japanese	Icefall	Avalanche
21	Tshering Tarkey	Sherpa	5 Apr 1970	Japanese	Icefall	Avalanche
22	Pasang	Sherpa	5 Apr 1970	Japanese	Icefall	Avalanche
23	Kunga Norbu	Sherpa	5 Apr 1970	Japanese	Icefall	Avalanche
24	Kami Tshering	Sherpa	5 Apr 1970	Japanese	Icefall	Avalanche
25	Kyak Tsering	Sherpa	9 Apr 1970	Japanese	Icefall	Falling seracs
26	Kiyoshi Narita	Japanese	21 Apr 1970	Japanese	Camp I (Icefall)	Heart attack
27	Harsh Bahuguna	Indian	18 Apr 1971	Internat.	West Ridge, 6900 metres	Cold, exhaustion
28	Tony Tighe	Australian	16 Nov 1972	British	Icefall	Falling serac
29	Jangbu	Sherpa	12 Oct 1973	Japanese	South-west Face	Avalanche
30	Gérard Devouassoux	French	9 Sep 1974	French	West Shoulder, 6400 metres	Avalanche
31	Lakpa	Sherpa	9 Sep 1974	French	West Shoulder, 6400 metres	Avalanche
32	Sanu Wongal	Sherpa	9 Sep 1974	French	West Shoulder, 6400 metres	Avalanche
33	Pemba Dorje	Sherpa	9 Sep 1974	French	West Shoulder, 6400 metres	Avalanche
34	Nawang Lutuk	Sherpa	9 Sep 1974	French	West Shoulder, 6400 metres	Avalanche
35	Nima Wangchu	Sherpa	9 Sep 1974	French	West Shoulder, 5800 metres	Avalanche blast
36	Wu Tsung-yue	Chinese	May 1975	Chinese	North-east Ridge, 8500 metres	Exhaustion, fall
37	Mick Burke	British	26 Sep 1975	British	Near summit	Disappeared
38	Terry Thompson	British	10 Apr 1976	British	Western Cwm (C II)	Falling in crevasse
39	Dawa Nuru	Sherpa	18 Apr 1978	Austrian	Icefall	Falling in crevasse
40	Ang Phu	Sherpa	16 May 1979	Yugo.	Hornbein Couloir	Fall
41	Ray Genet	American	3 Oct 1979	W German	South-east Ridge, 8400 metres	Cold, exhaustion
42	Hannelore Schmatz *(f)*	West German	3 Oct 1979	W German	South-east Ridge, 8400 metres	Cold, exhaustion
43	Wang Hong-bao	Chinese	12 Oct 1979	Chinese/Jap.	Below North Col	Avalanche
44	Luo Lan	Chinese	12 Oct 1979	Chinese/Jap.	Below North Col	Avalanche
45	Nima Thaxi	Tibetan	12 Oct 1979	Chinese/Jap.	Below North Col	Avalanche
46	Akira Ube	Japanese	2 May 1980	Japanese	North Face, 7900 metres	Avalanche
47	Nawang Kersang	Sherpa	6 Sep 1980	Italian/Nepal.	Icefall	Fall
48	Mario Piana	Italian	22 Sep 1980	Italian/Nepal.	Lhotse Face	Falling seracs
49	Noboru Takenaka	Japanese	12 Jan 1981	Japanese	Western Cwm, 6900 metres	Fall
50	Marty Hoey *(f)*	American	15 May 1982	American	North Face, 8000 metres	Fall
51	Peter Boardman	British	17 May 1982	British	North-east Shoulder, 8200 metres	Illness?
52	Joe Tasker	British	17 May 1982	British	North-east Shoulder, 8200 metres	Disappeared
53	Pasang Sona	Sherpa	31 Aug 1982	Canadian	Icefall	Avalanche
54	Ang Chuldim	Sherpa	31 Aug 1982	Canadian	Icefall	Avalanche
55	Dawa Dorje	Sherpa	31 Aug 1982	Canadian	Icefall	Avalanche
56	Blair Griffiths	Canadian	2 Sep 1982	Canadian	Icefall	Falling seracs
57	Lhakpa Tshering	Sherpa	27 Sep 1982	Spanish	West Ridge, 6770 metres	Internal haemorrhage
58	Nima Dorje	Sherpa	14 Oct 1982	Spanish	West Ridge, 8300 metres	Fall
59	Yasuo Kato	Japanese	27 Dec 1982	Japanese	South Summit area	Disappeared
60	Toshiaki Kobayashi	Japanese	27 Dec 1982	Japanese	South Summit area	Disappeared
61	Pasang Temba	Sherpa	8 Oct 1983	Japanese	South-east Ridge, 8600 metres	Fall
62	Hironobu Kamuro	Japanese	8 Oct 1983	Japanese	Hillary Step, 8800 metres	Fall
63	Hiroshi Yoshino	Japanese	9 Oct 1983	Japanese	Hillary Step, 8800 metres	Fall
64	Ang Rinji	Sherpa	26 Mar 1984	Indian	Icefall	Avalanche
65	Tony Swierzy	British	3 Apr 1984	British	North Face, 6150 metres	Avalanche
66	Hristo Ivanov Prodanov	Bulgarian	21 Apr 1984	Bulgarian	West Ridge, 8500 metres	Exhaustion
67	Craig Nottle	Australian	9 Oct 1984	Australian	Hornbein Couloir	Fall
68	Fred From	Australian	9 Oct 1984	Australian	Hornbein Couloir	Fall
69	Jozef Psotka	Slovak	16 Oct 1984	Slovak	Lhotse Face	Fall

No.	Name	Nationality	Date	Exp	Location	Cause
70	Ang Dorje	Sherpa	24 Oct 1984	Nepalese	South-east Ridge, 8400 metres	Fall
71	Yogendra Thapa	Nepalese	24 Oct 1984	Nepalese	South-east Ridge, 8400 metres	Fall
72	Juanjo Navarro	Spanish Basque	12 May 1985	Spanish	North Ridge, 7300 metres	Fall
73	Shinichi Ishii	Japanese	17 Sep 1985	Japanese	Below North Col	Avalanche
74	Kiran Inder Kumar	Indian	7 Oct 1985	Indian	South-east Ridge, 8500 metres	Fall
75	Vijay Pal Singh Negi	Indian	11 Oct 1985	Indian	South Col	Exposure
76	Ranjeet Singh Bakshi	Indian	11 Oct 1985	Indian	South Col	Exposure
77	Jai Bahuguna	Indian	11 Oct 1985	Indian	South Col	Exposure
78	M.U. Bhaskar Rao	Indian	11 Oct 1985	Indian	South Col	Exposure
79	Victor Hugo Trujillo	Chilean	16 Aug 1986	Chilean	Below North Col	Avalanche
80	Simon Burkhardt	Swiss	28 Sep 1986	Swiss	Lhotse Face	Avalanche
81	Geyalu	Sherpa	4 Oct 1986	Swiss	Icefall	Falling seracs
82	Dawa Nuru	Sherpa	17 Oct 1986	American	Below North Col	Avalanche
83	Tsuttin Dorje	Sherpa	30 Jan 1987	S Korean	South-west Face, 7700 metres	Fall
84	Roger Marshall	Canadian	21 May 1987	Solo	Hornbein Couloir	Fall
85	Masao Yokoyama	Japanese	2 Sep 1987	Japanese	East Rongbuk Glacier	Drowned
86	Mangal Singh Tamang	Nepalese	20 Oct 1987	British	Above Rongbuk Base Camp	Avalanche
87	Hidetaka Mizukoshi	Japanese	21 Apr 1988	Japanese	Base Camp	Heart attack
88	Michel Parmentier	French	20 Sep 1988	Internat.	North Face, 7700 metres	Probably exposure
89	Narayan Shrestha	Nepalese	21 Sep 1988	Spanish	West Ridge, 7200 metres	Avalanche
90	Lhakpa Sonam	Sherpa	13 Oct 1988	French	South-east Ridge, 8200 metres	Fall
91	Pasang Temba	Sherpa	13 Oct 1988	French	South-east Ridge, 8200 metres	Fall
92	Dusan Becik	Slovak	17 Oct 1988	Czech	South-east Ridge	Disappeared
93	Peter Bozik	Slovak	17 Oct 1988	Czech	South-east Ridge	Disappeared
94	Jaroslav Jasko	Slovak	17 Oct 1988	Czech	South-east Ridge	Disappeared
95	Josef Just	Slovak	17 Oct 1988	Czech	South-east Ridge	Disappeared
96	Ang Lhakpa Dorje	Sherpa	23 Dec 1988	Belgian	South Col	Cerebral thrombosis
97	Dimitar Ilijevski	Macedonian	10 May 1989	Macedonian	South-east Ridge	Fall
98	Phu Dorje	Sherpa	16 May 1989	American	South-east Ridge	Fall
99	Miroslaw Dasal	Polish	27 May 1989	Polish	Lho La area	Avalanche
100	Miroslaw Gardzielewski	Polish	27 May 1989	Polish	Lho La area	Avalanche
101	Waclaw Otreba	Polish	27 May 1989	Polish	Lho La area	Avalanche
102	Zygmunt Heinrich	Polish	27 May 1989	Polish	Lho La area	Avalanche
103	Eugeniusz Chrobak	Polish	28 May 1989	Polish	Lho La area	Avalanche wounds
104	Ang Pinjo	Sherpa	12 Dec 1989	S Korean	Western Cwm	Altitude sickness
105	Rafael Gómez-Menor	Spanish	12 Sep 1990	Spanish	Below North Col	Avalanche
106	Ang Sona	Sherpa	12 Sep 1990	Spanish	Below North Col	Avalanche
107	Badrinath Ghising	Nepalese	12 Sep 1990	Spanish	Below North Col	Avalanche
108	Ham Sang-Hun	South Korean	7 Oct 1990	S Korean	South-east Ridge	Fall
109	Rüdiger Lang	German	3 May 1991	Austrian	North-north-east Facet, 7850 metres	Exposure
110	Junichi Futagami	Japanese	27 May 1991	Japanese	North-east Ridge, 8700 metres	Fall
111	Deepak Kulkarni	Indian	2 May 1992	Indian	Below South Col	Exposure
112	Raymond Jacob	Indian	2 May 1992	Indian	Below South Col	Exposure
113	Subba Singh Tamang	Nepalese	11 May 1992	Spanish	Base Camp	Heart attack
114	Sher Singh	Indian	22 May 1992	Indian	Icefall	Fall
115	Manabu Hoshi	Japanese	23 May 1992	Japanese	North-east Ridge, 8350 metres	Disappeared

Of the victims' nationalities, 42 came from Nepal. Of these, 36 were Sherpas, while a further 7 Sherpas appear in the total of 17 from India, the second nation in the list. Subsequent figures are as follows: Japan 12; United Kingdom 8; China 6 (including 1 Tibetan); Slovakia, Poland 5; US, Australia 3; Canada, France, Spain, Germany 2; Italy, Bulgaria, Chile, Switzerland, Macedonia, South Korea 1. The list of locations confirms the lethal reputation of the Khumbu Icefall, with 20 deaths occurring there, although this is matched by the East Rongbuk Glacier/North Col and the South-east Ridge, also with 20 each. By far the largest single cause was avalanches, including falling rocks and seracs, with 51; falls (including into crevasses) accounted for 28, cold/exhaustion 13. There have been deaths every year since 1969, apart from 1977; the worst year was 1982, with 11.

EVEREST WITHOUT OXYGEN

There have been 51 ascents by climbers who said they had not used supplementary oxygen at any time, even to help them sleep, during their expeditions. Column 1 shows the number of the ascent, column 2 the number of the climber (where a climber has made more than one ascent, subsequent ascents are left blank in this column). In column 3 the age of climber is shown in brackets.

EVEREST WITHOUT ARTIFICIAL OXYGEN					
Ascents	No.	Name (age)	Nationality	Date	Route
1	1	Reinhold Messner (33)	Italian	8 May 1978	South Col
2	2	Peter Habeler (35)	Austrian	8 May 1978	South Col
3	3	Hans Engl (34)	German	14 Oct 1978	South Col
4	4	Mingma Nuru (24)	Nepalese Sherpa	16 Oct 1978	South Col
5	5	Ang Dorje (27)	Nepalese Sherpa	16 Oct 1978	South Col
6		Reinhold Messner (35)	Italian	20 Aug 1980	North Col to North Face
7	6	Larry Nielson (36)	American	7 May 1983	South Col
8	7	Ang Rita (36)	Nepalese Sherpa	7 May 1983	South Col
9	8	Haruichi Kawamura (35)	Japanese	8 Oct 1983	South Pillar to South Col
10	9	Shomi Suzuki (30)	Japanese	8 Oct 1983	South Pillar to South Col
11	10	Haruyuki Endo (26)	Japanese	8 Oct 1983	South Col
12	11	Hiroshi Yoshino (33)	Japanese	8 Oct 1983	South Col
13	12	Hironobu Kamuro (32)	Japanese	8 Oct 1983	South Col
14	13	Hristo Prodanov (41)	Bulgarian	20 Apr 1984	West Ridge
15		Ang Dorje (33)	Nepalese Sherpa	23 May 1984	South Col
16	14	Tim Macartney-Snape (28)	Australian	3 Oct 1984	North Face (Norton Couloir)
17	15	Greg Mortimer (32)	Australian	3 Oct 1984	North Face (Norton Couloir)
18	16	Jozef Psotka (50)	Slovak	15 Oct 1984	South Pillar
19	17	Zoltan Demjan (29)	Slovak	15 Oct 1984	South Pillar
20		Ang Rita (37)	Nepalese Sherpa	15 Oct 1984	South Pillar
21		Ang Rita (38)	Nepalese Sherpa	29 Apr 1985	South Col
22	18	Noboru Yamada (35)	Japanese	30 Oct 1985	South Col
23	19	Erhard Loretan (27)	Swiss	30 Aug 1986	North Face (Hornbein Couloir)
24	20	Jean Troillet (38)	Swiss	30 Aug 1986	North Face (Hornbein Couloir)
25		Ang Rita (40)	Nepalese Sherpa	22 Dec 1987	South Col
26	21	Stephen Venables (34)	English	12 May 1988	East Face to South Col
27	22	Michel Metzger (39)	French	26 Sep 1988	South Col
28	23	Marc Batard (36)	French	26 Sep 1988	South Col
29		Ang Rita (41)	Nepalese Sherpa	14 Oct 1988	South Col
30	24	Nima Rita (29)	Nepalese Sherpa	14 Oct 1988	South Col
31	25	Lydia Bradey (27)	New Zealand	14 Oct 1988	South Col
32	26	Jozef Just (33)	Slovak	17 Oct 1988	South-west Face
33	27	Sonam Tshering (29)	Nepalese Sherpa	10 May 1989	South Col
34	28	Carlos Carsolio (27)	Mexican	13 Oct 1989	South Col
35		Ang Rita (43)	Nepalese Sherpa	23 Apr 1990	South Col
36	29	Sergei Arsentiev (31)	Russian	7 May 1990	North Col to North-east Ridge
37	30	Grigori Lunyakov (35)	Kazakh	7 May 1990	North Col to North-east Ridge
38	31	Ed Viesturs (31)	American	8 May 1990	North Col to North-east Ridge
39	32	Andrei Tselishchev (26)	Kazakh	8 May 1990	North Col to North-east Ridge
40	33	Anatoli Moshnikov (37)	Russian	10 May 1990	North Col to North-east Ridge
41	34	Aleksandr Tokarev (30)	Russian	10 May 1990	North Col to North-east Ridge
42		Tim Macartney-Snape (34)	Australian	11 May 1990	South Col
43		Marc Batard (38)	French	5 Oct 1990	South Col
44	35	Battista Bonali (28)	Italian	17 May 1991	North Face (Norton Couloir)
45	36	Leopold Sulovsky (37)	Czech	17 May 1991	North Face (Norton Couloir)
46	37	Vladimir Balyberdin (41)	Russian	7 Oct 1991	South Col
47	38	Anatoli Bukreev (33)	Kazakh	7 Oct 1991	South Col
48		Ang Rita (45)	Nepalese Sherpa	15 May 1992	South Col
49	39	Alberto Iñurrategi (23)	Spanish Basque	25 Sep 1992	South Col
50	40	Félix Iñurrategi (25)	Spanish Basque	25 Sep 1992	South Col
51	41	Mario Panzeri (28)	Italian	28 Sep 1992	South Col

The figures confirm Ang Rita's pre-eminence in stamina and fortitude; all seven of his ascents were made without oxygen, while just four other climbers – Messner, Ang Dorje, Macartney-Snape and Batard – made two. Batard also made the fastest ever ascent, 22½ hours from Base Camp. Five climbers died during their descents: Yoshino (ascent number 12), Kamuro (13), Prodanov (14) Psotka (18) and Just (32). Only one woman appears on the list: Lydia Bradey (ascent 31).

WOMEN ON THE SUMMIT OF EVEREST

No.	Woman	Nationality	Date	Route	Leader
1	Junko Tabei	Japanese	16 May 1975	South Col	Eiko Hisano (f)
2	Phantog	Tibetan	27 May 1975	North Col–North-east Ridge	Shih Chan-Chun
3	Wanda Rutkiewicz	Polish	16 Oct 1978	South Col	Karl Herrligkoffer
4	Hannelore Schmatz	German	2 Oct 1979	South Col	Gerhard Schmatz
5	Bachendri Pal	Indian	23 May 1984	South Col	Darshan K Khullar
6	Sharon Wood	Canadian	20 May 1986	West Ridge from Tibet	Jim Elzinga
7	Stacy Allison	American	25 Sep 1988	South Col	James Frush
8	Peggy Luce	American	2 Oct 1988	South Col	James Frush
9	Lydia Bradey	New Zealander	14 Oct 1988	South Col	Rob Hall
10	Gui San	Tibetan	9 May 1990	North Col–North-east Ridge	Jim Whittaker
11	Yekaterina Ivanova	Russian	10 May 1990	North Col–North-east Ridge	Jim Whittaker
12	Christine Janin	French	5 Oct 1990	South Col	Marc Batard
13	Marija Stremfelj	Slovenian	7 Oct 1990	South Col	Andrej Stremfelj
14	Cathy Gibson	American	7 Oct 1990	South Col	Hooman Aprin
15	Ingrid Baeyens	Belgian	12 May 1992	South Col	Rob Hall
16	Santosh Yadav	Indian	12 May 1992	South Col	Hukam Singh

Hannelore Schmatz (2 October 1979) died of exposure after a bivouac on the South-east Ridge during her descent. She had reached the summit the day after her husband, Dr Gerhard Schmatz, the expedition leader. Maria Stremfelj (7 October 1990) and her husband Andrej (making his second ascent) were the first married couple to reach the summit of Everest together. They were followed a few moments later by Cathy Gibson and her Russian husband, Aleksei Krasnokutsky. US climbers lead the list of female ascents with 3; Tibetans and Indians have 2 ascents each.

PROGRESSIVE 'OLD MEN' OF EVEREST'

No.	Climber	Nationality	Birth Date	Ascent	Age
1	Tenzing Norgay	Indian Sherpa	Spring 1914	29 May 1953	39 years
2	Sonam Gyatso	Indian Sikkimese	Nov. 1922	22 May 1965	42 years, 6 months
3	Pierre Mazeaud	French	24 Aug 1929	15 Oct 1978	49 years, 52 days
4	Gerhard Schmatz	German	5 Jun 1929	1 Oct 1979	50 years, 118 days
5	Jozef Psotka	Slovak	12 Feb 1934	15 Oct 1984	50 years, 246 days
6	Chris Bonington	English	6 Aug 1934	21 Apr 1985	50 years, 258 days
7	Dick Bass	American	21 Dec 1929	30 Apr 1985	55 years, 130 days

PROGRESSIVE YOUNGEST EVEREST CLIMBERS

No.	Climber	Nationality	Birth Date	Ascent	Age
1	Edmund Hillary	New Zealander	20 Jul 1919	29 May 1953	33 years, 313 days
2	Jürg Marmet	Swiss	9 Sep 1927	23 May 1956	28 years, 257 days
3	Hans-Rudolf von Gunten	Swiss	12 Dec 1928	24 May 1956	27 years, 164 days
4	Luther Jerstad	American	28 May 1936	22 May 1963	26 years, 359 days
5	Sonam Wangyal	Indian Ladakhi	8 Jan 1942	22 May 1965	23 years, 134 days
6	Shambu Tamang	Nepalese Tamang	1954/55?	5 May 1973	18 years, approx.
7	Bertrand 'Zébulon' Roche	French	4 Mar 1973	7 Oct 1990	17 years, 217 days

The title of Everest's oldest summitter is one of the most cherished. Chris Bonington's tenure lasted just nine days. Dick Bass, who replaced him, was also completing the first ascent of the highest mountains on each of the seven continents.

The youngest Everest climber, Frenchman Bertrand Roche, went to the summit with his father Jean-Noël – the first father/son pairing to succeed.

CONVERSION TABLES

Metres	Feet	Feet	Metres	Feet	Metres
5,000	16,404	17,000	5,182	25,000	7,620
5,500	18,045	18,000	5,486	26,000	7,925
6,000	19,685	19,000	5,791	27,000	8,230
6,500	21,325	20,000	6,096	28,000	8,534
7,000	22,966	21,000	6,401	29,000	8,839
7,500	24,606	22,000	6,706		
8,000	26,247	23,000	7,010		
8,500	27,887	24,000	7,315		

PROMINENT EVEREST LANDMARKS

	Feet	Metres		Feet	Metres
Khumbu Icefall (*foot*)	18,000	5,486	First Step	27,880	8,498
Lho La	19,705	6,006	Second Step	28,200	8,595
Western Cwm (*lip*)	20,200	6,157	South Summit	28,750	8,763
Lhotse Face (*foot*)	23,000	7,010	Summit	29,028	8,848
North Col	23,000	7,010			
West Shoulder	23,800	7,254			
First Pinnacle (*foot*)	25,920	7,900			
South Col	26,200	7,986			
Third Pinnacle (*crest*)	27,630	8,422			

Bury/RGS, 24 Map Gary Cooke, 25 A. F. R. Wollaston/RGS, 26 George Finch/Dr and Mrs R. Scott Russell, 27 John Noel, 28 George Mallory/RGS, 29 George Finch, 30 Arthur Wakefield/Diadem Collection, 31 George Finch, 33 Captain C. J. Morris/RGS, 34 John Noel, 35 Howard Somervell, 36l Tom Holzel, 36r Howard Somervell, 37 Howard Somervell, 38 Salkeld Collection, 39 Alan Hinkes, 40 Noel Odell, 41 S. R. Bonnett/RGS, 43–46 all pictures Frank Smythe/RGS 47 Salkeld Collection, 48 Roger Mear, 49 Charles Warren/Salkeld Collection, 50/51 Galen Rowell/Mountain Light, 52/53, Eric Shipton/RGS, 54l Pilots of 684 Squadron/RGS, 53r 1951 Everest reconnaissance/ RGS, 54r 1951 Everest reconnaissance/RGS, 54 map Gary Cooke, 55l & r Eric Shipton/RGS, 56 Doug Scott, 57 Salkeld Collection, 58 Swiss Foundation for Alpine Research, 59 Swiss Foundation for Alpine Research, 60 Tom Bourdillon/RGS, 61 Alfred Gregory/RGS, 62 George Band/RGS, 63l George Lowe/RGS, 63r Alfred Gregory/RGS, 65 Edmund Hillary/RGS, 66 Salkeld Collection, 67 Gillman Collection, 68 Diadem Collection, 70 Dr Barry C. Bishop/© NGS, 72/73 Al Auten, 74 Dr Barry C. Bishop/© NGS, 75 Al Auten, 76 Dr Barry C. Bishop/© NGS, 77 Thomas J. Abercrombie/© NGS, 78l & r Indian Mountaineering Federation, 79 Salkeld Collection, 80/81 Doug Scott, 82–85 all pictures John Cleare, 86 Doug Scott, 87 Keiichi Yamada, 88 Chris Ralling, 89 Doug Scott, 90 Peter Boardman, 90/91 Doug Scott, 92 Peter Boardman, 93 Doug Scott, 94a Mountain Camera Collection, 94b Salkeld Collection, 95l Geoff Tabin, 95ar Pasang Gyalzen Sherpa, 95br Nigel Gifford, 97 Leo Dickinson, 98/99 Leo Dickinson, 100 Dickinson Collection, 101 Dickinson Collection, 102/103 Kurt Diemberger, 104 Bojan Pollak, 105 Tone Skarja, 106 Nejc Zaplotnik, 108/109 Stephen Venables, 110 Andrzej Zawada, 113 Andrzej Zawada, 114/115 Nena Holguin, 116 Reinhold Messner, 117 Reinhold Messner, 118 Chris Bonington, 119 Dag Goering, 120 Chris Bonington, 121 Chris Bonington, 123 Nick Kekus, 124–127 all pictures 1982 USSR Everest expedition, 128 David Cheesmond, 129 George Lowe, 130 Carlos Buhler, 131 Carl Tobin, 132 George Lowe, 133 George Lowe, 134 Lou Reichardt, 134/135 Carlos Buhler, 136 Lou Reichardt, 137 Lou Reichardt, 138 Andy Harvard, 139–141 all pictures Milan Ognjanov, 142–149 all pictures Colin Monteath/Hedgehog House, 150 John English Collection, 151 Carlos Buhler, 152 Stephen Venables, 153 Chris Bonington, 154/155 Bjorn Myrer-Lund, 156 Chris Bonington, 158/159 Dwayne Congdon, 160/161 Jim Elzinga, 162 Sharon Wood, 163 Dwayne Congdon, 164a John Cleare, 164b Yasuo Kato, 165 Kazuo Akimoto/Yomiuri, 167–170 all pictures Stephen Venables, 171 Ed Webster, 172 Dawa Tsering Sherpa, 173 Pedro Cacheco, 174/175 J. M. Boivin/Gamma, 175a J. M. Asselin/Vertical, 175b Alan Hinkes, 176l René Robert/Agence Freestyle, 176r Chris Bonington, 177 Dave Halton, 179 Leo Dickinson, 180 Pertemba, 182/183 Nick Kekus, 183 John English, 184/185 Roger Mear, 186/187 William Thompson, 187 Andy Harvard Graphics Phil Green, 189 Kurt Keller/Swissair Photo+Surveys, 190 Kurt Keller/Swissair Photo+Surveys, **back cover** Edmund Hillary/RGS.

EDITOR'S NOTE

I should like to register my immense gratitude to all those who assisted in preparing this anthology, listed below, and to the authors and photographers named in the lists of credits and acknowledgements. I should like to record special thanks to five people in particular: John Boyle, for the use of his unrivalled Everest library in San Francisco; John Cleare, for fielding a succession of photographic requests with such aplomb; Xavier Eguskitza, for his meticulous devotion to mountaineering statistics; Audrey Salkeld, for her depth of knowledge of mountaineering history and archives; and to my wife Leni, for her unflagging advice, encouragement and support.

Tetsuya Akiyama/Yomiuri Shimbun, Alex and Rachel Alexiev, Rick Allen, Werner Altherr/Swissair Photo+Surveys, George Band, Allen Auten, John Barry, Peter Bayley, Steve Bell, Barry Bishop, Geoff Birtles, Conrad Blanch, Dorothy Boardman, Margaret Body, Chris Bonington, John Boyle, Peter Clark/RGS, Charlie Clarke, John and Joey Cleare/Mountain Camera, Naomi Coke, Andrew Cook/India Office Library, Gary Cooke, Gary Crabbe/Mountain Light Photography, Frances Daltrey/Bonington picture library, Ingeborga Doubrawa-Cochlin, Rachel Duncan/RGS, Norman Dyhrenfurth, John and Andrew Frost, Dr Eugene Gippenreiter, Phil Green, Alf Gregory, Sheila Harrison, Andy Harvard, Liz Hawley, Sir Edmund Hillary, Claudia Hill-Norton, Roger Houghton, Peter Humphrey, Jane Insley/Science Museum, Sharon Joy, Pat Kattenhorn/India Office Library, Captain M. S. Kohli, Kunga Sherpa, Karma D. Lama, Bob Lawford, George Lowe, Mark Lucas, Col. K. S. Mall/Indian Mountaineering Foundation, John Mallory, Greg Mortimer, Bernard Newman, Mike Nicholson, Sue Parsons, Jo Ralling, Ralph Nodder, Lou Reichardt, Dr and Mrs R. Scott Russell, Bill Ruthven, Tseten Sandup, Doug Scott, Nicky Sherriff/RGS picture library, Nick Shipton, Tone Skarja, Ian Smith, Tony Smythe, Jim Somervell, Katherine and Pierre Tardivel, Bill Thompson, Stephen Venables, Charles Warren, A. Warrington/Swiss Foundation for Alpine Research, Bradford Washburn, Peter Wickman, Ken Wilson, Louise Wilson.

At Little, Brown: Martin Bryant, Hilary Foakes, Jenna Stych; Clive Hayball at The Image.

Index